Thurgood Marshall

Recent Titles in Black History Lives

W.E.B. Du Bois: A Life in American History
Charisse Burden-Stelly and Gerald Horne

Thurgood Marshall

A LIFE IN AMERICAN HISTORY

Spencer R. Crew

Black History Lives

An Imprint of ABC-CLIO, LLC
Santa Barbara, California • Denver, Colorado

Library of Congress Cataloging-in-Publication Data

Names: Crew, Spencer R., 1949–
Title: Thurgood Marshall : a life in American history / Spencer R. Crew.
Description: Santa Barbara, California : ABC-CLIO, 2019. | Series: Black
  history lives | Includes bibliographical references and index.
Identifiers: LCCN 2019019626 (print) | LCCN 2019021763 (ebook) |
  ISBN 9781440861451 (eBook) | ISBN 9781440861444 (print : alk. paper)
Subjects: LCSH: Marshall, Thurgood, 1908-1993. | Judges—United States. |
  African American judges—Biography. | United States. Supreme
  Court—Biography.
Classification: LCC KF8745.M34 (ebook) | LCC KF8745.M34 C74 2019 (print) |
  DDC 347.73/2634 [B]—dc23
LC record available at https://lccn.loc.gov/2019019626

ISBN: 978-1-4408-6144-4 (print)
      978-1-4408-6145-1 (ebook)

23 22 21 20 19   1 2 3 4 5

This book is also available as an eBook.

ABC-CLIO
An Imprint of ABC-CLIO, LLC

ABC-CLIO, LLC
147 Castilian Drive
Santa Barbara, California 93117
www.abc-clio.com

This book is printed on acid-free paper ∞

Manufactured in the United States of America

Contents

Series Foreword

The Black History Lives biography series explores and examines the lives of the most iconic figures in African American history, with supplementary material that highlights the subject's significance in our contemporary world. Volumes in this series offer far more than a simple retelling of a subject's life by providing readers with a greater understanding of the outside events and influences that shaped each subject's world, from familial relationships to political and cultural developments.

Each volume includes chronological chapters that detail events of the subject's life. The final chapter explores the cultural and historical significance of the individual and places their actions and beliefs within an overall historical context. Books in the series highlight important information about the individual through sidebars that connect readers to the larger context of social, political, intellectual, and pop culture in American history; a timeline listing significant events; key primary source excerpts; and a comprehensive bibliography for further research.

Preface

THURGOOD MARSHALL: A MAN WORTHY OF ADMIRATION

Thurgood Marshall retired from the Supreme Court more than a quarter of a century ago, and the memory of the importance of his contributions to African Americans and to the nation is beginning to fade. Most often, his name is currently brought up in comparison to his successor on the Supreme Court, Clarence Thomas, to contrast the very different views they have about interpreting the Constitution and protecting the rights of minorities. Marshall is also alluded to because he was the first African American to join the Supreme Court. But the focus on just these two points diminishes the significance of his contributions and breakthroughs, which are part of Marshall's legacy.

Thurgood Marshall was an icon even before he joined the Supreme Court. He worked for the National Association for the Advancement of Colored People (NAACP) in important legal capacities for twenty-seven years. During that time, he was involved in a myriad of court cases on behalf of African-American clients, with the goal of changing the biased legal environment in which African Americans had to function. Marshall was the embodiment of the belief of his mentor, Charles Hamilton Houston, that the lawyers Houston trained were social engineers. Their responsibility was to legally attack and change unjust laws discriminating against African Americans. During his NAACP years, Marshall was a tireless legal advocate, traveling to small towns in the South to defend African-American defendants. He did this despite the constant danger he faced in agreeing to make these trips. For example, he was nearly lynched in Tennessee for defending a group of men unfairly accused of inciting a riot and attempted murder. Even after this harrowing experience, he continued his mission.

The ultimate goal for Marshall was to seek cases that could make their way to the Supreme Court. There he hoped to obtain rulings that would have national impact. This did not preclude him from taking cases solely because of the injustice of the case. Discrimination angered him, and when possible, he sought to use whatever skill or influence he had to help however he could. His involvement resulted in several Supreme Court decisions that mandated that law schools and other higher education programs had to allow African-American applicants to matriculate to their schools in the absence of having truly separate *and* equal facilities to provide them. By the end of his career, including his two years as the first African-American solicitor general, Marshall had argued more cases before the Supreme Court than any other lawyer.

Even before the *Brown v. Board* ruling, Marshall had gained national notoriety for his legal efforts. The NAACP gave him their most prestigious award, the Spingarn Medal, in 1946, eight years before the *Brown* decision. On that occasion they hailed him an "American hero" for his efforts to end racial discrimination. It was his earlier legal work along with the victory in the *Brown* case that made Marshall the best candidate for nomination by President Johnson as the first African-American Supreme Court justice.

But this important prelude to his Supreme Court fame does not register as strongly in present-day popular memory. This amnesia is due in part to the dearth of more recent comprehensive biographies of Marshall. The most inclusive biographies of his life are *Dream Makers; Dream Breakers: The World of Justice Thurgood Marshall*, written by Carl Rowan in 1993; and *Thurgood Marshall: American Revolutionary*, written by Juan Williams in 1998. Each of their books sought to depict the evolution of Marshall from a youngster in Baltimore through his resignation from the Supreme Court. More recent books written about Marshall tend to focus more on particular aspects of his life. Larry Gibson's *Young Thurgood: The Making of a Supreme Court Justice* and Mary Dudziak's *Exporting American Dreams: Thurgood Marshall's African Journey* are good examples. They offer important insights into key parts of Marshall's life but do not examine Marshall's breath of accomplishments.

Understanding the full measure of Thurgood Marshall and his many accomplishments, especially before he joins the Supreme Court, is the heart of this study. The generation that immediately benefited from his work with the NAACP is disappearing, and with them is evaporating the overall significance of Marshall's contributions. Living conditions for African Americans in the South and the North were extremely circumscribed in the years before the *Brown* decision. African Americans faced violence, forced confessions, and capricious treatment by law officials on a regular basis. A strong belief that the legal system could change this environment and eventually rule against discrimination was necessary in order to sustain the years of effort put in by Marshall and the NAACP.

Books like *Before Brown* by Gary Lavergne, *Simple Justice* by Richard Kluger, and *The Devil in the Grove* by Gilbert King offer insight into the intensity of the challenges faced by Marshall and his colleagues. African Americans were not seen as equals and worthy of fair treatment. In many instances they were perceived as disposable and easy scapegoats to be manipulated by local officials. The death of a person of color was considered of little consequence and almost always justifiable. To maintain a belief in the legal system in the face of the roadblocks placed before Marshall was a remarkable accomplishment. His strength of character, belief in the rule of law, and determination while at the NAACP is important to remember and properly acknowledge. All these traits are evident in his speeches, writings, and oral interviews, as captured in Mark Tushnet's edited volumes, such as *Thurgood Marshall: His Speeches, Writings, Arguments, Opinions, and Reminiscences.* Marshall's commitment to the power of the law was evident in an essay he wrote for the NAACP publication *The Crisis*, in 1939, when he pointed out, "While it may be true that laws and constitutions do not act to right wrong and overturn established folkways overnight, it is also true that the reaffirmation of these principles of democracy build a body of public opinion in which rights and privileges of citizenship may be enjoyed, and in which the more brazen as well as the more sophisticated attempts at deprivation may be halted" (Tushnet, 2001, p. 77). Marshall hoped time was on his side and that eventually the courts and then the nation would extend full citizenship rights to African Americans.

The fact that Marshall's hopes and dreams as well as legal actions did bear fruit is an important reminder of the power of the individual. Determined people can effect change in a society, as exemplified in Thurgood Marshall. The world into which Marshall was born in 1908 changed significantly by the time he joined the Supreme Court. It continued to evolve while he sat on it, but important groundwork was in place before he arrived. Thurgood Marshall was one of the engineers of this evolving terrain. How that new environment emerged and the role Thurgood Marshall played in it comprise the central theme of this work and a story that should not diminish over time. He was a man who more than accomplished how he said he wanted to be remembered: "He did what he could with what he had" (Williams, 1998, p. 392). The nation owes him an enormous debt for prodding it to live up to its principles.

I feel extremely privileged to have had the opportunity to get to know Thurgood Marshall better. My respect for him and his work grew immeasurably as I discovered more about him. It has been both a joyous and a heartbreaking journey to follow his life and the challenges faced by African Americans during most of the twentieth century. They were not events unknown to me, but to journey through them with Marshall made the experience all the more real. It has made me more appreciative of him and of the privileges I have as a consequence of his efforts. I am also appreciative of the support of my friends and family who traveled through this journey vicariously with me. Their encouragement and sound suggestions along the way were invaluable. High on the list are my children, Alika and Adom Crew. They are not historians but are empathetic individuals who always have an encouraging word. But, most important is my longtime partner in life, Sandra Prioleau Crew. She was the person I could always count on to offer perspective as I worked on this project. She is a thoughtful observer of people, and her insights helped me understand Marshall more deeply. Without her, this work would not have been possible.

1

Early Influences

The parents of Thurgood Marshall decided to marry while his mother, Norma Arica Williams, was attending Coppin Normal College in Baltimore, Maryland. At the time, his father, William Canfield Marshall, worked as a porter on the Baltimore and Ohio Railroad. William and Norma married in 1905 when he was twenty-two and she nineteen. Norma's parents insisted that she finish college and get her teaching degree after she married. Her parents also insisted that William contribute to her college costs. The plan was that after graduating, Norma would begin a teaching career in the colored Baltimore school system.

A teaching livelihood was a logical choice for Norma. Her mother, Mary Fossett Williams, taught at a private African-American academy in Baltimore. Norma's sister, Avonia, was among the first African Americans hired to teach in the colored school system. This had been a major breakthrough, as it was only after a prolonged struggle that the Baltimore Board of Education had allowed African-American teachers to educate "colored" students. Teaching provided steady employment and reinforced the high value the family placed on education and economic stability. In fact, the families of both William and Norma had entrepreneurial spirits, as each owned a grocery business. Norma's father, Isaiah Williams, bought a home in West Baltimore and opened two stores after serving in the Civil War with the U.S. Colored Troops and then with the merchant marines. During his naval career, he traveled to South America and ports like Arica,

Chile, after which Norma got her middle name. In Baltimore, Isaiah was an activist who pressed Baltimore officials to admit African-American children to public schools. In his quest for equal treatment, he also protested the abuse of black Baltimore residents by the police.

William's father, Thurgood or "Thorney" Marshall, also enlisted. He joined the army and at one point was stationed in Texas as a Buffalo soldier, where he became ill and received a medical discharge. He used money from his time in the military and funds gained as a waiter to open a grocery in his home in West Baltimore. He married Anne Robinson from Virginia, and together they had seven children. William Canfield Marshall was their oldest son. William's education was cut short when he misbehaved in high school. When Thorney learned what his son had done, he came to the school and whipped William in front of his classmates. Embarrassed, William did not return to school and instead began working in the family grocery store as a delivery boy. He eventually left home and obtained a position with the Baltimore and Ohio Railroad as a porter. It was while working as a porter that he and Norma Williams fell in love.

William and Norma had two sons: William Aubrey, born in 1906, and Thurgood Marshall, born on July 2, 1908. Thurgood (sometimes called Thorney-good) was named after his paternal grandfather, Thorney Good "Thurgood" Marshall. The family lived in the West Baltimore neighborhood of the city, one of the primary sections of the town in which African Americans settled. The neighborhood grew in accessibility at the turn of the century as well-to-do whites moved out and left housing behind for occupation by the city's growing African-American population. The burgeoning working- and middle-class communities that developed in West Baltimore became centers of resistance against efforts by white politicians to restrict the rights of African Americans.

Two actions by local white citizens exemplified their campaign to segregate African Americans. The first was the 1889 decision to close access to the University of Maryland Law School to African-American applicants. After the graduation of two black law students the previous year, white students and faculty successfully lobbied the administration to turn away any future African-American applicants and to expel the current students. Seventeen years later, the Maryland legislature sought to further separate the races with the passage of Jim Crow laws that mandated racial segregation on trains and steamships. The legislature also tried, unsuccessfully, to follow the example of its sister state, Virginia, and disfranchise black voters, but the Democrats could not muster enough support from the Republicans, who saw this as a threat to their political base.

The issues faced by African Americans in Maryland reflected the challenges faced by African Americans throughout the South and, to a lesser degree, in other parts of the nation. While twenty African Americans were lynched in Maryland between 1890 and 1920, more than three thousand African Americans suffered a similar fate throughout the nation during the same period. The decision of the Supreme Court in the 1895 *Plessy v. Ferguson* case, which made separate but equal segregation statutes legal, emboldened legislators in Maryland and other states to pass more rigorous Jim Crow laws. The movement of African Americans from rural areas to urban centers like Baltimore resulted in growing tension between black and white residents, which at times resulted in riots directed toward the African-American community. While Baltimore avoided a major riot, others occurred in New York, New Orleans, and Atlanta. Most shocking was the Springfield, Illinois, riot of 1908, which lasted two days and resulted in the death of seven people and injured a hundred more. In its aftermath, a group of concerned black and white citizens met in New York City and subsequently formed the NAACP with the goal of "ensuring the political, educational, social and economic equality of minority group citizens of United States and eliminating race prejudice" (http://www .NAACP.org).

The national program of the NAACP reflected an agenda similar to that which local African-American organizations had promoted for many years. In Maryland, the return to power of the Democratic Party near the turn of the century marked a rise in anti-African-American rhetoric and legislation. Democrats declared Baltimore "a white man's city," in which they sought to "preserve in every conservative and constitutional way the political ascendancy of our race" (Callcott, 1967, p. 99). This push toward racial separation soon manifested itself throughout the city of Baltimore. A 1930 Urban League study of Baltimore labeled it the most segregated city in the nation. It had segregated schools, parks, and stores. Black customers could not go to department stores, and if one attempted to enter, Thurgood Marshall later noted, they told you "to get the hell out" (Ball, 1998, p. 15).

African-American residents of Maryland resisted both the rhetoric and the legislation that followed. Groups like the Colored Equal Rights League, the Suffrage League of Maryland, and the Mutual Brotherhood of Liberty of the United States of America formed to protest segregated schools, political discrimination, police mistreatment of black citizens, and other bigoted efforts directed toward the African-American community. The Constitution of the Brotherhood plainly set forth its goals for all to understand their resolve: "the avowed purpose of said Brotherhood shall be to use all legal means within our power to procure and maintain our rights as citizens of this our common country" (Fight for African American Teachers).

Thurgood Marshall's maternal grandfather, Isaiah Williams, was a part of this spirit of remonstration and resistance. When he organized a public protest decrying the beating of African Americans by the Baltimore police, it was the first such protest of its type in Baltimore (Ball, 1998, p. 15). Thurgood's paternal grandmother, Mary Forsett, also found her own way to fight. Marshall talked of how his grandmother's belief that with courage one could beat City Hall was put into action when she physically blocked the electric company from putting up a utility pole on the sidewalk outside of her grocery store. When they arrived to dig the hole, they found her seated in a kitchen chair exactly where they intended to excavate. She took this action in defiance of a court order. Grandma Mary argued she had paid for the sidewalk and that nobody had the right to put an electric pole in the middle of it (Rowan, 1993, p. 34). In the end, the electric company found another place to erect the pole. Her son, Thurgood's father, was a man who also always stood up for his rights, even if it cost him in the long run. He told Marshall as a boy, "Anyone calls you n—, you not only got my permission to fight him—you got my orders to fight him" (Columbia University Oral History Project). This imperative to resist social and political injustice was the legacy Thurgood inherited from both sides of his family.

All African-American parents are faced with the challenge of how to prepare their child to navigate an often unforgiving world. As much as they wish to protect their children and keep them in a safe cocoon of family and friends, they know that is not possible. Inevitably, their children will face the moment when they are told they are different and inferior. Consequently, parents can either teach their children to accept the way they are mistreated or to fight the injustices that confront them. Marshall learned his family did not meekly accept injustice but resisted it however they could. They expected him to follow their example. This approach of pushing back against racial injustice stayed with him throughout his life.

The birth of Thurgood's older brother, Aubrey, followed by the arrival of Thurgood two years later, put the teaching career of his mother on hold, as she elected to remain at home to care for her children. As a result, the family relied upon the income of William, which was not always adequate. Lured by the possibility of steadier work, the family moved to New York when Thurgood was two. Norma's older sister, Demedia, invited the family to join them in Harlem so that William could work with her husband, Clarence Dodson, as a waiter on the New York Central Railroad. She also offered to help her younger sister care for her two boys.

By accepting the invitation and relocating to New York, the Marshall family joined thousands of African Americans leaving the South and seeking better opportunities in the North. This Great Migration, as it was later called, fueled an explosion in the size of the African-American population in cities like Philadelphia, Chicago, and New York. Harlem's African-American population increased by more than 40 percent between 1900 and 1930. It was the fastest growth in its black population to date. It transformed a predominantly Italian and Jewish neighborhood into an African-American community of more than two hundred thousand residents. The newcomers also included Africans and immigrants of African descent from a myriad of Caribbean Islands. The diverse backgrounds of the new inhabitants turned Harlem into a rich mixture of geographic and cultural diversity reflected in the dialects spoken, foods eaten, religions practiced, and political perspectives expressed.

Harlem was an exciting place to live and very different from the Marshalls' former home of West Baltimore. Racial practices, in particular, were different in Harlem. Discrimination still flourished; it was a reluctance to live with African Americans that induced Harlem's white residents to sell their property to African Americans. Finding better-paying jobs was difficult for black workers and made it difficult to obtain affordable housing. Consequently, many of the newcomers had to live in cramped quarters in order to afford the cost of rent and food in their new city. The place the Marshalls shared with the Dodsons was, in Marshall's words, "a dingy tenement" (Rowan, 1993, p. 37). On the other hand, New York's department stores served black customers, and the schools, restaurants, and public transportation were not legally segregated.

To save on expenses, the Marshall family moved in with the Dodsons in an apartment on 140th Street and Lenox Avenue. The arrangement also made sense, as William's and Clarence's work as waiters for the New York Central Railroad took the men away from home for several days at a time.

THE GREAT MIGRATION

The start of World War I provided an incentive for African Americans in the South to look northward for greater opportunities. As war industries geared up and white men were drafted into military service, the need for laborers encouraged companies to recruit African-American workers to fill the gap. Given the discrimination and violence African Americans experienced in the South, moving North was enticing. Consequently, in the years during and after the War, a flood of migrants relocated to Northern cities, rapidly increasing the size of their African-American populations.

Their arrival in such large numbers challenged the capabilities of cities to provide housing and adequate services. The migrants frequently found themselves restricted to living in certain areas in these cities, such as Harlem in New York. This massive movement of people also altered the demographic profile of African Americans, making them more urban and more Northern. Their relocation made issues of race a national question rather than a primarily Southern one. Through organizations like the NAACP and the National Urban League, a more demanding African-American community pressured public officials to treat issues of race and discrimination differently.

For young Thurgood, it meant he spent much of his time with his mother and Aunt Medi, as they called her. With Aubrey old enough to attend school, large parts of the day focused primarily on Thurgood. Often the sisters dressed him up and took him on walks along the streets of Harlem to escape the apartment. All the attention spoiled the young boy, and he regularly took advantage of the situation. His aunt described "Goody" (their nickname for Thurgood) as a timid crybaby, always near his mother. The description was well deserved. He used this device as a means to get his way, breaking into tears when he wanted something. It worked several times until his mother caught on to his efforts to manipulate her and put a stop to it. But by then, Goody had talked her into letting him adopt several animals.

Over time, life in Harlem made Goody more self-reliant and hardy. His Aunt Medi noticed this change and attributed it to the neighborhood boys who introduced him to their rough-and-tumble world, where crying did not gain one any advantage. These lessons came when he went out with his brother, Aubrey, and his classmates. This introduced Goody to a different environment, beyond the walls of his apartment building. His meandering often resulted in his returning home with his clothes dirty and accompanied by stray animals and people he met, whom he asked his mother and aunt to feed. Norma said their home became known as the "Friendly Inn" because of the numerous strangers they helped due to her son's ability to connect with people and his desire to aid people in need of help (DeMille, 1954). It made the four years the family spent in Harlem both enjoyable and a period of growth for Thurgood. Harlem introduced him to a world very different from Baltimore. Harlem had a majority African-American population, more hectic lifestyle, and less rigidly defined rules of racial interaction. It illustrated that there were alternatives to the environment in Baltimore. Six-year-old Thurgood undoubtedly noticed the difference when the family decided to return to Baltimore.

Norma's mother's broken leg brought them back to Baltimore so Norma could help care for Grandma Mary. When the Marshalls returned in 1914, it was to a city where racial issues had worsened. The local black newspaper, the *Baltimore Afro-American*, published an editorial that year noting that relations between the races had never been worse (Williams, 1998, p. 26). Part of what inspired this lament was the use of restrictive covenants by the city to prevent African Americans from moving into certain areas. When a black lawyer bought a row house in a prestigious white neighborhood of the city, the Democratic-controlled city council proposed legislation to prevent African Americans from moving into predominantly white neighborhoods. The one African-American member of the city council protested vehemently on behalf of the black community, but the legislation passed anyway. It was the first law passed in the United States that mandated the segregation of each residential block. The stated goal of this residential segregation law, Ordinance 692, was "for preserving peace, preventing conflict and ill feeling between the white and colored races in Baltimore City and promoting the general welfare of the city" (Ordinances, 1910–1911, p. 378). African Americans saw it as racism, and the local branch of the NAACP contested the law in the courts. Ultimately, the Maryland Court of Appeals declared the law unconstitutional (Boger, 1979). But the conflict threw a spotlight on the attitude of white residents who agreed with *The Baltimore Sun*, which editorialized that "the white race is the dominant and superior race, and it will, of course, maintain its supremacy" (History of Baltimore).

Despite the racial turmoil in the city, the Marshalls sought to provide a protected and nurturing environment for their two boys. Upon their return, they moved in with Norma's brother, Fearless Mentor Williams. He received this name because as a newborn he had looked fearlessly into the eyes of his father. The Williams family lived on Division Street, part of a mixed neighborhood with Jewish, Russian, German, and Italian residents. Many of the stores in the neighborhood were owned by Jewish merchants, and while some served African Americans, others would not let them try on clothes before they bought them or would only serve very fair-skinned individuals.

Grandma Mary lived very close to the Williams family, which enabled Norma to tend to her needs. It also allowed Thurgood to spend extended periods with his grandmother, who cherished the time she spent with him. Thurgood valued the time together as well. He saw her as a very strong woman who had a great influence on him. During their time together, she talked to him about standing up for his rights and taught him how to cook. Like his parents, she hoped he would become a doctor or a lawyer but wanted him to have a practical skill to fall back upon if he needed employment. She pointed out to him that a black cook could always get a job.

Fearless and his wife, Flo, did not have children of their own, so they directed their parental instincts toward Aubrey and Thurgood. Because William's job with the railroad kept him away for extended periods, Uncle Fearless became an important male figure for the two boys. Fearless was the personal attendant to the president of the B&O Railroad. In this capacity he wore a coat and tie to work every day, as he set up meeting rooms for the president and served him lunch. His responsibilities put him in contact with key business and political figures from around the city. Consequently, he was one of the most influential African Americans working for the railroad because of his daily direct contact with the president.

The job also allowed Uncle Fearless to keep fairly regular hours, which meant he was home every evening. He used this time to interact with the two boys, playing games with them and discussing school issues and any other topics the boys had on their minds. His intent was to have a positive effect on the boys, to give them self-confidence, and to encourage them to take pride in their appearance and work. It was hard to tell if any of his personal examples or words of wisdom had the desired impact on Thurgood. As a youngster, Marshall did not always associate with the children his family preferred. He enjoyed hanging out with the roughnecks and tough kids in the neighborhood. Marshall once noted, "When it was time for dinner, my mother used to go to the front door and call my brother. Then she'd go to the back door and call me" (Goldman & Gallen, 1992, p. 24). This independent and somewhat rebellious spirit carried over to other aspects of Thurgood's life.

Thurgood began attending school when he was six. School 103 was one of the best colored elementary schools in Baltimore and only three blocks from the home of Uncle Fearless. Despite the pride the community took in the quality of the education the school's students received, the building itself was not in good shape. It was an older brick building with makeshift classrooms separated by sliding doors. Unfortunately, this was not unusual for colored schools since "Baltimore's black public schools were crowded and in disrepair, housed in the cast-off buildings left behind as whites moved to better facilities . . . no new black schools were built between 1898 and 1915" (Roberts, 2002, p. 28). In addition, the school year for African-American students was shorter than that for white students, as they were expected to get jobs on nearby farms in need of labor.

Early on in his school career, Thurgood made a major decision. While in second grade, he felt it was too hard to spell his given name, Thoroughgood, and decided to change it. He made everyone start calling him Thurgood and convinced his mother to change his name on his birth certificate. According to Marshall, the name Thoroughgood "was too damn long, so I cut it. I didn't have nobody's permission, I did it" (Williams, 1998, p. 26).

Thurgood's independent spirit showed up in other aspects of his school life. In elementary school he often was at the center of any disruptive activities that occurred in the classroom. One of his classmates later remarked that he was so "energetic that he had to sit in the front row so the teacher could keep an eye on him." He was not a very serious or good student as a result. One of the reasons his parents happily sent him to 103 was because his mother worked there and could also keep watch over her son.

After school Thurgood spent time at the nearby grocery store owned by a Jewish merchant named Mr. Hale. He played with the owner's son, Sammy, who became one of his best friends. Thurgood made deliveries for Sammy's father. He took items ordered by customers to their homes in his wagon. His compensation was ten cents a day and all he could eat. It was a good job for a ten-year-old.

As he got older, Thurgood's approach to education in junior high and high school did not change substantially. He maintained his relaxed attitude about studying, doing just enough to get by but not measuring up to his parent's expectations. His father felt his own lack of a high school education had relegated him to the service jobs he held with the railroad and later with a white country club. He wanted his sons to do better and believed education was the pathway to better opportunity. His mother tried to set an example for her sons by going back to college to renew her teaching certification. When Thurgood got to high school, his parents kept track of his actions through his father's brother, Cyrus Marshall, who taught math there. Anytime Thurgood misbehaved, other faculty told his uncle, who in turn, informed his parents. William then followed up by punishing his prankster youngest son. Thurgood's misbehaving mirrored his father's actions as a high school student. Like Thurgood, William did not fear his teachers and misbehaved regularly. The public punishment delivered by his father's hands was what prompted William to drop out and not finish high school. William's threats to his own son were probably intended to discourage Thurgood's rebelliousness and prevent him from suffering a fate similar to that of his father. The tactic had some effect, as the amount of trouble Marshall caused did decline.

But his father's threats did not entirely stop Thurgood from getting into trouble and having to meet with the principal on occasion. One of the creative punishments the principal devised was to send Thurgood to the basement of the school with a copy of the United States Constitution. He instructed Thurgood that he could not return to class until he had memorized a passage from the document. Marshall disliked the punishment, but it gave him firsthand knowledge of a document central to the legal system of the nation and one that would be important to him later in life. He said that by the time he left school he knew the whole thing by heart. This knowledge heightened his recognition of the discrepancy between the ideals of the nation and its selective application or denial to African Americans and other minorities. The best illustration of the abuses of the Constitution he observed came when Marshall described the scenes he witnessed from the window of his high school classroom. The school was located across the street from the Northwest Baltimore police station, which gave Marshall a front-row view of police mistreatment of black prisoners. He observed the questioning of black suspects and the beatings used to acquire a confession. These actions were not in accordance with the rights Marshall learned when memorizing the U.S. Constitution. The injustice of those scenes stuck with Marshall for the rest of his life.

Thurgood learned more about the law and how it operated in the courtroom from his father. The operation of the courts and the actions of the lawyers fascinated William Marshall. When not working, he spent long periods watching trials at the back of the courtroom. Sometimes both Thurgood and Aubrey accompanied him to the courtroom and the police station so they too could see firsthand how the legal system functioned. William carried home what they observed and challenged his sons to present their ideas in a logical, articulate fashion. This had to be the case no matter if the topic was politics or the weather. Their point of view needed sound proof and logical undergirding when presented. Their father and mother's insistence upon this rigor became the basis for many an intense discussion at the Marshall home. Both parents challenged ideas raised by their sons. They also made the boys read the paper every day to keep themselves informed about key issues. Thurgood later noted that these domestic debates helped turn him into a lawyer.

The debates at home served Thurgood well even before he became an attorney. In high school he joined the debate team and excelled. His natural skills as a conversationalist and the training in logical thinking he received at home served him well. The debate coach recognized his talents and pressed Marshall to do the work necessary to sharpen his skills and debate strategies. This combined with his enthusiasm made him a standout. His teammates recognized his skills and elected him captain as a freshman and again in his junior and senior year after he had to take a year off to improve his grades. The team was one of the best in Baltimore and accepted an invitation to compete in Delaware.

In general, Marshall was an adequate student. He was bright, tested into the better classes, but was indifferent about his schoolwork. Consequently, he did not measure up to the success of his older brother. His mother believed he did not work as hard as Aubrey did. He was popular with the students. He served on student council, played football, and had a lot of dates, which provided distractions. Another obstacle was the situation at home. His father developed a health problem that left him unable to work. Thurgood consequently worked part time as a porter to help supplement the family income and to pay his brother's college tuition. He also had to navigate his father's growing frustration with his illness and the barriers he faced without a high school or college education. William was angry with the world and vented his anger on Thurgood, his mother, and others with whom he came into contact. His anger also made him less tolerant of the restrictions of racial prejudice. Despite these challenges, Marshall graduated in the top third of his class, having never failed a course or arrived to school late. The influence of his parents was an important factor on his high school career.

His parents' influence also impacted how Marshall conducted himself when faced with day-to-day affronts directed toward African Americans. One example occurred as a result of one of his jobs. Fourteen-year-old Thurgood was a delivery boy for a dress company. On a Saturday before

Easter, he had a number of hats in hatboxes to deliver. The tall stack made it difficult to see where he was going or who was in front of him. He needed to take the streetcar to make the deliveries and headed to the streetcar stop and waited. When the car arrived, he grasped the boxes and began to step into the car. Before he could get aboard, a white male passenger grabbed his arm and stopped him. "N—, don't you push in front of no white lady again," he heard. Thurgood said that with the hatboxes, he never even saw the woman the man said he insulted.

Thurgood did remember his father's words to him about how to respond to the use of that pejorative word and "tore into him." As they fought, the hatboxes fell to the ground, and the hats were destroyed. One of Marshall's friends tried to stop the fight without success. Eventually, the police arrived and halted the fight before it escalated further. They arrested Thurgood and took him to the police station. The white man was not charged. When he heard what happened, the shop owner came to the station and paid Thurgood's bail. Marshall apologized for the damage to the hats, but the store owner was more concerned for Marshall's safety. The outcome could have been much more dire for Marshall, given the police brutality toward African Americans at that time in Baltimore, but the intervention of the store owner undoubtedly made a difference. However, Thurgood's reaction to the affront directed toward him reflected his family's history of refusing to accept racial bigotry. Marshall argued it was in his DNA.

As Thurgood matured, his confrontations with prejudice increased as his travels took him further afield. It also exposed him to a variety of tactics for responding to these affronts. His uncle Fearless offered him one alternative as he took Thurgood under his wing. Often he carried Thurgood on trips to the Eastern Shore of Maryland, which he very carefully planned. Fearless made certain he had extra gasoline in the trunk of the car and food for the travelers. The Eastern Shore had been the sight of several lynchings, and Fearless wanted to ensure they would not run out of gas or need to stop at a strange establishment for food. Thurgood did not realize the specific reason his uncle did this at first, but as he got older, he came to understand the need for precaution when African Americans ventured into rural areas of the South. The less contact one had with the local white residents, the better. For Uncle Fearless, caution and planning was the best alternative to possible confrontations in these circumstances. This was a strategy not lost on Thurgood.

Thurgood applied this more cautious and conciliatory approach himself on a separate occasion. It was when he applied for a position as a porter on the railroad. A white conductor interviewed him, decided to give him the job, and handed him a uniform. When Thurgood put it on, he pointed out to the conductor that the pants were too short. The conductor replied, "Boy, it easier to get another n— than another pair of pants. You want the job you wear the pants" (Smith & Ellis, 2011, p. 24). Thurgood wore the pants and took the job because he needed the money, despite the insulting attitude of the conductor. He later said incidents like that one motivated him to work to spare future generations from such insults.

The money Thurgood needed was to enable him to attend college. After his high school graduation, money remained a challenge for the Marshall family, especially with Aubrey still in college. His mother was working two jobs, and Thurgood had to work if he intended to attend college. By not reacting to the language of the conductor, he worked for six months for the railroad and earned enough money to enroll in Lincoln University, where he joined his brother.

Attending college was not optional for Thurgood. His parents and family had assumed this from early in his life. The only issue open to discussion was which college he would attend, although as an African American living in Baltimore, he had limited options. In 1925, local white colleges did not accept African-American students. The University of Maryland Law School had instituted segregation nearly fifty years earlier, and the University of Maryland banned African-American students as did Johns Hopkins University. Local schools available to African-American students included the Eastern Shore Branch of the Maryland Agricultural College, Morgan College, and Howard University in Washington, DC. The only other choice in the eyes of the Marshall family was Lincoln University.

HOWARD UNIVERSITY

An act of Congress in 1867 originally chartered Howard as a theological school. However it quickly broadened its educational mission by adding nontheological undergraduate, graduate, and professional programs. It was named after General Oliver Otis Howard who fought in the Civil War and was the commissioner of the Freedmen's Bureau. Until 1926, Howard only had white presidents. That year, it appointed its first African-American president, Mordecai Wyatt Johnson. During Johnson's tenure, Howard increased in stature through strengthening its professional schools, hiring prominent faculty, increasing federal support, and constructing additional buildings. One of Johnson's first projects was upgrading the law school.

The law school first opened in 1869 with six students. Classes were held in the homes and offices of the instructors. The program continued to meet off campus until 1936. To improve the law program, President Johnson hired Charles Houston first as vice dean and then dean of the law school and switched it from a night school for part-time students to a day program for full-time students in 1929. Subsequently, it gained accreditation and became a center for producing African-American lawyers focused on civil rights and social engineering.

Lincoln University had an impressive history. It began as the Ashmun Institute, charted in 1854 by the state of Pennsylvania. This made it the first degree-granting, historically black college. The goal of its founder, the Presbyterian minister John Miller Dicky, was to provide for the "scientific, classical and theological education of colored youth of the male sex" (Gibson, 2012, p. 83). In 1866, the school was renamed Lincoln University in honor of Abraham Lincoln after his assassination. The focus of the school also expanded as it sought to educate students of "every clime and complexion." By 1925, Lincoln's student body had grown into a diverse group, with students drawn from around the world and with a wide range of economic backgrounds. They came to Lincoln with the understanding that the school trained their students for a professional career and leadership roles in their communities. Due to the Princeton education of its founder, Presbyterian Church affiliation, focus on a classical education and school colors similar to Princeton, students and others often referred to the school as the black Princeton. The fact that most of the professors also graduated from Princeton added to this point of view. All these factors made Lincoln the Marshalls' preferred choice.

Furthermore, the advantages of choosing Lincoln included the fact that his brother Aubrey already attended the school, and as funds were a problem, Thurgood needed special consideration to overcome concerns about the family's ability to handle the tuition payments. Fortunately for Thurgood, a friend of the family was a minister and a graduate of Lincoln University. Initially, Lincoln hesitated to admit Thurgood. They suggested he take a year off to allow the family to finish paying Aubrey's bill and then have him reapply. But a letter from the alumnus Reverend W. W. Walker, vouching for Thurgood and the Marshall family, influenced the final decision. In the end, the school judged Thurgood's qualification for admittance on the merit of his academic record and not his financial standing and allowed him to matriculate. Thurgood's job with the railroad the summer before his first semester at Lincoln helped ease the financial burden.

When Aubrey returned to Lincoln in the fall of 1925, Thurgood made the car trip with him to begin his freshman year. Once they reached campus, the two brothers did not associate much with each other. Aubrey, very serious and studious, focused on preparing himself for medical school. Though his parents wanted him to become a dentist, Thurgood did not bring the same focus to his schoolwork as Aubrey. In many ways, his approach to college was opposite to that of his older brother.

Thurgood spent his freshman year at Lincoln enjoying college life. Unlike Aubrey, Thurgood was outgoing, loud, and engaged in a variety of campus pastimes. He devoted limited time to studying and more time to social activities around campus. Playing cards, going to movies, storytelling, and interacting with his fellow students occupied most of his time. He met a number of students who would later make marks for themselves, including Langston Hughes, Cab Calloway, and the future president of Ghana Kwame Nkrumah. Marshall and his roommate, a friend from Baltimore, regularly invited a stream of people to their room most nights. There Marshall bummed cigarettes while card games of pinochle and poker regularly occurred. Thurgood said he did well enough in those card games to help with his school costs. He also cofounded a group called the Weekend Club, which focused on leaving campus each weekend to go to Philadelphia in search of parties and other entertainment where women were present. They declared they never opened a book or studied on campus during the weekends. They only stayed on campus if there was a football game that weekend. Marshall later noted that during those early years, he did just enough to pass but had little interest in trying to do more than that (Rowan, 1993, p. 43).

One continuing concern was paying for college. Lincoln helped with that challenge by giving Thurgood a job in the school bakery. There he helped prepare bread, pies, and cakes for the school cafeteria. It was hard work, as he and other workers prepared pastry while working around the hot ovens. They sweated profusely, but their secret reward was their confiscation of some of the newly baked bread doused in butter. Years later, Marshall still had fond memories of those stolen treats.

The debate team attracted Thurgood's attention during his freshman year. His skill at analyzing data along with the expertise developed on his high school debate team served him well at Lincoln. He performed strongly enough in mock debates to make the school team as a freshman. Although he did not participate, Marshall traveled with the team when they had the opportunity to debate an Oxford University squad at Bethel AME Church in Baltimore. Returning home must have been exciting for him, especially in light of the crowd of more than a thousand people who turned out for the contest. Lincoln won the debate to the great joy of the audience. As he had in high school, Thurgood worked hard as a member of the Lincoln debate team. It was great training for his later career as a lawyer and manifested itself in his performances with the debate team later in his college career. Marshall quickly became one of the leading debaters for the team.

Thurgood successfully survived his freshman year, despite his lack of focus on his academic responsibilities. Fortunately, some of the worry about tuition money decreased. His campus jobs along with his father's improved health increased the ability of the family to cover the costs of attending Lincoln. Healthy again, William Marshall procured a position at one of the most prestigious country clubs in the area, the Gibson Island Club located a few miles outside of Baltimore. He was responsible for hiring and firing the African-American staff in the dining room of the club. He hired Thurgood as a waiter for the summer after his freshman year. The experience proved an important one for Marshall in light of the racism he encountered while there.

He faced his biggest dilemma with his mistreatment by one important customer: a U.S. senator from a western state. Showing off for the two women who accompanied him, the senator demanded immediate service at his table from Marshall. In the process, he used derogatory language, yelling, "N—, I want service at this table!" Although put off by the language, Marshall provided service for the senator that evening and several evenings that followed. What kept his temper under control was that each night the senator left a twenty-dollar tip for Marshall, which was a significant amount at the time. When his father observed the mistreatment of his son and his son's response, he scolded him for not standing up for his dignity and told him he was "a disgrace to the colored people" (Rowan, 1993, p. 42). He then threatened to fire Thurgood until his son offered an explanation of how much money he made each night serving the obnoxious but generous customer. He told his father for twenty dollars he could tolerate the customer treating him disrespectfully. But once the money ran out, he was no longer willing to tolerate the disrespect (Davis & Clark, 1992, p. 42). As a result of serving the senator, Thurgood earned enough to pay many of the bills he owed to Lincoln. The experience also illustrated the very pragmatic approach Thurgood adopted toward issues of racism and which strategies provided the most effective results in each circumstance. Sometimes the use of restraint proved most effective; at other times, more aggressive action was necessary. This perspective would serve him well in his future career.

With money issues now less of a concern, Thurgood returned to Lincoln for his sophomore year. It began much as his freshman year concluded. Social activities took precedence over academic demands. By his second year, any plans for a premed major and dental school disappeared. He got into a disagreement with his biology professor, which resulted in his failing the class. This grade and his general lack of interest in medicine doomed the plans his mother had for Thurgood following his brother into the health field. He found debates with his friends and debate team members much more interesting. He also enjoyed the socializing that went with it. This led him to join Alpha Phi Alpha, an elite fraternity, and get through its very demanding pledging process. Once he completed pledging, Thurgood thoroughly embraced fraternity life. He enjoyed the camaraderie with his fellow fraternity brothers and the tricks played on rival fraternities.

One set of pranks played on other students almost got him permanently expelled. He and other fraternity brothers decided to shave the heads of underclass students in spite of their protests. The school administration did not condone this and the other acts that Marshall and his companions executed. The school decided to expel them. According to one report, a group of them, too embarrassed to tell their parents, headed to New York with the goal of finding work aboard ships departing from there (Williams, 1998, p. 47). Hoping to have the administration change their mind, Langston Hughes, who was among the culprits, crafted a letter signed by each of them in which they acknowledged their misdeeds and asked for forgiveness. The letter worked. Lincoln rescinded the expulsion and instead fined them $125 and suspended Marshall, Hughes, and others for two weeks. Marshall later said that the experience "got the horsin' around out of my system" (Davis & Clark, 1992, p. 44).

Thurgood now redirected that energy toward other aspects of his college life. He kept his grades up and became one of the leaders of the debate team. While he was at Lincoln, the debate team flourished. They had exhilarating victories over white institutions, including Bates, Bowdoin, and Colby. He also began to engage more directly with issues of race. On campus he participated in a lively debate among the students about the composition of the staff. While it had a predominantly African-American student body, none of the professors at Lincoln was African-American. Bothered by this fact, a group of students began lobbying for the addition of African-American faculty members. They called for a referendum to gauge how the overall student body felt about this issue. A debate among the students followed with strong advocates on both sides of the issue. Marshall sided with the students opposed to adding black staff. They

---

BIRTH OF A NATION FILM, 1915

D. W. Griffin, the leading innovative filmmaker of his era, created the film *Birth of a Nation*. It purported to tell the Southern view of reconstruction, the necessary emergence of the Ku Klux Klan (KKK), and the rise of white supremacy. Griffin based it on an anti–African American book, *The Clansman*, by the segregationist Thomas Dixon Jr. The film negatively portrayed African Americans as illiterate, corrupt, uncouth former slaves, influenced by white Northern carpetbaggers. He also pictured them as lusting after Southern white women, which prompted the rise of the KKK to protect them. Critics widely praised it, with President Woodrow Wilson showing it at the White House and declaring it an accurate representation of the post–Civil War years in the South.

The NAACP protested the film and asked the courts to ban the film as racially inflammatory. Griffin successfully fought back against the efforts of the NAACP. It is estimated that 10 percent of the nation's population saw the film, and it was the most profitable film of its era. The film left a legacy of intensified racial strife, increased lynching, and the rebirth of the KKK.

offered three reasons for their position. First, they felt Lincoln operated well as it was and did not need to change. Second, they worried that an African-American professor might favor the student of one fraternity over another depending on his fraternal allegiance. And finally, they did not think the students would cooperate with a black professor (Williams, 1998, p. 48). The referendum supported the position of Marshall and his friends who did not want African-American faculty added. It was a surprising position for Thurgood to take, given the opposition of his family to any inferences that African Americans were inferior. It also surprised and angered Thurgood's friend, Langston Hughes, who strongly supported integrating the faculty. He and Marshall subsequently had lengthy conversations about this question and other issues about race. Hughes felt the refusal of students to support the idea of having African-American faculty revealed their own sense of inadequacy when compared to whites. When Marshall went to talk to his sociology professor, Robert Labaree, the professor also told him the right fight was to support the creation of an integrated faculty. These conversations caused him to think more deeply about issues of race.

Thurgood's perspective began to shift, in part, because of an incident suffered in the nearby town of Oxford, Pennsylvania. He joined a group of students who decided to attend the movie theater in the town. After paying for their tickets, they decided not to sit in the colored section in the balcony, but to take seats on the main floor in the white section. When the movie usher observed them, he instructed them that they were only to sit in the balcony, not on the main floor. The students pointed out they had paid their money and intended to sit anywhere in the theater. Rather than move, they asked for the return of their money, which the usher refused to do. Angry, the students proceed to cause a disruption by pulling down curtains and breaking the front door of the theater before heading back to campus. Later, they followed up with a series of protests pushing for the desegregation of the theater. Their efforts bore fruit, as the movie house eventually agreed to end having separate colored and white sections. Marshall later marked this activity as the start of his career as a civil rights activist.

His choice of reading material also shaped his new thinking. Thurgood began reading the publications of W.E.B. Du Bois and Carter G. Woodson. Du Bois was then the editor of *The Crisis*, the most important publication of the NAACP. The publication contained a variety of essays, many of which analyzed and criticized the racial environment in the United States. Woodson was the second African American to receive his PhD from Harvard. He highlighted the contributions of African Americans in his publication *The Negro in American History* and in his promotion of Negro History Week to make more people aware of the contributions of African

Americans. Marshall also read the writings of authors of the Harlem Renaissance, including James Weldon Johnson, Langston Hughes, Claude McKay, and Jessie Redmon Fauset. Their writings increased his appreciation for African-American culture and sharpened his thoughts about the place of people of color in the United States.

The evolving nature of his thinking was evident in the new position he adopted in the continuing debate concerning the inclusion of African-American faculty at Lincoln. His new position advocated for the integration of the faculty. Langston Hughes had continued his criticism of the old ways, even writing his senior thesis on the system of including only white faculty at Lincoln. Even Du Bois commented on the referendum in *The Crisis*, astounded that the students voted for segregation. After Hughes graduated, Marshall continued his campaign, and in the fall of 1929, when the school held a second referendum, the students voted to support the addition of African-American faculty. The first professor of color joined the staff the following year.

Thurgood's meeting of Vivian "Buster" Burney as a sophomore further accelerated his maturation process. School administrators encouraged Lincoln students to attend church regularly. Most often, Marshall frequented services at the Cherry Street Memorial Church in Philadelphia. Marshall said they went there because of the good-looking young women who also attended. It was in Philadelphia that Marshall met Vivian. He claimed they first met at an ice cream parlor. Vivian's memory was that they actually met earlier, but Thurgood was so busy debating with other people at the table that he did not notice her. But she certainly noticed him. What's certain is that when Thurgood did finally see her, Vivian grabbed his attention. At the time Vivian was seventeen and a freshman at the University of Pennsylvania in Philadelphia, majoring in education. People described her as having short, wavy hair; thin arms; fair skin; a sparkling smile; and an outgoing personality.

Vivian Burney was born in 1911 in Philadelphia to a middle-class family. Her father operated a catering business for hotels in Philadelphia and for country clubs in the region. She and Marshall dated during his sophomore year, attending movies at the theater he helped integrate in Oxford, Pennsylvania, and enjoying other activities in and around Philadelphia. They grew closer over time and began discussing marriage. According to Marshall, "First, we decided to get married five years after I graduated, then three, then one, and we finally did, just before my last semester" (Davis & Clark, 1992, p. 45). Even before they married, Vivian had a calming impact on Marshall. His campus antics came to an end, and he became more focused on his education. It was not unusual for Vivian to play the role of timekeeper to remind Marshall it was time to bring the evening to a close. The late evenings of playing cards and hanging out with his friends slowly faded to the background as a result.

An unexpected health issue also slowed Marshall's extracurricular activities as well as his graduation schedule. After a weekend trip to Baltimore with friends, they hitched a ride on a truck to return to campus. The truck broke down, and they had to push it to a garage in the town of Rising Sun, Maryland. While they waited for the mechanic to repair the truck, the young men stood outside the garage talking. When the local sheriff observed them, he first asked the mechanic how long the repairs would take, adding that they better be completed before five that evening. He did not want the students in his town after sundown. Rising Sun, in the eyes of the sheriff, was what was called a "sundown town." This meant local officials actively discouraged African Americans or other people they disliked from residing in or staying there for extended periods of time and especially after dark. The mechanic completed the repair before sundown, and the group boarded the truck for the ride home. Having wandered off, Marshall had to race after the truck or risk getting left behind. Although the driver slowed to allow him to jump in the back of the truck, getting aboard did not go smoothly. Marshall got one leg on, but caught one of his testicles in the gate of the truck, injuring himself. It was a very serious and painful wound. It was serious enough that the local doctor told them Marshall needed to go directly to a hospital in Baltimore to get the proper treatment. According to Marshall, the truck ride to Baltimore was extremely painful.

The accident resulted in the loss of one of Marshall's testicles. The recovery process prevented him from completing that spring semester at Lincoln. Marshall did not return until the fall semester of 1928, which put him a semester behind his classmates. This injury and his romance with Buster caused him to settle down and take his academic work more seriously.

The maturation process continued with his marriage to Vivian at the start of his senior year in 1929. Not everyone thought it was a good idea. Though his mother approved of Vivian, she thought they were too young to marry and should wait until Thurgood graduated. Vivian's parents agreed. On the other hand, Uncle Fearless approved of Buster but worried that marrying Thurgood would not benefit her. When she and her parents came to Baltimore to meet Thurgood's family, Fearless took Vivian aside and warned her about Thurgood. He told her, "You ought to beware of Thurgood. He always was a bum, he is a bum, and he always will be a bum" (Rowan, 1993, p. 45).

Vivian, who thought Thurgood had admirable qualities, did not take Fearless's advice. They loved each other and wanted to get married as soon as they could. The couple initially agreed to hold off marrying until

Thurgood graduated college. Because of his accident, Marshall was a semester behind Vivian, which postponed their marriage until 1930. This initial agreement did not hold up, and the pair married in 1929 before the start of Thurgood's senior year. They married in the First African Baptist Church, one of the oldest African-American churches in Philadelphia. The reception was held at Vivian's parents' home.

For the fall semester, Thurgood returned to Lincoln while Vivian lived with his parents in Baltimore. Marshall's schoolwork took higher priority during his senior year, and his grades improved. He graduated with honors in June 1930 with his bride and parents observing the ceremony from the front row. The service brought to fruition Norma's desire to have her son graduate from college. But her dream of Thurgood following his brother's career in medicine and becoming a dentist was no longer possible.

After graduation, Thurgood interviewed for a position at a New York bank, which they subsequently offered to him. He turned it down, though, because it paid him less than he could make as a waiter at the Gibson Island Club, where he worked previously. He did not intend to work there permanently but sought to save enough money to continue on to graduate school. Marshall wanted to be a lawyer. In the meantime, his parents offered to let Thurgood and Vivian live with them so they could save money. It was likely the only feasible way to generate enough funds to pay for law school.

Thurgood's desire to attend law school pleased his family and especially his mother. They all understood that his position waiting at Gibson Island had short-term utility. He had a wife to support, and waiting tables was the most likely way to acquire enough money for law school. The family could not help much, as Aubrey's bills for Howard medical school strained what resources they had.

Given their finances, the best choice for Marshall was the law school at the University of Maryland. As a resident of Maryland, Marshal's tuition would be less expensive than other out-of-state programs. The school was not very far from his parent's home. It was a short trolley ride to Redwood Street, the location of the law school campus. Plus, the training available there would provide good contacts and preparation for setting up practice in his hometown of Baltimore. The challenge was that the Maryland law school had stopped accepting African-American applicants many years earlier and did not seem likely to make an exception for Marshall. He explored possible pathways into the school by visiting a variety of African-American lawyers in Baltimore to see what advice they could offer. None of them had any encouraging suggestions. The law school steadfastly refused to admit African-American applicants.

The discouraging feedback he received sorely disappointed Marshall and angered him that the segregation policies of the law school interfered with his career plans. If he planned to go to law school, he would have to attend Howard University in Washington, DC. This option did not excite Marshall, as the Howard Law School had a very poor reputation. It was a program that one attended when you had no other choice.

Opening in 1869, the Howard Law School began as a part-time program in the evening. While it produced some notable graduates over the years, the program was not accredited by the American Bar Association or the Association of American Law Schools, who decided whether a law program met their standards. Without their approval, the program and its graduates were not considered of high-enough quality. The poor law library, inadequate classroom space, and minimal staffing put Howard's program in a vulnerable position. In a study of law schools, the highly respected Carnegie Foundation for the Advancement of Teaching described Howard Law School as without the resources necessary to provide quality legal training. Part of the challenge was lack of funding from Congress and neglect by previous Howard administrators.

The arrival of a new president of Howard in 1926 brought fresh energy to the campus. In Dr. Mordechai Johnson (1890–1976), Howard had its first African-American president. He was thirty-six years old and a Baptist minister, with degrees from several colleges and universities, including Atlanta Baptist College (now Morehouse College) and Harvard University Divinity School. He came to Howard after serving as a professor of economics and history at Morehouse. When he arrived, only the medical school and the dental program had accreditation. Johnson immediately set out to upgrade other programs at Howard and especially the law school. He understood the important role Howard played in the education of African-American students denied opportunities at other schools. He sought to do this by bringing major changes to the university. He aggressively lobbied Congress for additional appropriations for the school, discharged teachers who did not meet his strict academic standards, and recruited highly trained African-American scholars as faculty. He saw the law school as especially needing improvement and rapidly took steps to make it a source of pride rather than embarrassment.

To improve the law school, Johnson recruited Charles Hamilton Houston (1895–1950). Born and raised in Washington, DC, Charles was the son of Mary Hamilton, a hairdresser, and William Houston, a graduate of Howard Law School who had distinguished himself as a lawyer after graduating. As a couple, they took pride in their heritage and imbued in their son that same pride and repugnance to racial discrimination. His parents had high expectations for Charles, and after graduating from high school at the age of fifteen, he matriculated to Amherst College after turning down a scholarship to the University of Pittsburgh. He was the sole African American in his class. By his senior year, he had done well enough to win election to Phi Beta Kappa, an organization recognizing academic excellence, and was one of the commencement speakers at his graduation. After graduation, he taught English at Howard University until the United States entered World War I. Then he, along with other college-educated African Americans, lobbied the War Department to create a training camp for African-American officers. Bowing to public pressure, the War Department reluctantly set up a facility in Des Moines, Iowa. His experience there and abroad with the U.S. Army left him disillusioned by the discrimination he and others faced. Though he had no legal training, Houston represented several African-American soldiers falsely accused of various crimes. The prejudice of army officers and the mistreatment of soldiers left a strong impression on him.

Houston left the army with a desire to go to law school as a way to protect the rights often denied African Americans when using the legal system. In consultation with his parents, Charles applied to Harvard and gained admittance for the fall of 1919. There he excelled, becoming the first African American elected to the editorial board of the *Harvard Law Review*, one of the most prestigious journals focused on law scholarship in the country. It was an honor given only to the best students. After receiving his law degree, Houston won scholarships that allowed him to obtain his doctorate as well as travel to Spain to study civil law. While there, he had a chance for additional travel, and one of his trips was to northern Africa, which he found emotional. He called visiting there "a happy privilege" (McNeil, 1984, p. 55). He returned home with plans to make a difference.

After passing the bar exam allowed him to practice in the District of Columbia, Houston worked with his father in their firm, Houston & Houston. That same year, he also accepted a position teaching at Howard's law school. It was part of Howard's effort to upgrade the standing of the school and move it toward accreditation. From the very beginning, Houston expected a lot of his students. He believed that if they were properly trained, they could become first-rate lawyers, and he worked them with that standard in mind. His efforts caught the attention of President Johnson, and when the law school dean left, Houston became the resident vice dean in charge of a new three-year day law school and the law library. Houston brought to the job the belief that Howard had a special mission with regard to the training of lawyers. Since Howard produced 25 percent of the African-American lawyers in the United States, Houston believed these lawyers must serve the African-American community. They were social engineers tasked with guiding and protecting the advancement of the race. To accomplish this mission, they needed expert training to enable them to compete with lawyers trained at other law schools and win the cases they oversaw. This also would improve Howard's academic standing and move them along the path to accreditation. The problem, however, became that as the day school increased in enrollment and importance, the night school shrank.

The issue that faced both Houston and President Johnson was that the path to accreditations for Howard lay through the promotion of the day school. It also meant ending the long and utilitarian tradition of the night school. Even with its problems, the night school had served as a vehicle for economic advancement for many men with families and day jobs who could only go to school in the evening. It was how William Houston, Charles's father, had gotten his law degree. Despite this tradition, in 1930, the Howard trustees voted to abolish the evening school and directed resources to the day school. They also kept on Houston as the vice dean for the day school. This decision met with criticism from some alumni, who decried the "Harvardization" of the law school, but Houston and President Johnson pushed forward with their plan to improve the quality of the program and the students it trained. This was the state of affairs greeting Thurgood Marshall when he began classes at Howard in 1930.

2

Thurgood Marshall Becomes a Social Engineer

Even with both Thurgood and Vivian working steadily after his graduation from Lincoln, Marshall did not have enough money to pay his tuition for Howard. Consequently, Marshall thought he might have to delay attending Howard for a year. But Naomi had different ideas. She did not want her son to delay his education. She pawned her engagement and wedding rings to give him the additional money he needed. While he obtained enough money for tuition, Marshall could not afford to live at Howard or in Washington, DC. Instead he commuted each day, rising at five in the morning for the train ride to the district and the walk from Union Station to the law school building. After class, he returned home to various jobs: waiting tables, working as a bellhop, and helping at a local bakery. Studying his law books had to wait until later in the evening. The next day, he repeated the routine. The schedule proved hard on Thurgood physically, as he lost forty pounds during his first year studying law. According to Marshall, "I heard law books were to dig in so I dug deep . . . . I was at it twenty hours a day, seven days a week" (Davis & Clark, 1992, p. 48).

The demanding expectations Charles Houston had for his students motivated Marshall. Marshall's class represented the first year Howard transitioned to a full-time day law school and the closure of the night school. Houston's goal was to train excellent students and to attain accreditation for the law school. The first day of class Houston set the tone. He told the new students to "to look at the man on your right and look at the man on your left, and bear in mind that two of you won't be here next year" (Williams, 1998, p. 53). Marshall took Houston's words seriously and put aside the fun-loving Lincoln University undergraduate for a serious student of law. For the first time in his life, according to Marshall, he really studied (Kennedy, 1997, p. 415).

If he hoped to succeed, Marshall had little choice. Houston set up a rigorous program for the day school. He assembled an impressive faculty, which included Harvard Law School graduate and later the first African-American federal judge, William Hastie. Houston expected maximum effort from his students and precision in their work. To reinforce this point, he had a law clerk make a presentation to the class in which he stated he could always tell the difference between a brief created by an African-American lawyer and a white lawyer by the quality of the writing and argument. Houston drilled into the students that they had to be better than the white lawyers whom they might face in the courtroom. No one would take pity on them because they were African-American. To reinforce the necessity of putting in extra effort, Houston installed a rule called "the cutback." This option allowed a professor to deduct five points from a student grade arbitrarily. It made the students work extra hard to ensure they passed the assignment or attained the grades they desired. Marshall responded by reading and taking copious notes while riding the train in the morning and in the evening. After work, he typed his notes up in preparation for the following day. His efforts paid off, as he was the top student after his first year. His work in legal bibliography earned him the Callaghan Prize for obtaining the highest grade in the class.

As the top student, Marshall received financial support for his second year from Howard. He became the student assistant in the law library. It paid for one-half of his tuition and provided him with more time to study and use of the casebooks located there. He used the study time wisely and continued to thrive as a student. In recognition of his hard work and grades, his fellow students elected him to the Court of Peers. This was a special honor, as the task of the court was to hear legal arguments presented by other students and judge their quality. Eventually, they promoted him to the position of chief justice of the court. His work as a student assistant also brought him into daily contact with Houston, who could be abrupt and demanding. Some of the students called him "Iron Pants" or "Cement Pants" because of his unbending expectations of his students. According to Houston, as African-American lawyers, they had a responsibility to be "social engineers" working against the inequities of society and not simply getting a law degree so they could earn a good living. They had to give something back to their community (Rowan, 1993, p. 47). Rigorous training was the pathway to reaching that goal, which Houston intended to provide. But, at the same time, he cared a lot about his students and their success. The other side of Houston, according to Marshall, was a compassionate man whose door was always open and who treated you fairly (Davis & Clark, 1992, p. 55). Thurgood found in Houston a mentor who molded him into a first-rate lawyer.

Houston exposed his students to many of the best legal minds of the time. They included professors from Harvard such as Felix Frankfurter, later a Supreme Court Justice, as well as Clarence Darrow. As a civil rights lawyer, Darrow's most noteworthy legal victory was the 1925 *Scopes* trial in Tennessee. There he defended a high school teacher accused of breaking state law by presenting the Darwinian theory of evolution in his classroom. The Howard students also attended sessions of the Supreme Court to observe its workings and to listen to the presentations of lawyers to the justices. For Marshall, the most impressive of these lawyers was John W. Davis of West Virginia. Davis had run for president in 1924, but even more importantly, was famous for the powerful arguments he made before the Supreme Court. Many thought of him as the best attorney in the United States.

The students also made visits to the U.S. Attorney's Office and the Federal Bureau of Investigation as well as local police stations, courts, jails, and law firms. Houston wanted them to see the people they might represent and what happened to them after their trials, especially when they were found guilty. As lawyers, the future of their clients would depend upon the quality of their preparation and presentations in the courtroom. Houston did not want them to forget that point. The lives of the people they represented depended upon the outcome of their cases.

As a result of their visits and reviews of local statutes, the students made an important discovery. The Code of the District of Columbia created by Congress did not include civil rights legislation. This omission meant that technically African-American district residents did not have the legal right to vote. With this discovery, the students began lobbying Congress to correct this omission. Their efforts resulted in Congress passing legislation that rectified this gap in the original district codes. Their discovery and subsequent lobbying gave the students and Marshall a hands-on opportunity to understand Houston's philosophy about the social impact lawyers could have.

Houston further illustrated this concept for Marshall in his second year, when he allowed Thurgood to work on a North Carolina school case with Howard faculty member and brilliant lawyer William Hastie. Thomas R. Hocutt had been denied admission to the pharmacy school of the University of North Carolina because of his race. Hocutt believed this violated his right to equal protection under the Fourteenth Amendment and sued. His suit against the university was the first legal action to desegregate higher education in the South. He lost his first suit brought against the university but hoped to win on application to the North Carolina Appeals Court. Given the similarity of the position of the North Carolina Pharmacy School to that of the University of Maryland Law School, this case must have resonated with Marshall. To Hastie and Marshall's disappointment, they lost their appeal, as North Carolina University lawyers contended Hocutt was poorly trained and not qualified. They also argued Hocutt only brought the case at the urging of outside agitators trying to force integration on the school. The appeals court agreed based on a technicality, notwithstanding what many described as a brilliant argument by Hastie. The court case, despite the loss, was an important experience and lesson for Marshall. While losing the suit proved disappointing, Howard University did receive good news on another front that year, when the law school received accreditation from the American Bar Association. This was an important milestone in the long-term goals of both Houston and Howard president Mordecai Johnson.

Houston provided Marshall additional litigation experience during his third year at Howard. The NAACP's legal arm at that time often turned to Houston and Howard's Law School for support on key civil rights cases. Local lawyers usually litigated the cases but looked to the NAACP and Howard for help in formulating their arguments. Periodically, Houston or

---

FOUNDING OF THE NATIONAL ASSOCIATION FOR THE ADVANCEMENT OF COLORED PEOPLE, 1909

In August 1908, the worst riot in a Northern city in fifty years took place in Springfield, Illinois. The violence heavily damaged African-American homes and businesses. Eight African Americans were killed and thousands more driven from the city. Shaken by Springfield's racial violence, an interracial group gathered in New York early in 1909 to discuss the hostility and discrimination directed toward African Americans. A new organization, the National Association for the Advancement of Colored People (NAACP) emerged from that meeting. Its charter committed to advancing "the interests of colored citizens" by demanding equal rights and ending racial prejudice. Their main efforts focused on voting rights, legal justice, access to better educational opportunities, and improved employment prospects.

The NAACP became the leading national organization focused on improving conditions for African Americans. They employed legal challenges in the courts, peaceful protests, and lobbying as their main tactics. The early issues on which they focused included voting discrimination, passage of an antilynching law, and halting the showing of the film Birth of a Nation. The stature and influence of the organization steadily increased as the century progressed.

Hastie took a more direct role in higher-profile cases. The trial of George Crawford in Loudoun County, Virginia, was one of those high-profile lawsuits.

George Crawford stood accused of the murder of a prominent Virginia woman, Agnes Boeing Ilsley, and her maid, Mina Buckner. Virginia extradited him for trial from Boston after several appeals that eventually reached the Supreme Court, which refused to overturn a lower court order sending Crawford back to Virginia. Walter White, the executive secretary of the NAACP, asked Houston to handle the case in an effort to save Crawford's life. Houston assembled an all–African American team to litigate the case and asked Marshall, his favorite student, to assist in the preparation process. They hoped to undercut Virginia's case by highlighting Loudoun County's tradition of excluding African Americans from the jury pool. They believed this policy of exclusion denied Crawford equal protection under the law as guaranteed by the Fourteenth Amendment of the U.S. Constitution. The team did not expect to win the case in Virginia but hoped to win on appeal before the Supreme Court. The *Crawford* case was the first time the NAACP assembled an all–African American legal team to handle a lawsuit.

Thurgood Marshall's role was to research the many issues involved in the case for the team. The NAACP legal team hoped to strike a blow to the legal system in Virginia and other states that systematically excluded African Americans from jury duty, thus depriving African-American defendants of a trial by a jury of their peers. They also sought to throw out Crawford's confession, challenging its validity on the grounds that it had been coerced by the authorities. Marshall also had the opportunity to travel to New York to join in the debates over strategy. He did so energetically, unafraid to question the ideas of Houston and other members of the team, according to Walter White, who also joined the sessions. Although Marshall did not join the team when it traveled to Virginia for the case, his input proved valuable.

Another lesson Marshall learned in the course of the trial was the danger connected to threatening long-standing racial traditions and mores. The trial team could not stay in Loudoun County, as no hotel would accommodate them because of their race. Likewise, African-American residents refused to house them because of threats from local whites against anyone helping the legal team. White residents resented the presence of the African-American lawyers who sharply questioned their local officials and did not defer to them in the way locals thought they should. As a result, the team had to travel eighty miles each day from Howard to defend Crawford. When the trial ended, state police guarded the team to ensure they safely left Loudoun County.

In the end, the local jury found Crawford guilty of first-degree murder. But, unexpectedly, instead of asking for the death penalty (the sentence usually recommended for African-American defendants in murder cases), the jury recommended life imprisonment. While naturally disappointed by the guilty verdict, both the defense team and Crawford found solace in the life sentence. As Marshall later noted, "If you get a life sentence for a Negro charged with killing a white person in Virginia, you've won . . . because normally they were hanging them" (Williams, 1998, p. 59). It was a small victory in a larger effort to gain fairer treatment of African Americans in the courts.

Marshall did not neglect his classroom work while providing support for the Crawford team. He had found his calling and enjoyed the challenges of preparing to become a lawyer and a "social engineer." His graduation in June 1933 was a major accomplishment. Of the thirty-six students who began with Marshall, only six survived the three years under Houston's demanding regime. Marshall finished at the head of that graduating class. His wife and family attended the ceremony, proud that all their aspirations for him had been fulfilled. He then had to decide what he would do next with his training.

One option was to accept an opportunity to go to Harvard and follow in the footsteps of Charles Houston. Dean Roscoe Pound of Harvard, who met Marshall while speaking at Howard, offered Thurgood a scholarship to obtain an advanced law degree. The scholarship provided him with a stipend and a chance to earn his doctorate in law. He and Vivian could move to Boston and have enough extra money to live comfortably. But Marshall decided to turn it down. His time at Howard under Houston infused him with the desire to begin his own practice and apply the skills he had acquired working with Houston and the Howard faculty. He might not make as much money, but he might make a difference in the lives of the people he represented. To do this, he first had to apply for, study for, and pass the Maryland bar examination. He also wanted to contribute to the household expenses of his parents' home where he and Vivian still lived. After graduation, he began the summer by returning to work as a waiter back at the Gibson Island Club. Since no white law firm in Baltimore hired African-American associates and black firms primarily were one-man operations, returning to Gibson Island provided Marshall with the money and the time he needed to prepare for the bar exam. It was important in the short term to recognize the need to earn what he could as a waiter to help his family. He could stop waiting tables once he passed the bar and began the work he hoped to accomplish as a Charles Houston–trained lawyer.

If Marshall had any doubts about the importance of that work, Houston resolved them by asking Marshall to join him on a tour of African-American schools in the South on behalf of the NAACP. The tour was part of the effort by the NAACP to construct a strategy to undermine

---

BALTIMORE AFRO-AMERICAN

Founded in 1892, the *Baltimore Afro-American* was one of the many important and influential twentieth-century African-American newspapers. At the height of its influence, it was the most widely circulated African-American newspaper in the country, with editions printed in Baltimore; Washington, DC; Philadelphia; Richmond; and Newark. The publishers offered an alternative perspective to that of mainstream newspapers on news inside and outside the African-American community. The *Baltimore Afro-American* was owned and operated by the Murphy family and consistently campaigned for racial and economic equality for African Americans. The Murphy family also philosophically and financially supported efforts to legally challenge or protest discriminatory public policies. They worked with Thurgood Marshall and the NAACP to bring about the acceptance of Donald Murray to the previously segregated University of Maryland Law School. They also supported economic boycotts in Baltimore to demand jobs in businesses where African Americans were a major clientele. Papers like the *Baltimore Afro-American* were critical organs for ensuring African Americans were informed about key issues and encouraged to demand their rights as American citizens.

---

segregation. Several years earlier they received a one hundred thousand-dollar grant from the American Fund for Public Service, or Garland Fund, which supported progressive social and economic causes. Their instructions were to use the funds "to secure for Negroes in this country a fuller and more practical enjoyment of the rights and privileges and immunities theoretically guaranteed them by the Constitution of the United States." The grant gave the NAACP the flexibility to set aside time to consider long-term strategies as they continued to respond to immediate crises among their constituents (Davis & Clark, 1992, pp. 63–64). There were various schools of thought within the organization about the best path to follow, but in the end, the course that won out was to pursue a legal attack on segregation. This was the strategy advocated by Arthur Spingarn, chief lawyer for the NAACP, and Charles Houston, among others.

The man selected to study this concept and recommend a litigation strategy was Nathan Ross Margold. Margold knew Houston from Harvard and was highly recommended by Felix Frankfurter, who was a mentor to both Houston and Margold. Nathan Margold wrote a 218-page report crafting a plan for attacking segregated public education in the South. The heart of the plan was to press for strict application of the "separate but equal" decree of the Supreme Court in the 1896 *Plessy v. Ferguson* case. In the *Plessy* case, the court ruled segregation constitutional as long as the facilities provided were separate *and* equal. However, in the years that followed the ruling, facilities provided for African Americans rarely equaled those provided for whites. Margold argued that by forcing Southern governments to provide equal educational facilities for African-American students, the NAACP would cost Southern educational systems thousands of dollars they did not want to spend or could not afford. In the end, desegregation, he believed, would prove more cost effective than segregation for the South. Not long after finishing his report, Margold accepted a solicitor position in the Department of the Interior in the Roosevelt administration. The task of implementing his ideas eventually fell on his friend Charles Houston.

Before accepting a position at the NAACP, Houston decided to examine the issues firsthand by traveling to the South to observe educational facilities provided for African-American students. He asked Thurgood Marshall to accompany him on this fact-finding trip during the summer of 1933. Their task was to document the significant differences between resources provided for white and black schoolchildren. The trip took them from Washington, DC, to New Orleans by way of South Carolina, Georgia, Alabama, and Mississippi. Along the way they stayed with African-American families and friends of Houston's, or they slept in Houston's automobile. They carried fruit and other food in the car in order to tide them over between meals at homes or restaurants that would accommodate them.

The trip carried them down back roads in the South where they took pictures and film of the shocking educational conditions for African-American children. They also interviewed parents and students to further document the depressing conditions of their schools. The men accepted this assignment at great personal risk. Two African-American men traveling in a car, asking questions about segregation, and taking photographs was unacceptable in the eyes of many white Southerners. The danger of lynching, still a frequent occurrence in the South in the 1930s, was ever present.

The conditions faced by the African-American schoolchildren they observed stunned both Houston and Marshall. They recorded their findings through photographs and notes typed in the back seat of Houston's car. One example they noted was the irony of an abandoned white school in one county located within a mile of a black school. African-American students there sat crowded together on benches, with "no desks, no chairs, just one old piece of blackboard" (James, 2010, p. 58). The abandoned white school building contained desks and other unused equipment, which school officials refused to allow the black students to use. In addition, many African-American schools were required by law to have shorter school years so that the children could help with the crops. For white officials, the labor of African-American children was more important than their education.

Even though both Houston and Marshall were Southern-born and edu-cated, they were not prepared for what they saw in the rural areas of the South. The poverty and educational conditions were unimaginable. Mar-shall would go on to describe an encounter with a young boy outside a school as Marshall sat eating an orange. The boy stood staring at Mar-shall's orange until Marshall offered him one of his own. The boy had never seen an orange before and did not know how to eat it. Rather than removing the skin, he bit right into the orange peel. For Marshall, this encounter spoke volumes about the deprived educational and economic conditions under which the children they observed struggled. Their report would testify to the "separate and unequal" educational conditions they found. Their travels provided a foundation for Margold's legal strategy of attacking educational segregation that would be followed by the NAACP in the years to come.

But before he could mount any legal assaults, Thurgood Marshall first had to pass the Maryland bar examination. The training he received from Howard law school and the studying he conducted before taking the exam paid off. Marshall passed the bar on his first try. Marshall would later cor-rect a statement in the *Baltimore Afro-American*, which implied he passed the exam with flying colors. He pointed out "it was about one point above the passing mark of 210" (Davis & Clark, 1992, p. 69). But, however nar-rowly, he had passed, and he now had the credentials to practice law in Maryland. At the time Marshall took the bar exam, Maryland credentialed only two new African-American lawyers per year. He had joined a very small cadre of individuals. Of the more than twenty-seven hundred law-yers practicing in Maryland, only thirty-three of them were African-American (Gibson, 2012, p. 125).

The next challenge would be to launch his practice and start acquiring clients—a difficult proposition in the midst of the Great Depression. For suggestions, he talked with African-American lawyers in Baltimore and, in particular, with Warner McGuinn, a graduate of Yale Law School. McGuinn could not hire Marshall but encouraged him to open an office near his and that of another African-American lawyer, William Alfred Hughes Jr. The three of them decided to rent four rooms together on the top floor of the Phoenix Building, becoming the first African-American lawyers to rent in that part of Baltimore. Marshall occupied one office and gained access to a waiting room for clients. This arrangement also put him in a position to get advice when needed from McGuinn and Hughes, which proved invaluable.

The office was a small, sparsely furnished space on East Redwood Street near the downtown section of the city. The University of Maryland Law School was not very far from where Marshall began his practice. The fact that they would not accept him still aggravated Marshall, but he now had the satisfaction of joining the ranks of attorneys despite Maryland's intransigence regarding the acceptance of African-American law students. But earning a living as an African-American lawyer was difficult. The economic crash of the Great Depression hit black Baltimore very hard. Two-fifths of African Americans in the city needed help from relief agencies to survive. The mainly lower-paying, unskilled positions previously gained in the local steel and shipbuilding industries had evaporated, which meant few people had money to pay lawyers (Farrar, 1998, p. 89). Moreover, the unemployment rate for African Americans was twice that of white residents. Those African Americans who could afford lawyers often turned to white lawyers instead of African-American attorneys, assuming that the biases of the court system and the networks in which white lawyers circulated greatly increased their likelihood of success. Consequently, Marshall struggled to earn money in his practice. In his first year practicing law, he claimed that he lost more than three thousand dollars.

To create a cash flow, Marshall happily accepted any case that appeared at his door no matter how small. But even small cases appeared only sporadically. Even with the help of local judges and other lawyers who sometimes referred people to him, Marshall struggled to find clients. This state of affairs made keeping the office open an ongoing challenge, to the degree that Marshall and his secretary alternated bringing lunch to the office for each other. He'd bring leftovers one day, and she'd bring sandwiches the next. A check for services rendered was cause for celebration, with the two of them and their spouses splurging on a home-cooked steak dinner. Business was so slow that when his mother and wife came to see the office, Norma felt it was so sparse that she went home and took the rug from her floor and brought it to Thurgood's office to improve the impression it made. A lack of clients also forced Marshall to accept a position as a clerk in Maryland's Bureau of Communicable Diseases in order to better contribute money to his family. He and Vivian still lived with his parents and his brother's family, as they could not afford a place of their own.

One positive aspect of the slow pace of his legal career in Baltimore was that it allowed him to accompany Charles Houston on another trip investigating educational conditions in the South. This time they traveled to Virginia, Missouri, Tennessee, and Kentucky. It was an opportunity for Marshall to bond more closely with Houston as they journeyed through these states recording their findings for the NAACP. They were reminded of the possible dangers they faced on their mission when in Mississippi the NAACP state president provided an armed escort to travel with them. He understood the violent reaction white residents might have to the task of these two African-American outsiders, and he wanted to ensure the safe completion of their mission.

THE NIAGARA MOVEMENT, 1905

Unhappy with the increasing mistreatment of African Americans, a group of twenty-nine men met in Niagara Falls in Ontario, Canada, to form a new protest organization. Led by scholar activist W.E.B. Du Bois and newspaper editor Monroe Trotter, the group opposed the ideas of Booker T. Washington, the president of Tuskegee Institute. A decade earlier, Washington had given his "Atlanta Compromise" speech, in which he spoke against political and social activism by African Americans. The Niagara Movement members strongly disagreed with Washington's philosophy of accommodating discrimination and waiting patiently for better treatment. The organization's "Declaration of Principles" demanded immediate equal rights for African Americans. They also insisted on an end to segregation, the opportunity to vote, and access to economic opportunity.

The organization eventually grew to over 170 members. Unfortunately, the group did not have the impact it hoped, as Washington used his influence to stifle their efforts. In 1908, key leaders left the Niagara Movement to become a part of the interracial National Association for the Advancement of Colored People (NAACP), which had greater access to finances and the media. The Niagara Movement members, however, brought their ideals with them, and they became an important influence on the goals of the NAACP.

While traveling together, Houston shared with Marshall his strong belief that integration was the key mechanism to ensure African-American children received an education equal to their white counterparts. He hoped it would provide a pathway to ending racism in the country as black and white children attended school together, got to know one another, and recognized what they had in common. He hoped this intermixing would undercut racial stereotyping and create a generation not poisoned with the biases of the previous generation. These discussions made a strong impression on Marshall, and their travels provided the NAACP with valuable information it would use in the future.

The trip with Houston served to further reinforce Marshall's resolve to embrace the philosophy of his mentor and become one of the African-American lawyers "dedicated to fighting for equal rights under the Constitution in the courts" (Tushnet, 1994, p. 433). He did this by taking on cases for the Baltimore NAACP and other organizations. The Baltimore branch that formed in 1912 was one of the oldest local NAACP organizations. Among the most active NAACP branches in the country, the Baltimore group fought vigorously against disfranchisement and housing segregation. Unfortunately, by the early 1930s, it had lost steam. The election of Lillie Mae Carroll Jackson as president of the Baltimore chapter in 1935 reversed its decline. Prior to accepting that role, she had partnered with her daughter, Juanita Jackson, to form the City Wide Youth Forum in the city. Directed toward providing regular gatherings for African-American youth in Baltimore, the forum hosted nationally known speakers, including W.E.B. Du Bois, Walter White, and Charles Houston. It also sought to "create opportunities for employment for efficient and qualified young people." In support of this last goal, in coalition with the Baltimore Urban League, they brought about the hiring of sixteen African-American social workers by the Baltimore Emergency Relief Commission (Franklin & McNeil, 1995, pp. 67–69).

The forum also joined the effort to launch a "Buy Where You Can Work" campaign. Kiowa Costonie, a local activist and an early client of Marshall, organized the first campaign. Working the youth forum alongside two women's organizations, the Opportunity Makers Club (presided over by Vivian Marshall) and the Housewives League, Costonie focused his attention on one store in particular. The Great Atlantic & Pacific (A&P) grocery store chain had never hired African-American workers. They followed this policy despite the fact that in some stores African Americans represented the majority of their customers. When discussion with management proved fruitless, forum members supported by the African-American community launched a boycott of those stores. They also created picket lines and spread the news of their actions through the *Baltimore Afro-American*. The effort proved effective, as revenue at the stores measurably decreased. Forty churches supported the effort, and more than five hundred people picketed the A&P stores to make their point. The loss of revenue quickly convinced the store managers to alter their policy. By the end of the boycott, they had hired thirty-eight young men as part-time and full-time clerks.

Buoyed by their success, the group turned its attention to white merchants located along the 1700 block of Pennsylvania Avenue in Baltimore. The businesses there depended heavily upon African-American customers, but they too refused to hire African-American employees. The coalition targeted these stores for their next attack. Thurgood played an important role in these efforts. He provided legal advice and worked with the local police commissioner in planning the picketing so as to minimize arrests. The efforts on Pennsylvania Avenue did not go as well as the previous efforts. Initially, the coalition tried to negotiate with the owners, but they refused to cooperate. The coalition then began picketing the stores. After twelve days, the store owners, faced with a 60 percent drop in their sales, took the picketers to court, declaring they illegally disrupted their businesses. The merchants also claimed the coalition harassed their customers and wanted them to fire all their white employees. Marshall, who attended every day of the picketing to ensure they obeyed the law, testified in rebuttal to the charges of the merchants. The judge conducting the trial agreed with the merchants, ruling the picketing illegal and the picketers as agitators (Moreno, 1999, pp. 32–33). Although the coalition did not attain all its goals, many merchants did change their policies with regard to hiring African Americans. The campaign energized Marshall, who threw himself into the effort. As a result, his commitment to civil rights work increased even more and was noticeable to his family. As his cousin Charles Burns observed, "I think that's when he really got charged up in the area of civil rights. That's the first time I knew where he got physically or actively involved" (Gibson, 2012, p. 165).

His participation in the "Buy Where You Can Work" campaign led to Marshall working on other civil rights cases in Baltimore and other parts of Maryland. His efforts led to increased recognition for his skills, both locally and nationally. Three cases in particular played an important role in bolstering his reputation. The first involved the tragic death of Kater Stevens. A resident of Washington, DC, Stevens had a minor accident, hitting the car of a white woman while out driving with his wife in Maryland. The police arrived and arrested him for reckless driving and intoxication. They then transported him to a justice of the peace, who decided to hold him without bond. They told Stevens's wife to go home. She never saw him alive again. According to the officer transporting him to the county jail, Stevens died accidentally. The officer, Charles Flory, reported that Stevens jumped out of the car at a traffic light and began running away. While chasing him, Flory said he tripped and accidently shot Steven in the back.

A white witness to the shooting offered a different story. He said Flory chased Stevens into an alley, firing three shots. As Stevens walked back out of the alley, Flory shot once more, hitting Stevens. From the perspective of the witness, Flory shot Stevens in cold blood. In light of this testimony, Stevens's wife Mildred retained attorney Belford V. Lawson, another graduate of Howard Law School, in order to sue. Lawson had an independent autopsy performed on Stevens, which contradicted Flory's story. He then sought to have Flory held accountable for his actions. Not surprisingly, the coroner in Prince George's County, Maryland, where the incident took place, cleared Flory. Angry African-American residents of the county held a meeting in which they pushed for further legal action on behalf of the widow. Lawson sought help from the NAACP, and the New York office asked Thurgood Marshall to look into the matter to see if they should get involved. Marshall assessed the situation and decided to join Lawson on behalf of the NAACP.

One of the first steps taken by Marshall was to discuss the case with a local judge and the county prosecutor. From his work in Baltimore, Marshall understood the value of developing a relationship with local officials to get the best possible outcome for his case. He found the conversations informative and useful as the case moved forward. Eventually, Prince George's County law officials agreed to hold a grand jury hearing to determine whether Flory should stand trial. After reviewing the evidence, the grand jury voted to indict Flory for manslaughter. The trial took place in May 1935, ten months after Stevens's death. Neither Marshall nor Lawson was allowed to directly participate in the trial, but the local prosecutor did allow them to join him at his trial table. In presenting his argument, he used a great deal of material Marshall had prepared for the case. Their presence as African-American lawyers working with the prosecutor was a first for the county. The outcome of the trial was disappointing, as the jury, including one black man, found Flory not guilty.

Marshall and Lawson then initiated a civil case of wrongful death against Flory. Despite a key witness not arriving in time, the lawyers convinced the jury to find in favor of Mrs. Stevens. They awarded her the sum of twelve hundred dollars, a sizeable sum in 1935. Unfortunately, Flory did not have the money to pay the award, so the verdict was only a moral victory. The case further cemented Marshall, in the assessment of NAACP officials, as a resourceful and dependable lawyer they could turn to for other cases.

In Baltimore, the local branch of the NAACP under the leadership of Lillie Mae Jackson had already begun turning to Marshall when they needed legal advice or help with their activities. During the "Buy Where You Can Work" campaign Marshall worked tirelessly to get local citizens behind the campaign. He went to the poorest neighborhoods to talk and engage with the residents. His card-playing skills from college, his ability to tell a good story, and the logic of his ideas made him a respected individual in those communities (Davis & Clark, 1992, p. 75). His efforts not only developed support for the boycott but also helped increase the membership of the Baltimore NAACP. Lillie Jackson appreciated Marshall's skills and support, as she sought to mount campaigns for the benefit of Baltimore African Americans. She turned to him more and more and came to think of him as her lawyer, although she rarely paid him for his services. John and Carl Murphy, the publishers of the *Baltimore Afro-American*, used the paper, which published weekly not only in Baltimore but also in Washington, Philadelphia, North Carolina, and South Carolina, to promote improved civil and political rights for African Americans. Together, they and Jackson frequently enlisted Marshall's legal skills as they developed strategies aimed at attacking discrimination.

The Murphys also understood that Marshall was struggling to earn enough to keep his legal practice solvent. His only steady clients were two large African-American Baltimore businesses that he came to represent due to the influence of his uncle, Fearless Williams. One client, the Ideal Building and Loan Association, was the largest black-owned bank in Baltimore. Fearless Williams sat on its board of directors. The other account,

Druid Laundry, cleaned and pressed laundry for Fearless's employer, the B&O Railroad. The laundry's owner also was the brother-in-law of Fearless. Aside from these accounts, Marshall had no steady clients and often found himself short of cash and behind on his bills. With this fact in mind, and wishing to keep Marshall engaged in important but not profitable civil rights cases, the Murphys decided to have him handle some of their legal work. This new work did not solve Marshall's money problems but helped to make them a bit less pressing.

While Marshall needed to make more money, he also felt compelled to continue his civil rights work. His continued association with Charles Houston only served to reinforce the importance of his social engineering work. As he told Houston in a letter, "Personally, I would not give up these cases here in Maryland for anything in the world, but at the same time there is no opportunity to get down to really hustling for business" (Long, 2011, p. 17). In part, he could not give up the cases because they often had personal resonance for him. This was particularly true in the case of the University of Maryland Law School and its continued refusal to admit African-American students.

Marshall never sent a letter of application to the law school because of its segregation policies. But their policies continued to infuriate him. It was a concern he often brought up in correspondence with Houston. He sought to move forward with a case, but Houston did not share Marshall's impatience. Eventually, two events caused Houston to finally support action on that front. One catalyst was a not-quite-accurate headline in the January 1933 *Baltimore Afro-American*, which indicated that two men had applied to the Maryland law school and to its graduate school. At the time, they had not yet applied but planned to do so. The other was an initiative of the national fraternity Alpha Phi Alpha, which planned to bring a suit against the University of Maryland at College Park seeking to desegregate it. This action in particular concerned both Marshall and Houston as it ran counter to the NAACP plans to attack educational segregation initially at the graduate level, not the undergraduate level. Marshall sought to dissuade the fraternity from their idea, but they elected to move forward in their planning. Their decision prompted Marshall and Houston to bring a suit against the University of Maryland Law School.

Harold Seaborne, the applicant identified in the *Baltimore Afro-American* article, did finally apply to the law school in July 1933. As expected, he received a letter of rejection from Raymond Pearson, the president of the university. Several other African Americans also applied to the law school and also received rejection letters. Marshall looked to identify the best candidate possible to use as a court test case against the university. The person Marshall and Houston found was Donald Gaines Murray, the grandson of Wesley John Gaines, a prominent bishop in the African Methodist

Episcopal Church. A recent honors graduate of Amherst College, Murray submitted a letter in coordination with Marshall to President Pearson, inquiring about applying to the law school. He received a form letter in return discouraging his application. The rejection letter also pointed out a partial state scholarship fund set up to help defray the costs of attending an out-of-state institution. Murray ignored Pearson's suggestion and formally applied to the law school and received a formal rejection letter. The letter indicated that the university only accepted Negro students at its Princess Anne Academy. After sending copies of the letter to the board of regents and after receiving yet another rejection, Marshall and Houston filed a lawsuit against the university. The case *Murray v. the University of Maryland* held opening arguments in June 1935.

Marshall offered opening remarks, but Houston conducted most of the case brilliantly. Expecting the university to point to the Princess Anne Academy as an alternative, Marshall visited the campus prior to the trial and documented the poor conditions at the school. He also verified that only one faculty member there had a master's degree, and none had a doctorate. Houston used this information to undermine information presented by President Pearson and Law School dean Roger Howell when testifying. The strategy of the team was to prove that Maryland did not provide "separate but equal" education for African-American students.

After both sides presented their arguments, the judge, Eugene O'Dunne, immediately issued his decision. In his opinion, Maryland did not offer equal education at the Princess Anne Academy and consequently Murray should start at the law school that fall. Maryland University lawyers appealed the judge's decision. They asked the Maryland Court of Appeals to hear the case quickly to prevent Murray from actually attending classes should they overturn O'Dunne's ruling. They claimed that if Murray attended classes, scores of white parents would remove their children and especially their daughters from the school. Marshall had the task of preparing the brief opposing the appeal by Maryland. The appeals court decided not to expedite the hearing, which allowed Murray to attend classes that September.

For Marshall and the NAACP, the pressure now was to ensure that Murray started school on schedule and was successful. But late in the summer, Murray communicated that he did not have the money to start school and needed a loan to pay his expenses. To solve the dilemma, the publisher of the *Baltimore Afro-American*, Carl Murphy, arranged a loan from a wealthy philanthropist. Murphy, in turn, forwarded the tuition money to Murray. Walter White, the executive director of the NAACP, felt the Murrays were more likely to repay the publisher of an important local newspaper than an anonymous donor they did not know. With the loan in hand, Donald Murray began classes on schedule, accompanied his first day by Marshall. The law school dean initially suggested seating Murray separately from the other students, which Marshall firmly rejected. After other suggestions were made and declined, it was finally agreed to treat the day like any other one and have Murray attend classes like a normal student. Once the semester began, things moved smoothly for Murray, as the *Baltimore Afro-American* reported he was treated cordially (Williams, 1998, p. 79).

To ensure Murray did well in the law program, Marshall checked in with him regularly. They could not afford to have Murray fail any of his classes. The Maryland administration vehemently opposed Murray's presence, and failure on his part would allow them to claim that African Americans were not capable of competing with white students and should only attend their separate schools. Leading up to the day Murray reported for class, the president of the University of Maryland, Henry Clifton Byrd, discussed resisting the court order. He even wrote about his willingness to go to jail if necessary, which in the end he did not do (Gibson, 2012, p. 261). Even after Murray entered the law school, Byrd unsuccessfully sought permission from the state attorney general to have Murray removed and sent to Howard or another school. To ensure Murray's success, Marshall had a member of the Howard Law School faculty work with him to make sure he did well and had a successful semester and first year. During that time, the appeals court sustained Judge O'Dunne's decision, guaranteeing Murray's place at Maryland. The law school had its first African-American student since the last quarter of the nineteenth century. It was a first step by the NAACP to break the barrier of segregation in America's education system. But, Charles Houston understood this was the start of a much longer struggle and that resistance was not over. As he noted in the title of an article he wrote for the NAACP publication *The Crisis*, "Don't Shout Too Soon," he knew more battles lay on the horizon.

In fact, Marshall's efforts on behalf of school segregation in Maryland did not end with Donald Murray. The *Baltimore Afro-American* noted other issues that needed attention as well. They wanted equal pay for African-American teachers, the same length of school term for black and white students, equal education facilities, and transportation provided for colored schoolchildren commuting to schools from rural locations (*Afro-American*, 1935). To begin action on these issues, the Baltimore NAACP sought to have a high school for African-American students constructed in nearby Baltimore County, which surrounded the city of Baltimore. While in the city of Baltimore, African-American students had the choice to attend Douglass High School, Booker T. Washington High School, or Dunbar High School, their counterparts in Baltimore County, a separate school district, did not have access to any high school. There were ten public high schools in the county, but none for African-American students, even though African Americans constituted about 10 percent of the population. If students wished to continue school beyond the seventh grade, they had to leave Baltimore County and travel to Baltimore city. Students had to pass an examination administered by the county in order to qualify to receive money set aside to pay for their tuition as out-of-city students. But these funds did not cover the cost of their daily transportation (see testimony of Clarence G. Cooper).

After a discussion with parents in Baltimore County, Marshall agreed to bring a suit against the County Board of Education. The parents of two students, Margaret Williams and Lucille Scott, agreed to serve as the focus of the suit. Both families lived in the southwestern portion of the county in Cowdensville, near Arbutus, Maryland. Through the seventh grade, Margaret Williams, on whose behalf the final lawsuit was brought, attended School 21, a small one-room building of the type frequently provided by the county for African-American students. After completing seventh grade, Williams took the test to attend high school in Baltimore and failed. She repeated seventh grade and failed the test once again. With the encouragement of Houston, Marshall had both Williams and Scott go to Catonsville High School, the high school nearest to where they lived. Accompanied by Reverend James E. Lee and Mr. Williams, Margaret and Lucille met with the principal, David Zimmerman, who denied them admission. He cited the policy of the county, which prevented black and white students from attending the same public schools. Zimmerman did admit that if Margaret and Lucille were white, their grades qualified them for admittance (see testimony of Joshua B. Williams Jr.).

Marshall then sent Margaret's application to the superintendent of Baltimore County Schools, Clarence Cooper. In the material accompanying the application, Marshall pointed out that despite her desire to attend the high school, the principal refused to admit her. This, Marshall argued, violated her constitutional rights. Cooper refused to take steps to change the situation. Marshall then sent a letter to the Baltimore County Board of Education, asking them to allow Margret to attend Catonsville High School. They too ignored Marshall's letter. Finally, Marshall appealed to the Maryland State Board of Education to step in and allow the admittance of Williams and Scott. They refused, saying it was a local matter in which they could not interfere. At this point Marshall, having done all he could through school channels, decided to initiate legal action.

After consulting with Houston, Marshall considered bringing two suits at the same time. One suit would seek to have Williams admitted to Catonsville High School. The second suit, with Scott as the plaintiff, looked to pressure the county to build a high school for African-American students. The challenge facing Marshall was his ability to adequately pursue both cases simultaneously with his limited resources. With some financial help from the national NAACP office, Marshall pressed forward with the two suits and the investigations needed to present both of his cases. As part of this evidentiary effort, he crafted a questionnaire for past and present African-American students about their experiences in the system. He also gathered statistical evidence about the student population, school buildings, and the grading system. As he organized to gather this material, Marshall created a first draft of his petition to the court, which he shared with Houston, who had since left Howard to work at the NAACP national office. Part of Houston's recommendation back to Marshall was to urge him to generate positive press coverage of Williams and the case as he moved forward with the suit. Houston wanted to counterbalance the coverage of white Baltimore papers like *The Baltimore News*, which characterized Marshall and the NAACP as troublemakers going against tradition in seeking the attendance of black students at white schools. Houston believed the support of moderate and progressive whites would give the case a greater chance of success. Houston also encouraged the execution of the survey on educational circumstances for African-American children in Baltimore County.

For the survey, Marshall enlisted the help of Juanita Jackson, the daughter of the head of the Baltimore NAACP, Lillie Mae Carrol Jackson, and his fellow attorney, Robert McGuinn. The selection of McGuinn had a strategic aspect, as Marshall felt that his light skin color would make it easier to get information from white school officials. Together with Marshall, they traveled the county and gathered the material needed to prepare for the case. As they assembled the information and thought about next steps, Marshall and Houston faced a dilemma. Their long-term education strategy focused on using "separate but equal" as a tool to move toward integration of school systems. Consequently, they wanted to avoid a demand for a separate black high school as the centerpiece of the NAACP litigation. But they also understood that a positive short-term remedy for Baltimore County African-American students was the construction of a separate black high school. As a solution, they had a local organization, the United Parent Teacher's Association (UPTA), send a report to the press. The report used the data accumulated by Marshall to highlight the inadequate school facilities for black children in the county. For the UPTA, the best immediate solution was the construction of a separate black high school.

On the heels of the *Murray* case against the Maryland law school, Houston felt it best not to make integration of the schools the main objective. With this in mind, the suit filed by Marshall charged the school principal, the county superintendent, and the school board with abrogating the civil rights of Margaret Williams. As a remedy, Marshall wanted her admitted to Catonsville High School. He did not expect them to agree to admit her but hoped they would agree to the construction of a separate but equal black high school. To deflect criticism that the NAACP sought black and white students going to the same school, Marshall had African-American parents write to white-owned newspapers indicating they did not want integration, only to have their own properly equipped schools.

Litigating the case proved challenging for Marshall and his team. The lawyers for Baltimore County treated Marshall and the other lawyers disrespectfully. Marshall told Houston that they were "mean, nasty and arrogant" (Williams, 1998, p. 80). They took the position that the NAACP suit sought to break a long-held tradition in the county that kept black and white children's education separated. They also argued that Williams was not admitted because of her color and that she did not pass the test administered to all Baltimore students, black and white, seeking to enter high school. Her failure to pass the test illustrated the inferiority of African Americans and justified the discriminatory practices of the county. Marshall felt their legal position gave him an advantage, as they admitted Williams's race was a key issue for refusing her acceptance, which constituted denial of due process under the Fourteenth Amendment. Marshall also felt sure that not all students had to take the high school entrance test, only African-American students. These things he felt were significant issues in determining whether Williams and other black students were treated equally.

Unfortunately, the judge for the case, Frank Duncan, chose not to address the issue of the equality of education for African-American students. In addition, whether or not only black students had to take a high school entrance examination was irrelevant for him. He believed the only issue of importance was whether Margaret Williams had passed the test. This view undercut the essence of Marshall's case, which sought to prove the illegality of Williams having to take a test only administered to African-American students. Neither the testimonies of Margaret's father nor the expert witnesses presented by Marshall impacted Duncan's position. Very quickly Marshall surmised that Judge Duncan would find in favor of the county, and he changed his tactics to focus on crafting a record he hoped would have greater impact on the court of appeals. Duncan's decision to deny the petition of Marshall and Williams did not surprise Marshall and his team. They hoped the court of appeals might see the county's actions and the judge's ruling differently. But it did not and refused to overturn Judge Duncan's decision. The NAACP felt the case was not strong enough to take before the U.S. Supreme Court, so they decided not to pursue it any further. They did take solace in the language of the ruling of the appeals court, which made reference to the reality that "the mere existence of a separate system in itself imports inequality" (Gibson, 2012, p. 290). For the NAACP and Marshall, it was recognition by the courts that race-based separate-but-equal activities were, by their nature, unequal.

While disappointed by the outcome of the *Williams* case, observers were not disappointed by Marshall's effort. Professor Leon Ransom from Howard, who assisted with the case, issued a very favorable report on Marshall's expertise and composure in the face of a judge who favored his opponents at every turn. Marshall certainly appreciated the recognition of his work, but he faced a financial crisis while prosecuting both the *Murray* and *Williams* cases. Preparing and trying these cases, which paid him very little, took him away from his own practice, which itself generated only minimal cash flow. He already held a position at the Baltimore City Department of Health as a night clerk, but that was not money enough to solve his financial challenges. Marshall desperately needed to secure a more consistent source of revenue. To that end, Marshall inquired about a position at Howard's law school. As an alumnus of the school, he felt at least one member of the faculty should have been trained there. When a position did open, Marshall hoped to get the job but found himself in competition with another Howard graduate. In the end, neither of them got the position, and Marshall's money issues continued.

Despite his financial challenges, Marshall continued his work with the Baltimore NAACP. Antilynching legislation was an important issue for President Lillie Mae Jackson, and she turned to Thurgood to work with her on it. The goal focused on persuading Maryland elected officials at the national level to support the adoption of the bills coming before Congress. They sent a series of letters to them requesting their support during the spring and fall of 1936. The bill did not come to a vote, but the members of the Baltimore NAACP and the national office appreciated Marshall's efforts. They also appreciated his efforts on behalf of Baltimore's hosting of the NAACP national convention during the summer of 1936. As the largest national convention to date, successfully organizing the gathering placed great pressure on the Baltimore members. Marshall coordinated several aspects of the convention as well as copresented on the issue of combating educational inequalities. In appreciation for his work, the NAACP sent him twenty-five dollars for his "valuable assistance" during the convention.

His participation in the Baltimore convention allowed Marshall to meet delegates from across the country and increase his profile within the organization. He also spent time with the executive director, Walter White; his assistant, Roy Wilkins; and Charles Houston, the head of the NAACP's legal department. He made a good impression on both White and Wilkins, and when Houston lobbied for an assistant to help him with the growing responsibilities of his job, both White and Wilkins agreed to hire Marshall for the position. While Houston traveled around the country fundraising, giving speeches, and attending meetings, Marshall was to handle the day-to-day legal issues back at the office. They offered Marshall an initial six-month contract for two hundred dollars per month. Marshall accepted. In preparing to leave Baltimore, he shared many of his clients with other lawyers and moved to New York with Vivian to live for a while with his Aunt Medi and Uncle Boots Dodson. They eventually found their own place on 149th Street, giving them a space of their own for the first time. In addition, Marshall could finally work directly with his mentor, Charles Houston; concentrate on the work he valued most; and earn enough money to help his family in the process. As he wrote to Walter White about his new position, "I have the opportunity now to do what I have always dreamed of doing! That is to actually concentrate on the type of work the Association is doing" (Zelden, 2013, p. 30). In his new position, Marshall's responsibility, according to the announcement of his hiring in *The Crisis*, was to perform special research for the NAACP campaign for educational equality.

The move to New York did not free Marshall entirely from issues back in Baltimore. Things took a turn for the worse with his family as he was preparing to leave. The persistent cough of his brother, Aubrey, was diagnosed as tuberculosis, which increased the strain on the resources of his family. In addition, there remained clients and cases Marshall looked to finish himself as he transitioned to New York. For a period of time, those cases had him traveling back and forth to Baltimore and maintaining an office in the home of his parents. One of these cases, in particular, had the potential to make a major difference in the lives of African-American teachers in Maryland and elsewhere.

The salary of African-American teachers in Maryland trailed substantially behind that of their white counterparts, which was in accordance with the law. Everywhere in the state, school boards adhered to this policy and paid African-American teachers lower wages. Baltimore was an exception to the rule, as all teachers there operated on the same pay scale as a result of a lawsuit won in 1925. This disparity in pay outside Baltimore infuriated the Baltimore NAACP and Carl Murphy, who sought to change that policy. They looked to Marshall to help them take this issue to the courts. The difficulty was identifying a teacher willing to challenge their school system's pay policy. Anyone who accepted the challenge risked losing their job during a period when finding any work was difficult, and teaching, even at a reduced salary, provided steady employment. The most likely candidate needed to work in a county that provided tenure and job protection for a teacher bringing suit against their board of education. They initially identified one candidate who taught high school but lost him when he received an offer to become a principal in a neighboring county. There was suspicion that the promotion was a tactic to have the teacher give up his tenure for a higher-paying position and to drop his lawsuit, but it was an offer too tempting for him to reject. Two years later he was fired from the principal position as was feared might happen.

As a result of losing their first plaintiff, the NAACP identified a second person, William Gibbs Jr., who worked in Montgomery County. As an acting principal in the "colored" county school system, Gibbs earned less than half of what white principals earned. On behalf of Gibbs, Marshall and the NAACP petitioned the county board for back pay and an equal pay scale for African-American employees, which the school board refused to approve. Marshall then filed a lawsuit requesting equal pay and back pay for African-American teachers in Montgomery County. The lawyers for the school board filed papers objecting to the NAACP's demand but were rebuffed by the court, which insisted they respond to the accusations. This ruling marked the first time that any court had acknowledged that equally qualified black and white professionals had the right to equal pay (Gibson, 2012, p. 318).

In response to the ruling of the court, officials in Montgomery decided to negotiate with Gibbs and his lawyers. The final agreement committed the Montgomery County School Board to equalizing teacher salaries within a year. This represented a significant victory for African-American teachers and the NAACP. In light of this ruling, the Colored Teachers Association, urged by Marshall, looked for potential plaintiffs in other counties in Maryland. The goal was to mount a county-by-county initiative to equalize the pay scale throughout Maryland. After the NAACP filed suit, Cecil County also agreed to equalize teacher pay, and several other counties followed suit. By late 1938, nine Maryland counties had agreed to pay equalization, which increased support for the NAACP throughout the state and the nation. In subsequent years, this became an important effort by the NAACP, as they looked to equalize teacher salaries wherever they could. The teacher salary successes also served to reinforce the view of Charles Houston and the NAACP that focusing on inequalities in education represented an effective pathway for attacking segregation.

This approach became a critical aspect of the efforts of the NAACP after the presentation of the Margold report and Houston's travels through the South accompanied by Marshall. The NAACP announced the framework of this strategy in a press release in the fall of 1936 announcing, "Educational Inequalities must go!!!" (Ball, 1998, p. 50). Charles Houston had developed the specifics of the plan, which became the first long-term focused concerted legal endeavor of the organization. The plan included six main goals toward which the NAACP intended to direct its legal efforts. It sought equality of school terms, equal pay for teachers, equal transportation for students, comparable buildings and equipment, equivalent expenditures for African-American students, and similar access to graduate and professional training. To accomplish these ends, the NAACP sought to legally compel segregated educational systems to fully enact the concept of "separate but equal" as enunciated in the *Plessy v. Ferguson* ruling of 1896. As Houston described the parameters of the effort, "All we can insist upon is equality of treatment. The state can separate the races provided it kept the educational opportunities equal" (ibid., p. 51). They did not seek desegregation under this plan according to Houston, just equal access. But the agenda underlying this strategy was the belief that the segregated systems could not afford to create two truly separate and equal educational operations. In the end, faced with court rulings demanding equality of opportunity, the states would face economic reality and allow for the integration of their educational facilities.

The other part of the NAACP effort was to provide African Americans greater access to political and legal rights due, but often denied, to them as citizens. In the 1930s, discriminatory laws and legal treatment remained the norm for African Americans in many parts of the country. The ill treatment by police Marshall observed out of his classroom window as a young boy in Baltimore still characterized relations between police and African-American communities in much of the nation. Confessions of guilt extracted through beatings or other means of intimidation still commonly occurred. African-American travelers faced segregated facilities on trains, boats, buses, and other forms of transportation they used. And, the most basic right of citizenship in a democracy, the right to vote, was denied African-American residents in most Southern localities. Attacking these injustices along with other challenges faced by African Americans throughout the country constituted the core efforts of the NAACP, as Marshall assumed his new role as special assistant to Houston when he moved to New York.

3

At the NAACP

When Thurgood Marshall joined the New York offices of the NAACP, it was a modest operation. Marshall and Houston constituted the legal team, and Walter White and Roy Wilkins comprised the executive team. But they all dedicated themselves to the advancement of colored people as highlighted in the mission of the organization. Adhering to this goal kept all of them constantly busy tending to the essential business of the organization. Houston spent much of his time traveling, attending meetings with local groups, and seeking opportunities to initiate cases testing discriminatory laws and practices. Marshall's key task was to develop legal briefs and other legal materials as needed. He also traveled through parts of the South looking for candidates to serve as plaintiffs in suits seeking equal pay for African-American teachers or the right to vote. In addition, he and Houston sought out Howard law school graduates to convince them to provide the legal representation needed to bring suits in local districts. This was necessary, as Marshall and Houston did not have the time or resources to plead every case themselves, nor were they certified to serve as lawyers in a number of states. Marshall and Houston made a good team. Their personalities differed but complemented one another. Houston was detailed, reserved, a taskmaster, and the better writer of the two. Marshall was outgoing, congenial, practical, and the better public speaker. They had a healthy respect for each other's strengths, which made them effective. Marshall especially treasured the opportunity to work with Houston on a daily basis.

Their personal lives did not mesh as well. Houston lived alone in a room at the 135th Street Harlem YMCA while his estranged wife remained in Washington, DC. Marshall lived with Vivian, and they took advantage of life in Harlem. They regularly attended the shows and entertainment available in New York, which was then in the midst of an African-American cultural renaissance. After work they could go to places that hosted entertainers like Duke Ellington and Katherine Dunham. With Marshall's outgoing personality, they became a popular couple, spending time with a variety of friends. Vivian helped launch a social/civic club called the Girl Friends, for whom Thurgood crafted a charter. The frustrating part of their marriage was their inability to have a child. During the time Thurgood worked for the NAACP, Vivian had three miscarriages and never was able to carry a child full term.

Interacting with their friends after hours offered a welcome change of pace from the daily workload Marshall faced. The NAACP received numerous requests asking for help in solving often heartrending challenges. The NAACP was careful to focus its efforts on cases that might result in legal precedents on a national level. Considering their limited resources, they felt this approach would make the biggest legal differences. Consequently, when Houston learned of the rejection of Lloyd Lionel Gaines's application to the University of Missouri Law School, it represented exactly the type of case he believed they should pursue.

A graduate of Lincoln University, an African-American college in Missouri, Gaines decided to apply to the law school at the University of Missouri. The registrar at the university at first refused to even respond to his application, but the NAACP forced him to make a decision. The registrar then rejected Gaines's application based upon his race. The university also argued that although they had no in-state law school for African-American students, they did provide money for students to attend other schools out of state. They believed this put them in conformity with the "separate but equal" guidelines previously issued by the U.S. Supreme Court. Disagreeing, the NAACP filed a brief in the Missouri courts charging the university violated Gaines's Fourteenth Amendment rights by excluding him based upon his race. The Fourteenth Amendment provided that laws passed should protect all U.S. citizens equally. The remedy in the eyes of the NAACP was to admit Gaines to the law school or have the state create an equal law school for African Americans with the same facilities, law library, and quality of professors available at the main campus.

The NAACP lost the first court decision, as expected, and then appealed to the Missouri Supreme Court as they had planned. Because this case was based on interpreting the Fourteenth Amendment and the U.S. Supreme Court, by law, hears lower court cases based on constitutional issues, it went to that venue for a final ruling. A favorable decision there would have nationwide implications. The U.S. Supreme Court heard the case of *Missouri ex rel. Gaines v. Canada* in November 1938. Silas W. Canada was the registrar who originally denied Gaines's application. In their brief, Houston and Marshall put into operation their plans emerging from the Margold report. They did not seek to have the concept of "separate but equal" overturned but demanded that Missouri live up to the letter of that law. They insisted the state had to immediately create an accredited law school for Gaines and other African Americans truly equal to the white law school to be in compliance. Sending him to a law school in another state did not meet that requirement, as it would not prepare him as well to become a lawyer in the state of Missouri. Moreover, just promising to create such a school at some point in time in the future was not acceptable. Gaines wished to attend law school as soon as possible. In this instance, his Fourteenth Amendment right to an equal education could only be met by immediately admitting him to the University of Missouri Law School. The U.S. Supreme Court justices accepted the NAACP argument, ruling in their favor and noting the importance of "equality of rights" for both black and white citizens of the state. This decision resembled the decision of the *Murray* case in Maryland, but because it had reached the U.S. Supreme Court, the ruling impacted graduate education nationally, not just in Maryland.

Just as the University of Maryland had done, the administration in Missouri sought to circumvent the court ruling. The next year they created a law school for African-American students at Lincoln University, Gaines's alma mater. With the new school in place, the Missouri officials proclaimed the state now had a "separate but equal" law school for Gaines to attend. The NAACP protested in court that the new law school would not be ready by the fall semester and that Gaines should instead be admitted to the white law school that fall. The Missouri State Supreme Court agreed and ordered the school to admit Gaines, noting "that he was entitled to the equal protection of the laws, and the State was bound to furnish him within its borders" (Goldman & Gallen, 1992, p. 42).

The one problem now for the NAACP was Gaines himself. The notoriety of the case caused Gaines to demand special treatment from the NAACP and others who came into contact with him. To placate him, the NAACP provided money to allow Gaines to go to the University of Michigan to work on a master's degree in economics. They could not afford to have him abandon the case as it worked its way through the courts, or they would have to find another client and begin the process all over again. Unfortunately, that is just what happened. In September 1939, on the first day of classes at the University of Missouri Law School, Gaines was not available. He had disappeared. There was a lot of speculation about what happened to him, ranging from his being murdered to his accepting a bribe not to appear. Whatever the cause, Gaines never reappeared, and the NAACP had to drop the case when the lawyer for the University of Missouri moved to dismiss it for want of prosecution. Marshall, who saw the case as one of the NAACP's greatest victories in its attack on "separate but equal," was sorely disappointed at Gaines's disappearance and the wasting of the time of so many people (Rowan, 1993, p. 78). They would need to find another person to lead the charge in their attack on graduate education inequality for African-American students.

As the *Gaines* case worked its way through the courts, changes occurred within the NAACP. Charles Houston divorced his wife, remarried, and then decided to return to private law practice at his father's firm in Washington, DC. The bureaucracy of the NAACP frustrated him. He did not enjoy working for Walter White or having to report to the board of directors. The low salary he received also persuaded him to return home. Houston departed the organization in the summer of 1938, leaving Marshall in charge of the legal activities. In compensation for his new responsibilities, the board awarded Marshall a two-hundred-dollar raise, which still was less than they had previously paid Houston. The raise also did little to ease financial circumstances for him and Vivian. She pointed out to him that the raise amounted to about four dollars a week, which meant they still had to watch their finances closely. Although Marshall appreciated the board's confidence in him, Houston's absence placed more responsibility on his shoulders and on making the right choices of cases to accept moving forward.

An immediate problem faced by the NAACP and its new legal leader was a ruling by the Internal Revenue Service (IRS). The IRS declared that money donated to the NAACP to support legal cases was not tax deductible because they saw the NAACP as a lobbying entity that was not tax exempt. For the NAACP's law operation, the IRS ruling was potentially disastrous, as they depended on outside donations to prosecute their cases. To solve the dilemma, Marshall persuaded the IRS to allow the legal arm of the NAACP to become a separate entity, thus making it tax exempt. This resulted in the incorporation of the NAACP Legal Defense and Educational Fund, Inc. (LDF) in the spring of 1940. Its mission was simple: "To render free legal aid to Negroes who suffer legal injustices because of their race or color and cannot afford to employ legal assistance" (Goldman & Gallen, 1992, p. 43). Thurgood Marshall became head of this new entity. Working with a board of directors and with Walter White did not frustrate Marshall as it had Houston. Marshall developed a good working relationship with both of them. His outgoing personality and ability to work with people served him well in his new responsibilities. One issue that, at times, did irritate Marshall was the tendency of White to interject himself into legal matters and offer ideas on how Marshall or other NAACP lawyers should handle cases.

White's interference, however, did not distract Marshall from the work he needed to accomplish. As the replacement for Houston, his travel increased. He logged several thousand miles each year journeying to different regions of the country. There he met with local chapters and lawyers to rally support for the national organization and to discuss their local issues. His contact with them provided intelligence to the New York office about the concerns and aspirations of the membership. He also conferred with local lawyers about cases they were litigating and stood in as counsel for cases he thought important enough for the national office to prosecute. For many of these groups, Thurgood Marshall became the face of the NAACP. They rarely had any personal contact with Walter White or Roy Wilkins, especially if they did not attend a national meeting or live in a big city. Marshall came to the small towns and localities to talk with them, swap stories, share a drink, and think about strategies to combat the challenges they faced on a daily basis. He made the NAACP more human and approachable for those who turned to it for help. "Thurgood is coming" meant help was on the way for many people.

The travel was physically and psychologically draining. It meant riding by train to many locations or driving by automobile when the occasion demanded it. Often Marshall had to make these trips by himself. When in the South, he usually stayed and ate at the home of local residents, as most hotels and restaurants would not accommodate African Americans. It also was safer, as news of his coming to town oftentimes angered white residents, who saw the NAACP as an outside agitator seeking to disrupt traditional black and white relationships in their community. This especially was the case if Marshall arrived to try a case. In the courtroom he was a lawyer out to defend his client and willing to badger and publicly embarrass white officials who sought to preserve segregation. This did not sit well with local white residents, and they often hoped to punish "that fancy New York lawyer" or more derogatorily "that n— lawyer" Marshall for his arrogance. Thurgood described the many nights he lay in the bed of the home of local families willing to put him up, despite the danger, worrying if the KKK might come, drag him out, and kill him. This was a real possibility, as this frequently happened to African Americans deemed out of line in the South. Sometimes he would stay in a different house each night, and armed black citizens would sit outside to prevent any trouble.

His concerns emerged out of real moments of jeopardy he faced during his travels. Two, in particular, illustrate the opposition he encountered. In a Dallas, Texas, case, Marshall learned the local sheriff had declared publicly that he would personally teach Marshall a lesson when he arrived in town. Concerned about this declaration, Marshall contacted the Texas governor, who promised to protect him by assigning a Texas Ranger as his bodyguard. True to his word, the governor had a ranger waiting for Marshall upon his arrival. The relationship did not get off to a great start, as the ranger repeatedly referred to Marshall as "boy." A call to the governor ended that practice, though Marshall still worried if this was the right person to serve as his bodyguard. It turned out he was exactly the person Marshall needed. After leaving the courthouse one afternoon and walking to the car where the ranger waited, Marshall found himself confronted by the local police chief with his gun drawn menacingly and declaring, "You black s—, I've got you now" (Williams, 1998, pp. 103–104). Marshall was not sure what to expect next. But, the ranger calmly drew his own gun and warned the sheriff not to come any further. He and Marshall then drove off in the car. It was a harrowing moment for Marshall and a reminder of how local law officials often resented his work and that of the NAACP.

An even more frightening episode unfolded as the result of a case Marshall litigated in Columbia, Tennessee. After successfully defending two accused African-American men, Marshall had to drive to Nashville, Tennessee, to catch a train back to New York. Marshall left in a car with three other men, but they were followed and stopped by a group of state troopers

---

PLESSY V. FERGUSON, 1896

In 1890, Louisiana passed the Separate Car Act, which required that white and African-American train passengers sit in separate cars, but that the accommodations should be equal but separate. Unhappy, African Americans challenged the law by having mixed-race Homer Plessy purchase a train ticket and take a seat in the white coach. When asked to leave the coach, Plessy refused and was arrested and charged with breaking the law. At his trial, Plessy contended that the law was unconstitutional, but the judge John H. Ferguson ruled against him. Plessy appealed to the Louisiana State Supreme Court and lost again. He then appealed the case to the U.S. Supreme Court. Plessy's lawyers argued the Separate Car Act violated the Thirteenth and Fourteenth Amendments to the Constitution, which barred slavery and granted equal citizenship rights to African Americans. They also argued that by separating the two races, the law implied one race was inferior to the other.

The justices provided their decision in May 1896. Separate but equal accommodations were constitutional in their view. The *Plessy v. Ferguson* decision thus made the doctrine of "separate but equal" constitutionally acceptable and provided the foundation for segregation laws for the next fifty years.

and city police. They declared they had a search warrant to look through the car. Marshall gave permission but watched them closely to make sure they did not "plant" liquor in the car, as it was a county that banned alcohol. Finding nothing, they let Marshall and his colleagues leave. But the police stopped them again further down the road. This time they took Marshall into custody and told the others to drive away.

The police put Marshall in the back of one car and drove him off the main road toward the nearby Duck River where a crowd of men waited for them. Marshall feared for his life, but fortunately for him, his friends refused to leave him and followed the police car. Not wanting witnesses to what they were planning, the officers returned to the highway followed by his friends and took Marshall to Columbia. Looking for an excuse to harm Marshall, an officer told Marshall to cross the street to the judge's office, who they hoped would put him in jail. Marshall refused to walk ahead of the officer fearing getting shot in the back for trying to escape. Instead, he insisted that the officer walk next to him to see the judge.

In the judge's office, the officer wanted Marshall jailed for drunk driving even though he had not been driving the car. They hoped once they had him in the city jail they could punish him for his arrogance in the courtroom. The judge asked to smell Marshall's breath and then declared he could detect alcohol easily but did not detect any from Marshall and told the officer to let him go. Even then Marshall was not safe, and this time when he left Columbia, another man drove off in a decoy car while Marshall took another one. Marshall made it back safely to Nashville, but the driver of the decoy car was stopped and so badly beaten by the police he was in the hospital for a month.

Despite these harrowing experiences, Marshall continued to travel through the South. Even though he worried about his safety, his work was much too important to stop. It was part of the baggage that came with his mission as a social engineer. Plus, Marshall understood that his resolve was more than matched by the African Americans who lived in the places he traveled to and had to stay behind after he left town. They were the ones with courage because they "dared to stand up, to file lawsuits, were beaten and sometimes murdered after I spoke my piece and took the fastest goddam train I could find out of the area" (Rowan, 1993, pp. 113–114). If they could stand up for their rights with the risks that accompanied that decision, he too could take risks in order to support their resolve.

The courage of the people willing to stand up for their rights, and the perspective Charles Houston constantly advocated about the duty of African-American lawyers, proved a strong motivation for Marshall. He reflected it in the way he drove himself as the lead lawyer for the NAACP. In preparation for cases, he normally worked twelve-hour days or more, combing through the data and ensuring the legal papers were accurate and well written. It was not unusual for him to return home from work around ten or eleven o'clock at night. Marshall wanted to ensure all the applicable legal precedents were reviewed and the relevant ones included in the briefs. His goal was to ensure that he always entered the courtroom well prepared or that the lawyer presenting the case on behalf of the NAACP had all the information necessary. He knew that often they faced hostile environments where biased officials sought ways to use anti–African American sentiment to undermine cases.

Not all of the cases accepted by the LDF focused on injustices in the South nor was all the racial opposition faced by their clients found there. One case in Connecticut concerned the accusations of a highly respected, wealthy white woman named Eleanor Strubing that her African-American butler had raped her. According to Strubing's story, her butler, Joseph Spell, armed with a knife, forced himself on her four times, had her write a ransom note, tied her up, and drove to a reservoir where he threw her into the water. She survived by playing dead and swimming to the shore after he left.

Spell offered a different story. In his version of events, he came to Strubing's room to borrow money and found her dressed only in a thin robe. Stimulated by her attire, he propositioned her. Strubing agreed as long as he promised not to reveal their liaison. Worried about being surprised in her bedroom, they decided to go to the garage and use the car. In the car she became nervous, and he suggested they go for a drive. She agreed but became increasingly worried that someone might see them. They finally stopped near a reservoir where she ran from the car and jumped into the water when he tried to calm her down.

The NAACP took the case because they believed Spell innocent despite his past criminal record. He claimed police had coerced him into signing a confession he did not fully understand. They also recognized the panic the case triggered among wealthy white Connecticut employers who began firing their African-American helps for fear that something similar might happen to them. The possible economic impact on African Americans in the region could be devastating if many of them lost their jobs because of false accusations made by Strubing. Refuting Mrs. Strubing's story was important to the economic well-being of many New York and Connecticut supporters of the NAACP. The 1941 trial of Spell with Marshall as cocounsel with local lawyer Samuel Friedman resulted in an important victory for the NAACP. It reminded observers that racial injustice did not happen only in the South, and supporting the organization had benefits for people all across the nation.

The fact that racial injustice was a national problem across the United States came through even more clearly in the summer of 1943 in Detroit, Michigan. There, racial tensions had increased over competition for jobs

---

THE NEW NEGRO RENAISSANCE

The New Negro Renaissance, or the Harlem Renaissance as it also has been called, was an important period of African-American artistic, cultural, and intellectual flowering. Its leading figures embraced their African heritage and African-American expressions endemic to their culture. They conveyed their pride in many forms, including literature, art, theater, music, and dance. In their works, they rejected traditional aesthetic standards that negatively classified African-American and African cultural traditions. Instead, they embraced the cadence, colors, and world views that were part of their lives and of their richly diverse communities.

They further refused to acquiesce quietly to the violence and racism in society. Their racial pride compelled them to write and speak out against it. They were a new generation of African Americans who demanded their proper place in society not sometime in the far distant future but during their lifetimes. The work of these creatives served to illustrate the resolve of a generation more urban and less accommodating than the preceding generation. It was a generation that resisted when rioters came into their neighborhoods and were unafraid to demand their rights as human beings and American citizens.

---

and housing. Whites had burned a cross at an African-American housing development built in a white neighborhood, and white workers had stopped working because of the promotion of an African-American employee. Finally, a fight broke out between black and white residents at an amusement park called Belle Island. Afterward, rumors spread in the African-American community that a black woman had been thrown off a bridge by a white mob. In the white community, another rumor spread of the rape of a white woman. Rioting broke out again in the city lasting twenty-four hours. Violence took place in both black and white communities with people getting pulled from vehicles and being beaten or attacked while walking down the street. The fighting only stopped when President Franklin Delano Roosevelt sent federal troops into the city. The police did little to stop the violence and often sided with the white rioters when they did act. Nine whites and twenty-five African Americans died from the violence. Several hundred people were injured as well. The Detroit police killed seventeen African Americans during the riot, justifying their deaths by claiming the victims were looters. No whites were killed by police.

On behalf of the NAACP, Roy Wilkins sent a telegram to the governor of Michigan condemning the actions of the police and proclaiming they were not protectors of the African-American community but deadly enemies of its residents. In response, the county prosecutor and the Detroit chief of police placed the blame for the riots on the local African-American newspaper, the *Michigan Chronicle*, and the NAACP for creating dissension. Angered by this response, Walter White and Thurgood went to Detroit to talk with African-American residents and provide their perspective on the events. Their conversations and investigation produced a document based on their findings titled "What Caused the Detroit Riot?" In it, Marshall agreed with local African-American leaders that among the contributing factors were the lack of African Americans on the police force and chronic police brutality toward African Americans over the years. In Marshall's eyes, this bias evidenced itself during the riot, as police ignored white rioters while beating and arresting African Americans. Consequently, the "weak-kneed policy of the police commissioner coupled with the anti-Negro attitude of many members of the force helped make a riot inevitable" (*Detroit News*, 1999). His strong language highlighted Marshall's ongoing distrust and disappointment with the actions of police toward African Americans across the nation. He could see it in the way law officials treated him when trying cases in the South, with the treatment of Joseph Spell in Connecticut, in the cases he argued fighting against forced confessions of black prisoners, and in the unequal treatment of black soldiers willing to fight for their country but treated unfairly by the military.

The insulting treatment of African Americans in the U.S. military carried a special sting of its own. When African Americans volunteered to serve in times of war, they hoped to show their loyalty to the United States and to prove they were worthy of full citizenship rights. But the culture of the military refused to see or treat them as equals and instead sought ways of demeaning their valor and accomplishments. Blacks in the military found themselves accused of misconduct and punished for it much more frequently than their white counterparts. Marshall found this bias operating in World War II and again in Korea, as the NAACP received numerous letters, calls, and telegrams from servicemen and their families about prejudicial treatment. During World War II, the volume of letters for help from African-American military personnel and their families was so extensive that Marshall hired three additional lawyers. One of them, Ralph Carter, was a military veteran whom Marshall came to depend upon increasingly in subsequent years.

One of the cases that clearly highlighted the biases of the military occurred in California. Operating in segregated units and consigned mainly to supply duties, black sailors were assigned the task of loading ammunition. After an explosion in Port Chicago, California, in July 1944 resulted in the destruction of two ships and the death of over three hundred men, a few weeks later, the men refused to continue loading ammunition under similar conditions. What prompted the action of the sailors was the manner in which the officers in charge approached the work. They created a competition between units loading the dangerous material to see who could finish first. In the process, they threatened the sailors if they did not work quickly enough. Sometimes the workers were told to toss the boxes of ammunition as they loaded them. Tragically, one box missed its mark, hit the ground, and a deadly explosion followed.

Survivors of the Port Chicago explosion were reassigned to work with African-American sailors working at Mare Island, California. They told their new coworkers why the explosion had happened. The group then requested new procedures to enhance their safety. When the navy officers in charge refused to alter the procedures, the sailors declined to continue loading the dangerous cargo. When the sailors refused to load the ammunition, the military charged them with mutiny.

Marshall wrote to the secretary of the navy asking for an unbiased investigation into the events. The preliminary investigation of the NAACP led them to the conclusion that the men did not mutiny, did not believe they were disobeying a direct order, and the sailors were being put on trial because of their race (Long, 2011, pp. 141–143). Marshall then sat in with the defense team for the sailors and believed they had a good case for acquittal. To his surprise, after a twelve-day trial, the men were found guilty of mutiny. Marshall decided to personally handle their appeal in Washington, DC. There he pointed out to the judge advocate general why the men had stopped working, why they had not in fact mutinied, and why they should be acquitted. Refusing to obey an order and not "mutiny" was the worst thing of which they were guilty, according to Marshall. But despite pressure from First Lady Eleanor Roosevelt and the secretary of the navy, James Forrestal, the men again were found guilty of mutiny. Fortunately, after the NAACP and others placed more pressure on Forrestal, the men were not punished. Instead, the navy quietly released them and returned them to active duty. It was an important victory for Marshall but showed him once again the unfair treatment faced by African-American military personnel.

This antipathy toward the rights of African-American soldiers by the military was apparent in another case revolving, in part, around how the police and other officials obtained confessions. This was an issue that perturbed Marshall throughout his legal career. In this instance, three soldiers stationed in Louisiana at Camp Claiborne in 1942 were arrested for raping a white woman. The men insisted that the woman was a prostitute and they had paid her for her services. But the police who arrested them came forward with a confession of rape signed by the soldiers. Based primarily on the confession, a Louisiana federal court found them guilty. Wary of police-produced confessions, Marshall interviewed the men after they asked for help. From them he learned they provided the confession only after a beating by the police and the fear of being lynched by a white mob gathering outside the jail. The police threatened to turn them over to the group if they did not admit their guilt.

Based on his discussions with the men, Marshall filed an appeal of their conviction. He felt they were wrongly charged and that their trial was conducted in the wrong venue. Either a military court or a state court had jurisdiction over the case, not the federal district court that convicted them. He also was skeptical of the validity of the confession produced by the police. A new trial took place before the U.S. Circuit Court of Appeals, which agreed that the original trial was improper and returned it to a military court for retrial. Following the pattern often occurring in military trials of African-American soldiers, the military court found the men guilty and sentenced them to death. Fortunately, upon appeal, their sentences were reduced, and they gained their freedom after five years. Throughout the process, one of the key pieces of evidence leading to a guilty verdict, their confession, remained questionable. The circumstances under which the police extracted the confession did not influence the consideration of the judges, and for Marshall, it offered yet another instance of the corruption of the legal system when it came to African Americans charged with a crime. Sadly, the military was only a reflection of the larger society.

What also troubled Marshall about the treatment of African Americans during President Roosevelt's four terms in office was his reluctance to take steps to improve the issues faced by African Americans. Roosevelt depended upon Southern democratic votes to keep him in office and to support his programs, so he did not directly take on racial issues for fear of their possible negative reactions. Marshall and the NAACP sent numerous letters to the administration about African-American issues. While some of his cabinet members were sympathetic, Roosevelt often chose to ignore the correspondence. A report card prepared by the NAACP in 1940 on what Roosevelt had done for African Americans was telling. It pointed out his failure to condemn lynching, segregation in his agencies, and a refusal to integrate the armed services. This attitude by Roosevelt caused Marshall to see him negatively. From Marshall's perspective, "he was not [worth] a damn so far as Negroes were concerned . . . When it came to just Negroes, Roosevelt was not a friend" (Ball, 1998, p. 131).

The issue of coerced confessions, like in the Louisiana military case, troubled Marshall a great deal, and he often accepted civilian cases where convictions were based on what he believed were illegally extracted confessions obtained after several days in isolated police custody. One of the most notorious of these cases took place in Oklahoma in 1941. There, a farmer, his wife, and one of their children were brutally murdered in the town of Hugo, Oklahoma. Afterward, their house was set afire to destroy any evidence. Only one family member, a nine-year-old son, survived the attack. Initially, the authorities arrested two men from the nearby prison out on unsupervised leave for the murders. The men even confessed to committing the crime. But as the warden of the prison and the governor received sharp criticism for allowing the men to leave the prison unsupervised, things changed. In response, the governor sent an aide to further investigate the events. He decided the convicts were innocent, despite their confession, and released them. He then launched a search for the "real" murderer.

Soon they arrested a twenty-one-year-old African-American sharecropper, W. D. Lyons, who had been hunting in the vicinity of the farm. Although he said he had nothing to do with the crime, they arrested him. The authorities did not charge him with anything for several days and then held him in custody for more than a year before bringing him to trial. During that time, they extracted two confessions from him. The first they obtained after bringing him to the prosecutor's office, where he was beaten mercilessly with a nightstick. The second confession they extracted by taking Lyons to the scene of the murders and placing a pan of bones of the murdered woman in his lap. Later that day under questioning, he offered a second confession according to the authorities (Rowan, 1993, pp. 3–13).

Local African-American residents skeptical of the accounts of the white law officials raised the necessary money to have Marshall come to Oklahoma and defend Lyons. Marshall arrived hoping to use the precedent created by the NAACP in earlier cases in Mississippi and Florida where the Supreme Court had overturned convictions based upon coerced confessions. Given the hostile racial climate surrounding the case, Marshall had to alternate where he slept each night to ensure his safety. When the trial ended, the jury found Lyons guilty, and he was sentenced to life imprisonment. Even so, the hope remained that the Oklahoma Criminal Court of Appeals would overturn the verdict based upon the earlier Supreme Court decree.

But to the disappointment of Marshall and the NAACP team, the Oklahoma Court of Appeals refused to authorize a new trial for Lyons. The NAACP team then appealed to the U.S. Supreme Court, still believing they might win the appeal. Marshall's hopes were buoyed by another ruling by the U.S. Supreme Court earlier that year that had overturned a similar case based upon a coerced confession. But the decision of the U.S. Supreme Court surprised the NAACP team. The court agreed that the first confession was coerced but decided the second confession was not. As a result, they denied the request for a new trial and upheld the guilty verdict of the lower court. The guilty decision greatly affected Marshall. It illustrated painfully to him the difficulty for a person of color or the poor to get a fair trial in the American legal system. The case showed how the rich and powerful could manipulate the system to protect themselves by framing an innocent individual. Years later, the case continued to gnaw at Marshall, who felt Lyons was innocent. It was a sad commentary on the state of justice in the country, which Marshall fought against throughout his career.

Unfortunately, as head of the LDF, Thurgood rarely had the luxury of working on just one case at a time. As they fought to free Lyons in Oklahoma, the LDF fought a different civil rights case on another front in Texas. There, they sought to have the right to vote fortified. At issue was a long history in Texas and other Southern states to create devious means of excluding black voters. The Fifteenth Amendment to the U.S. Constitution forbade denying a citizen the right to vote because of their race, color, or previous condition of servitude. To skirt that amendment, states seeking to restrict the right to vote for African Americans created new laws that did not refer to race, color, or previous condition of servitude. They employed other devices like poll taxes, literacy tests, and grandfather clauses to control who might vote. The combined impact of these laws meant that by 1940 only 3 percent of African Americans were registered to vote throughout the South (Ball, 1998, p. 79; Davis & Clark, 1992, p. 112).

Texas employed a different device to disfranchise African-American voters. They allowed African Americans to vote in the general election but prevented them from voting in the Democratic primary elections. In states like Texas where Democrats won the majority of the time, the winner of the Democratic primary became the de facto winner of the general election. Only registered Democrats could vote in the primary, and the Texas Democratic Party did not allow African Americans to join. It was a very effective device for restricting the most important elections in the state. After some early success in the courts fighting this device in 1927 and 1932, African Americans suffered a setback when the U.S. Supreme Court ruled in 1935 that the convention to elect Democratic candidates in Texas was a private group activity that could restrict participation and did not violate the Fourteenth Amendment.

Marshall decided to mount an attack on this Texas practice at the Texas State NAACP conference in 1940. In order to proceed, he needed financial support from the NAACP's state branches and to identify a good candidate to file against the state. The person they ultimately identified was Dr. Lonnie Smith, a dentist from Houston and an officer in Houston's branch of the NAACP. Smith attempted to vote in the Democratic primary election, and as expected, the precinct judge, S. E. Allwright, turned him away. Marshall then filed suit for Smith in the federal court. Marshall accepted this challenge under great pressure. The Texas chapter and the national NAACP office raised a great deal of money to prosecute the case and expected success. Winning the case would change African Americans' ability to impact politics at the local, state, and national levels. As Marshall rightly noted, "Without the ballot, you have no citizenship, no status, no power in this country" (Zelden, 2013, p. 46).

At the district court and court of appeals, Marshall lost. But Thurgood argued the case so that the U.S. Supreme Court could review it and provide its own ruling. The *Smith v. Allwright* case represented one of the first nationally significant cases Marshall argued before the U.S. Supreme Court. Consequently, he faced great pressure to properly prepare and to provide an effective presentation. The position taken by Marshall revolved around a previous decision by the court, *Louisiana v. Classic*, in which they ruled that all primary elections were not private endeavors. Therefore, forbidding selected people from participating in them violated their rights under the Fourteenth Amendment. Marshall adopted the position that the same logic applied to the primaries in Texas and that they were therefore unconstitutional. Texas officials argued their primaries did not parallel those in Louisiana and that the precedent did not apply.

The U.S. Supreme Court supported Marshall and the NAACP. It viewed the primaries in each state as similar and unconstitutional. The court ruled that the primaries in Texas were not private but were connected to national election results and consequently fell under federal regulations and the Fifteenth Amendment. By preventing African Americans from voting, they had breached the rights guaranteed under that legislation. With the court ruling in their favor, everyone in the NAACP's New York office celebrated, as did friends of the NAACP from around the country. Marshall was personally uplifted by the decision. He felt momentum was on the side of African Americans, and they needed to continue pressing forward. In a speech later in Chicago, he sounded a call to action: "We must not be delayed by people who say 'the time is not ripe,' nor should we proceed with caution for fear of destroying the status quo. Persons who deny to us our civil rights should be brought to justice now" (Davis & Clark, 1992, p. 117).

Texas and other Southern states seeking to stop African Americans from voting, though losers in the *Smith* case, did not given in easily. They continued to devise devices to prevent African Americans from voting. Local voting registrars throughout the South persisted in arbitrarily turning away African Americans seeking to register to vote. The Department of Justice regularly received complaints and legal statements about the voting discrimination. Marshall had to take the state of South Carolina to court in 1947 to negate legislation that allowed local registrars to discriminate. Several years later in 1953, the LDF struggled with Texas again when they sued the Jaybird Democratic Association in Fort Bend County, which declared itself a private club and refused to register African-American voters in its Democratic primary. The Supreme Court again ruled against them. But it was another reminder for Marshall and the LDF of the importance of both the right to vote and the necessity of resisting impediments to African Americans exercising that right whenever circumstances demanded it.

Marshall's legal successes in defending the rights of African Americans in both civilian and military cases made him a highly regarded person within the African-American community. Black and white publications regularly highlighted his accomplishments. In 1946, the NAACP decided to honor their chief counsel by bestowing on him their highest honor, the Spingarn Medal. This was given yearly by the organization "for the highest or noblest achievement by a living American Negro during the preceding year or years." It was a wonderful surprise and honor for the thirty-seven-year-old Marshall, who became the second youngest person to receive the award. At the 1946 ceremony in Cincinnati, they proclaimed him an American hero whose efforts impacted hundreds of thousands of lives around the nation. It was a wonderful event and moment for Marshall.

The ceremony greatly lifted Marshall's spirits and came at a good time. His strenuous schedule, poor eating habits, drinking, and chain smoking were all taking their toll on his health. A month later he became ill with pneumonia, which eventually forced him to enter the intensive care unit at Harlem Hospital. He remained there most of June and July before he began feeling better and slowly recovering from his struggles with the respiratory disease. Even then, the decision was made to take more time off by way of an extended leave away from the constant pressure of the caseload at the office. Thurgood and Vivian left New York for an extended vacation to the U.S. Virgin Islands. His friend and colleague William Hastie was the governor there as a result of an appointment by President Harry Truman. Hastie's presence helped ensure a warm welcome and good treatment. While they were away, the couple also visited Haiti, Jamaica, and Cuba. It was the first time in many years Marshall agreed to set aside time to spend alone with Vivian. The rest served its purpose, as Marshall's health improved during their time away. This was despite the fact that he could not completely divorce himself from work and regularly communicated with the lawyers litigating a case in Columbia, Tennessee, where they faced hostile local officials and a biased presiding judge. Upon returning, Marshall joined the team and successfully helped defend two men accused of attempted murder of a policeman.

Though chastened somewhat by his illness, Marshall remained committed to bringing legal challenges to instances of injustice and civil rights discrimination. One of the issues that greatly concerned him was the segregation faced by African-American travelers in the South. On the most frequently used forms of transportation, such as trains, buses, and boats, black travelers had to occupy separate seating while paying the same fare as white travelers. The civil disobedience of Irene Morgan in protest of being forced to give up her seat while traveling by bus provided the perfect opportunity to contest this practice. A married resident of Baltimore, Maryland, Mrs. Morgan worked in an airplane factory during World War II. In July 1944, she visited her mother in Gloucester County, along the eastern shore of Virginia. After seeing her mother, Irene boarded a Greyhound bus for the return trip home to Baltimore. As per local custom, she took a seat in the colored section of the bus. After traveling more than twenty miles, the crowded bus made a stop near Saluda in Middlesex County, Virginia, where two white passengers boarded. The bus driver asked Mrs. Morgan and another African-American woman with a baby in her lap to give up their seats to the new passengers and move to the very back of the bus. Mrs. Morgan refused to relinquish her seat and tried to prevent her seatmate from relocating as well. Morgan said later, "I didn't do anything wrong. I'd paid for my seat. I was sitting where I was supposed to" (McCain, 2007).

Greyhound's company policy gave the driver the authority to control seating and to relocate passengers at his own discretion at any time. Drivers could also eject resistant passengers and even make arrests when they saw fit. Refusing to obey the directions of the driver constituted a misdemeanor crime with a possible fine between five and twenty-five dollars. In addition, Virginia state law required segregation of seating on buses, trains, boats, and other forms of transportation. Since Mrs. Morgan refused to move, the driver went to the local sheriff to have her forcibly removed. When the sheriff arrived and informed Mrs. Morgan that he planned to arrest her, she did not argue. However, when he presented her with an arrest warrant, she tore it into pieces and threw it out of the window. When he attempted to drag her from her seat, she retaliated by kicking him below the belt. She was brought in and charged with resisting arrest and breaking state laws on segregation.

Originally, Spotswood Robinson, an African-American lawyer from Richmond, took her case, with the support of the national NAACP office. Their strategy was to avoid litigating based on the issue of separate but equal and to look instead to the commerce clause in the Constitution. In the past, courts had ruled the commerce clause to mean that states could not control passengers or commerce traveling across state lines. The mistake made by the arresting officers in Morgan's case was to charge her not only with resisting arrest but also with breaking state segregation laws. The charges against Morgan allowed Robinson the opportunity to directly attack the application of segregation in interstate travel. Robinson took the position that under the commerce clause, the state of Virginia could not force Morgan to use segregated seating. After hearing the case, the Virginia Supreme Court ruled against Morgan, taking the position that she had violated Virginia law and was guilty. That fall, Morgan's defense team, now led by Marshall, appealed the case, *Morgan v. Virginia*, to the U.S. Supreme Court. They presented the argument that the courts in the past protected federal control over interstate travel and that Virginia had violated federal law. Virginia lawyers countered that desegregation would deprive white passengers of their equal protection under the law. They argued that whites and blacks needed to remain separate because of their natural dislike of one another. It was not up to government to try and oppose this antipathy.

The U.S. Supreme Court ruled in support of Morgan. They felt the Virginia law did interfere with interstate commerce by forcing transportation companies traveling through the state to make different operating rules while within its borders. The court would not allow Virginia or any other state to place this illegal burden on these companies. This legal triumph was heralded within the African-American community as an important blow against segregation. It also had special significance for Marshall, as Vivian had come to Washington to watch him argue before the Supreme Court for the first time. Marshall called the verdict one of the most momentous decisions in the history of the country (Zelden, 2013, p. 50).

But Thurgood did not have the luxury to bask very long in his victory of the *Morgan* case. Additional calls for legal help poured into the NAACP that Marshall had to review and decide if his office could provide the help needed. The choices were not easy, as cases of false criminal accusations against African-American men, in particular, were a common occurrence, especially in the South. Many times these individuals faced death sentences, and their best hope to live lay in help from the NAACP. When he accepted these capital cases, Marshall had to use creative legal strategies to try and win either an acquittal or at least a reversal of the death sentence. One strategy Marshall used he had learned working with Charles Houston while still in law school. Thurgood had provided legal research for the *George Crawford* case in Virginia where part of Houston's defense was to hammer on the issue that African Americans were excluded from the jury pool, thus depriving Crawford of his right of due process. Thurgood turned to this strategy a number of times, including a key case in Mississippi that wound up before the U.S. Supreme Court.

The case involved Eddie Patton, an African American who was accused of killing a white man in 1947. While Eddie denied the crime, the jury found him guilty of murder and sentenced him to death. He appealed the conviction based, in part, upon jury selection and composition. No African Americans sat on the grand jury or the trial jury, nor were any African Americans in the selection pools. Systematic exclusion of African Americans from jury lists, jury boxes, and jury service had been common practice in Mississippi for decades, and Patton argued this tradition prevented him from receiving a fair and impartial trial. This argument was central to the presentation made by Marshall before the Mississippi Supreme Court. That court did not find that Patton's rights were abridged, and the appeal was denied. Marshall then immediately appealed to have the case presented before the U.S. Supreme Court.

As was the plan with most of the cases Marshall argued before the Supreme Court, the long-term goal was to obtain a ruling, setting precedents for future similar cases. The *Eddie Patton* litigation was no different. If the court supported Marshall's argument, it would force local officials to create more diverse jury lists and juries or face overturning of the results of their trials. The Supreme Court ruled in favor of Patton's petition. They believed that the systematic exclusion of African-American jurors was unconstitutional and the argument offered by the state of Mississippi unconvincing. They sent the case back to Mississippi to redress the issues that concerned them. For both Patton and Marshall, the decision of the court was a happy one. It meant Patton would receive a new trial with a more diverse jury. For Marshall there was satisfaction in seeing the strategy he worked on with his mentor Charles Houston supported by the U.S. Supreme Court. The ruling in the 1948 case of *Patton v. State of Mississippi* became a tool to use in the future where parts of the population were excluded from the jury lists because of their race.

Thurgood needed as many strategies as he could muster to help him in the numerous lawsuits the NAACP took on to help individuals they felt were unjustly accused and facing death sentences. There were times when pointing out that a confession was obtained under duress or the problem with having an all-white jury judging the case was not enough to win an appeal. Then Marshall had to turn to other avenues to save his clients' lives. Such was the circumstance of the 1949 Groveland, Florida, case. Four men had been chased and beaten by a mob that accused them of raping a young white woman. One man died from the beating, and the other three survived but suffered terrible physical punishment. The police claimed the men confessed while in custody, though they had no written statement. The men denied having confessed and consistently professed their innocence. The jury for their trial found them guilty and sentenced two of the men to death and the youngest, who was sixteen, to life in prison. Marshall and the NAACP appealed their conviction, and the Supreme Court ruling of *Shepard v. Florida* in 1951 upheld their appeal noting the prejudicial events that surrounded the trial. Before the retrial, two of the men, Samuel Shepard and Walter Lee Irvin, were shot by the sheriff who claimed self-defense while transporting them back to Groveland for retrial. One died, and the other was badly wounded. Irvin was again found guilty at the retrial and once again sentenced to death. The other young man, Charles

Greenlee, had decided to accept his original life sentence rather than risk retrial and a possible death verdict.

Marshall again appealed the decision to the U.S. Supreme Court, but this time the court upheld the lower court's decision. With his legal options exhausted, Marshall used NAACP connections to bring public pressure on Florida's governor. They contacted the Florida state legislature and the Justice Department seeking mercy for their client. They also used the African-American press to generate public pressure on behalf of their case. The governor consequently received hundreds of letters asking for clemency for Walter Irvin. As a result, the governor commuted the death sentence to life imprisonment, and eventually both men received their release from prison. It was a long, sometimes desperate, struggle that called upon all of Marshall's experience and political connections to gain the release of both men. And it highlighted the pressure he and his colleagues regularly confronted in terms of the life and death issues faced by the people they represented. The case also illustrated Marshall's resourcefulness and commitment to protecting the civil rights and lives of unjustly accused or convicted individuals.

Criminal cases constituted many of the litigations handled by Marshall and the LDF, but they were not the only issues of interest to the organization. Injustices directed toward African Americans were embodied in a wide variety of actions taken by government officials and by private individuals. These actions also captured the attention of the LDF. One of the most aggravating of these actions for Thurgood Marshall were restrictive covenants, which prevented African Americans and other groups from purchasing property in certain locations. Marshall believed that the policy of restrictive covenants deprived African Americans of the right to choose where they might live. Black ghettoes were one result of these policies.

This perspective within the NAACP was a view enunciated by one of its earliest members, Arthur Spingarn, who observed that as "a wave of residential segregation laws swept the country . . . no one for a moment believed that they were anything but the initial steps in an attempt to create Negro ghettoes throughout the United States" (Ball, 1998, pp. 83–84). In their initial efforts to combat these ordinances, the NAACP launched a letter-writing campaign to the press to highlight the trend, in the hope of generating a public outcry against residential segregation. They soon found that letter writing had little impact, as cities in the South and in border states continued to enact these laws. Baltimore was one of these places, as it tried to corral the influx of African-American migrants into its midst.

The first successful case brought to the U.S. Supreme Court by the NAACP against segregation ordinances was not in Baltimore but in Kentucky. In Louisville, the law prevented African Americans from moving into white neighborhoods and whites from moving into African-American neighborhoods. In 1915 when challenged in the local courts, they ruled the legislation legal. But when argued before the U.S. Supreme Court in 1917, the justices unanimously ruled in *Buchanan v. Warley* against the legislation. They believed it interfered with the rights of an owner to dispose of his property as he desired. This barrier they noted clashed with the rights of citizenship guaranteed in the Fourteenth Amendment. This ruling by the court allowed for the overturning of similar laws in other cities. The positive aspect of the decision was that it stopped the creation of legislation decreeing residential segregation. The limitation of the decision was that it did not speak to private agreements like restrictive covenants, which also supported residential segregation.

Litigation seeking to attack restrictive covenants did not fare as well for the NAACP when they brought forward a case from the District of Columbia, where the neighbors sued another resident, Irene Corrigan, for agreeing to sell her home to an African American. They contended she had signed a covenant agreeing not to sell, lease, or give the property to "any person of the negro race or blood" and thus her action was illegal and void. The NAACP lawyers in *Corrigan v. Buckley* cited the Fifth and Fourteenth Amendments to the Constitution as reason to rule against the neighbors. This time in a unanimous decision, the court ruled against them. They did not believe the amendments had an impact upon agreements between private individuals and how they disposed of their property. This ruling by the court in 1926 opened the door for the use of restrictive covenants in cities throughout the nation not just in the South. In many places the documents signed when purchasing a home in certain sections of the city contained restrictive covenants preventing its future sale to African Americans, Jews, or Asians.

Even the federal government utilized restrictive covenants as it constructed public housing. In 1940, Thurgood Marshall sent a letter to President Roosevelt concerning the stance taken by the Federal Housing Administration (FHA). It had adopted a policy for building public housing that followed the principle that "if a neighborhood is to retain stability, it is necessary that properties shall continue to be occupied by the same social and racial classes" (Kluger, 2004, p. 246). The FHA would ensure that the housing was "separate but equal," but not integrated. This meant, in application, that even if white housing units remained unoccupied while African-American units had waiting lists, the white units would remain unused. To Marshall, this policy resulted in forced racial segregation in housing even in states where segregation went against their public policy. In his eyes, the federal government should not reinforce such actions (Long, 2011, p. 75). In part, due to the efforts of the NAACP, the FHA did alter its policy on restrictive covenants, giving the NAACP a victory. But this did not solve the bigger problem of the growth in private restrictive covenants. A broader-based creative plan of attack was necessary if Marshall and others hoped to bring about its demise.

To formulate a coordinated attack among the lawyers around the country bringing suits against restrictive covenants, Marshall called for a national meeting organized by the LDF in Chicago in 1945. He called it a "Meeting of N.A.A.C.P. Lawyers and Consultants on Methods of Attacking Restrictive Covenants" (Vose, 1967, p. 58). Thirty-three lawyers attended, including Charles Houston, who was involved with a case in Washington, DC. William Hastie presided over the meeting while Marshall provided the framework for their discussions. They were to work to get the question of restrictive covenants before the U.S. Supreme Court again. The new, innovative, and complex strategy argued that when state officials used their resources to enforce restrictive covenants, enforcement made it a public not a private action. This made the act of enforcement subject to federal review and therefore within the jurisdiction of the Fourteenth Amendment. The NAACP believed that the Fourteenth Amendment consequently made restrictive covenants unconstitutional. As the meeting ended, Marshall promised the NAACP would pay special attention to the issue of restrictive covenants going forward and would assign a staff member to focus full-time on housing (Vose, 1967, p. 64). The goal was to maintain national coordination as individual cases moved forward.

In the months that followed, none of the active litigations came before the U.S. Supreme Court, which caused Marshall and Hastie to call a second meeting at Howard University in 1947. Marshall believed the court was moving in a direction to entertain a review of appropriate cases brought before it concerning restrictive covenants. The key was to get the strongest possible cases before the court, and Marshall wanted to try and ensure that would happen. Cases in process in Missouri, Michigan, and the District of Columbia seemed to have the best prospects, and the goal was to coordinate their progress. However, one lawyer, George L. Vaughn (1885–1950), a St. Louis lawyer and justice of the peace, was determined to push his case forward as fast as possible even if it did not fit the NAACP plan. Soon after the meeting, he persuaded the court to review his Missouri case of *Shelley v. Kraemer*. In this instance, a white neighbor sought to prevent an African-American family from purchasing property in their community. The court later included cases from Michigan and the District of Columbia for their judicial review.

Marshall and the LDF prepared the legal brief for the Michigan case while Charles Houston represented the District of Columbia cases and Vaughn prepared the Missouri brief. A challenge facing everyone was how to present data that would convince the court that previous decisions supporting private restrictive covenants were incorrect. The concept that state or court enforcement of restrictive covenants no longer made them a purely private matter offered one path to present. What the litigants also decided to include was data highlighting the negative social ramifications of restrictive covenants on African Americans. As part of their briefs, they included scholarly published material illustrating these issues. The group also worked to coordinate the friends of the case amici curiae briefs submitted to the court to ensure they were helpful and not repetitive. In particular, they sought to have the Department of Justice provide an amicus brief in which they provided their legal views on the case. With Truman as president, they felt they had a sympathetic presence in the White House supportive of their effort. Truman did allow the Department of Justice to write in support of the NAACP position. It was the very first time the federal government filed a brief supporting the NAACP.

Once the legal teams filed their briefs, Marshall organized a review and rehearsal session at Howard University as was his practice for other U.S. Supreme Court cases. Law school faculty served as the surrogate court justices while second-year law students and other knowledgeable individuals questioned Marshall and the other presenters to the court. It was a rigorous session that readied them for the kind of questions the justices might pose. Because of segregation rules in Washington, the various legal teams had to stay in an African American–owned boarding house, where they had to eat all of their meals, as no white restaurant would serve them. And as no white cabs would stop for them, they rode to the U.S. Supreme Court in black-operated cabs (Motley, 1998, p. 68).

To the surprise of the legal teams, on the day of their appearance before the court, three of the justices disqualified themselves because they lived in places with restrictive covenants. Marshall gave the final presentation to the court on behalf of the anti–restrictive covenant lawyers. His well-rehearsed presentation and response to questions from the justices was "elegant and articulate," according to one of the observers (James, 2010, p. 194). In May 1948, the court rendered its *Shelley v. Kraemer* decision. In a 6–0 vote, they agreed with the argument of Marshall and others that judicial enforcement of restrictive covenants was invalid under the Constitution. Both the sociological data and the view that court enforcement took restrictive covenants out of the realm of private actions protected by the Constitution proved persuasive to the justices.

The decision gave Marshall, the LDF, and the legal teams involved a tremendous victory. Until the court handed down its ruling, they were unsure as to how the justices might view the case. Marshall later said they "were all scared to death" about the decision. Once he heard the verdict, Marshall took the public position that it justified thirty-one years of effort by the NAACP to outlaw housing discrimination. He also said it "gives thousands of prospective homebuyers throughout the United States new courage and hope in the American form of government" (Long, 2011, p. 235).

As a headline in the *Pittsburgh Courier* overly optimistically announced, it meant African Americans "Can Live Any Where You Can Buy" (Vose, 1967, p. 212). The decision also meant the African Americans sued for purchasing homes in white neighborhoods did not have to leave and lose their investment. The court's verdict launched several hours of celebration in the New York headquarters of the NAACP and continued to elevate the reputation of Thurgood Marshall as a civil rights lawyer.

Two additional important precedents also emerged from the process of assembling the case. The briefs presented by Marshall made extensive use of sociological data illustrating the negative social and economic impact that restrictive covenants had upon African-American access to property ownership. Ghettoes with all the attendant problems of overcrowding, overpriced costs, and health issues emerged in part because of restricted access to housing according to the data. This information, Marshall believed, had an influential impact on the thinking of the justices. The successful use of sociological data in these cases established a strategy that Marshall saw as a powerful tool for use in future cases.

The other important precedent set was the decision of the federal government to provide a friend of the court brief on behalf of the NAACP. The decision to issue the brief was the result of extensive lobbying by the NAACP and other sympathetic groups directed toward President Truman and the attorney general Tom Clark. This lobbying tactic had been used in the past but had previously elicited tepid White House support at best. With Harry Truman as president, the federal government became more supportive of protecting the rights of all citizens. As civil rights became an issue of emphasis under Truman's leadership, it would come to work to Marshall's advantage in the future.

4

The Truman Years

When Marshall and the legal team working on the restrictive covenant cases requested a brief from the attorney general supporting their efforts, they expected a positive response. On a case of this magnitude, they knew the attorney general would confer with the president about whether to get involved. After inheriting the presidency with the death of Roosevelt, the new president, Harry S. Truman (1884–1972), had done several things indicating his support for protecting African-American civil rights.

A year earlier in 1947, Truman spoke at the national conference of the NAACP at the invitation of Walter White. It was the first time a sitting president had done that. Franklin D. Roosevelt only had reluctantly sent written messages to some of the past national meetings of the organization. Truman did not just send a written message but decided to speak in front of the Lincoln Memorial, joined there by Eleanor Roosevelt, Supreme Court justice Hugo Black, and Chief Justice Fred M. Vinson. Nationally broadcast on radio and presented to an audience of ten thousand at the site, Truman's appearance indicated his respect for the NAACP and his interest in civil rights. In the presentation he spoke to the need for a more proactive stance by the federal government on civil rights. For him, the government's role was to serve as "a friendly, vigilant defender of the rights and equalities of all Americans" (Truman, 1947). *The Crisis* described the presentation as the most comprehensive speech on minority rights ever given by a president (Shogan, 2013, p. 101).

This speech came several months after Truman had proposed the creation of the President's Committee on Civil Rights. This decision resulted from a discussion with Walter White and other civil liberty activists. They came to Washington to talk about the rise in lynchings and hate literature around the nation. Their presentation stunned Truman and spurred him to create his committee. Its task was to investigate civil liberties violations and to contemplate ways to reduce racial tensions around the country. After completing its work, the committee was to make recommendations to the president and the nation. It was a plan White and the NAACP found exciting, and they provided suggested nominations for the committee. That same year, Truman appointed William Hastie, who had long connections to the NAACP, as the territorial governor of the Virgin Islands, the first African American to hold that job. In addition, in his 1947 State of the Union address, Truman decried segregation and discrimination as "attacks upon the constitutional rights of individual citizens as a result of racial and religious bigotry." These actions marked an important difference between Truman and Roosevelt on human rights issues.

As president, Roosevelt had avoided public positions regarding civil rights and African-American issues for fear of offending Southern democrats whom he needed politically. It was an issue that Marshall and other civil rights advocates found frustrating and, at times, obstructive. Roosevelt's initial refusal to take steps to force companies receiving government war contracts to follow nondiscriminatory hiring practices was one example. It took the threat of a massive march on Washington in 1941 by A. Philip Randolph (1889–1979), an African-American activist, to push him to create the Fair Employment Practices Commission to watch over the hiring process. Once Truman became president, he almost immediately adopted a different stance. He quickly included mention of civil rights issues in speeches during his first year in office, including a speech given at the United Nations Conference on International Organizations in 1945 and in special messages he gave to Congress that same year. While some criticized Truman as talking more than taking concrete actions, he did create an environment where civil rights was a key issue under discussion. This encouraged Marshall, Walter White, and the NAACP. They were optimistic that Truman would provide support for their lawsuit opposing restrictive covenants.

Some of Truman's responses to civil rights violations early in his administration also caused Marshall to reevaluate his early opinion of him. When Isaac Woodward, an African-American veteran, was beaten and blinded by South Carolina police for moving too slowly according to a white bus driver, Truman condemned the actions of the police and had the Justice Department launch an investigation into the incident. In addition, Truman had his attorney general, Tom Clark, take an active interest in pursuing other violent civil rights violations. Although it proved difficult to get convictions in Southern courts, the support of Truman and his attorney general was a welcome change from the Roosevelt years. Truman also gained Marshall's approval when he backed legislation in 1945 for comprehensive universal health coverage. Marshall felt the legislation would help address the inequities in health care faced by African Americans (Long, 2011, pp. 156–157). In the end, the bill did not pass, but Truman's backing was appreciated.

For Marshall, the creation of the President's Committee on Civil Rights further enhanced his opinion of Truman. After the selection of the fifteen-member interracial committee, they met ten times and called in numerous people to talk to them. Marshall was one of the citizens invited to appear. During his conversation, Marshall proposed several issues the committee should investigate and recommend for action as part of their conclusions. Their final report, *To Secure These Rights*, contained many of his ideas. When Truman endorsed the report and brought to Congress a ten-point plan for improving civil rights, it resonated with Marshall. Likewise, Truman's Executive Order 9981, desegregating the armed services, also impressed Marshall. It meant the resolution of a long-standing concern of the NAACP. The timing of these actions especially impressed Marshall, as he knew Truman offered the plan on the eve of the Democratic National Convention to determine their nominee for president. Truman faced a difficult challenge there and in the general election. It was a courageous and calculated decision on Truman's part, as he recognized the importance of the support of African-American voters to enhance his chances of winning the national election. The work of Marshall and the LDF against white primaries, and allowing more African Americans to register to vote in South, had made them a significant bloc of voters for the upcoming presidential election. Truman wanted to pull African Americans away from their traditional support of the Republican "party of Lincoln" and into his camp, which offered concrete action on civil rights issues.

During his two terms as president, Truman created a supportive environment for Marshall and the NAACP to pursue their goals. He made it clear his administration stood for civil rights and against efforts to limit them for African Americans. As Marshall put it, "Well, you knew you had somebody to rely on. Who would go the whole hog . . . It's a warm feeling, you just can't put your hands on. But you know he's there when you need him" (Kennedy, 1997, p. 456). As a consequence, Marshall felt he had an ally in the federal government when he sought to fight unjust convictions or overturn laws violating the civil rights of African Americans.

It was Truman's very public expressions concerning civil rights that made Marshall and the LDF feel optimistic about the Department of Justice supporting their appeal of the restrictive covenant cases. Their optimism regarding Truman only increased after his 1948 presidential campaign and reelection. His campaign platform included pro–civil rights language, which prompted Southern Democrats to withdraw their support of him. He actively campaigned for African-American votes and in the process made the first ever appearance of a sitting president in Harlem. After winning the election, Truman invited African Americans to his integrated inaugural events and made sure they had access to hotel rooms. This was the first integrated celebration by any president. He also sent to Congress bills against lynching and poll taxes, promoting fair employment practices, and proposing a Civil Rights Act. His presidential appointments included several prominent African Americans, among them Edith S. Sampson as a delegate to the United Nations, Anna Arnold Hedgeman to work in the Health, Education, and Welfare Department, and William Hastie to the Third Circuit Court of Appeals, making him the first African American to serve as a judge at that level.

Thurgood Marshall also came under consideration by Truman for a position as a federal district judge. The possibility of a tenured life position was a tempting consideration for Marshall. A number of issues weighed in favor of seeking the position. His father's death caused him to think about his own health, which the constant travel, poor eating habits, smoking, and long working sessions for the NAACP all adversely impacted. His travel kept him away from home most of the time, leaving Vivian on her own. Often Vivian was then left to cope with the sadness and frustration alone because of Thurgood's LDF responsibilities. While Thurgood was away, Vivian occupied herself by working with civic groups like the Urban League and with family she had living in New York. She also would go to social events with friends when Thurgood was not available to accompany her. It was, at times, a frustrating and lonely existence, even though she understood the importance of his work.

As Truman deliberated on who to appoint for the judgeship, lobbying increased to have him seriously consider Marshall as one of the best-known African-American lawyers in the country. Both former first lady Eleanor Roosevelt and the president of the NAACP board, Arthur Spingarn, sent letters to Truman highly recommending Marshall. They noted he strongly supported Truman in meetings where others sought to criticize the president by stating Truman "has done more up to date for civil rights than all the other presidents put together" (Long, 2011, p. 255). However, the location of the position in New York became a complication when considering Marshall. Local black and white Democrats resisted Marshall's nomination because he was not part of the network there. He had not paid his political dues in New York by working for the party and rallying voters. Faced with this resistance, Truman decided to make a different choice rather than get entangled in New York politics. Not receiving the nomination certainly disappointed Marshall, but the constant demands for help directed to the NAACP allowed him to focus on other issues.

When Truman issued his 1948 executive order desegregating the armed forces, he anticipated resistance on the part of the military. To guide the transition, he created the President's Committee on Equality and Treatment and Opportunity in the Armed Services. Their task was to determine what military rules might hinder the desegregation process and to propose steps to implement his executive order. Truman let them know he wanted concrete results from their work so that the process would move forward. If, in the end, they found tough measures were needed on his part, he was ready to do what was necessary. It took the efforts of the committee, strong pressure from the secretary of defense, and the determination of Truman to move the process forward. The air force, navy, and marines led the way in implementing the integration of their units. Although not all their operations were integrated, they made steady progress toward the enactment of Truman's order. More resistant to making any changes, the army moved much more slowly down the path of desegregation. In part, the heritage of much of its leadership fueled this resistance, as many of the officers had Southern backgrounds and disliked the idea of integrated units. They consequently found innumerable reasons to delay the process.

A strategy used in the past became a key plan of attack against desegregation: discrediting the bravery and fighting ability of African-American

---

SCOTTSBORO BOYS

In 1931, nine young African-American men were arrested and accused of raping two white women in Scottsboro, Alabama. They were put on trial and quickly found guilty. Eight were sentenced to death, and one, a thirteen-year-old, was sentenced to life in prison. The American Communist Party (ACP) took on their case and made it a national issue. After they inevitably lost to an all-white jury, the ACP mounted a major national campaign to overturn the convictions and oppose racism.

The National Association for the Advancement of Colored People and other civil rights groups belatedly joined in the effort to save the young men and formed the Scottsboro Defense Committee. The Committee then appealed the case to the Supreme Court. They also worked to build public outrage over the legal system in Alabama and the South in general. During the appeal process, one of the women accusing the young men recanted her story and joined the campaign to spare their lives. The Supreme Court agreed to hear the case in 1937 and overturned the convictions. The boys spent several years in prison before their release. While their ordeal resulted in a blow to Southern judicial injustice, it was a personal tragedy for the young men.

soldiers to prove they should not be allowed to fight alongside their white counterparts. According to the army leadership, it would damage the morale of the white troops as well as put them in danger. During an NAACP board meeting in 1951, Marshall described the pattern the NAACP had seen previously during both the first and second world wars. Early in the conflict, African-American troops fought bravely and won commendations for their valor. But the positive attention they received worried the military, as it challenged their claims concerning the deficiencies of black soldiers. The traditional argument was that African Americans were cowards and would wilt in the heat of battle, but the early bravery shown by black troops weakened that claim. To undercut their successes, the military sought to discount their accomplishments and find fault with their service by arresting them and putting them on trial for questionable reasons. This pattern appeared in World War I and again during the World War II, as the military accused black troops of cowardice. As Marshall described it, "The heroes of yesterday were now cowards: the same men, the same outfits—brave one day and frightened the next" (Davis & Clark, 1992, p. 126).

When North Korea crossed the 39th parallel into South Korea launching the Korean War, the pattern described by Marshall appeared once again. One of the first units sent into combat was the 24th Infantry's African-American Third Battalion. They received positive press coverage for their courage in places like Yechon and Bloody Ridge. For example, Private First Class William Thompson held back the enemy by himself while his platoon withdrew. He subsequently died from the wounds he suffered, and received the first of two Congressional Medals of Honor presented to African-American soldiers in the Korean War. But this kind of success by black soldiers did not sit well with the army, according to Marshall. Almost overnight, the number of courts-martial of these soldiers increased dramatically and were out of proportion to the percentage of African-American soldiers fighting. The charges ranged from cowardice to misbehavior to failure to perform their assigned duties. As reports of these arrests and trials came back to the NAACP, Marshall announced the readiness of the LDF to come to the defense of these individuals who they felt were victims of racial discrimination. The response was overwhelming, as dozens of oftentimes desperate letters arrived. Many letters were from mothers of soldiers requesting Marshall do something to save their sons, whom they believed were unjustly accused.

After World War II, when the NAACP sought to help African-American soldiers, the military made it difficult for them to find information or informants to build their cases. Expecting even more difficulties with cases in a distant place like Korea, the organization believed they needed someone to travel to the Korean front to conduct a full investigation.

Thurgood Marshall was the logical choice to make the trip to investigate the circumstances behind the arrest of thirty-six African-American soldiers in Japan, who were in jail, on various charges. When Marshall first applied for a passport to travel to Japan and Korea, his request was denied by General Douglas MacArthur, the general in charge of the United Nations Command. He did not want Marshall to launch an investigation and persuaded the FBI to refuse Marshall travel clearance. He even sent a letter to Marshall in which he claimed no discrimination of African-American soldiers existed and that Marshall need not make the trip. When Marshall appealed to Truman, the president acquired clearance for him to travel to military headquarters in Japan and to Korea. The mission, Marshall believed, was one of the most important tasks of his career. He felt he was about to launch a full-frontal assault on discriminatory practices in the military. Just as significantly, undercutting discrimination in the army, in the view of the NAACP, was an important step toward undermining discrimination in the civilian sphere. If desegregation could work in the military, it would provide a positive example that could be emulated in other aspects of American life.

Upon his arrival in Japan, in January 1951, Marshall met with General MacArthur, whom he questioned about the process of desegregation under his command. MacArthur stated he was working on it, but that it would take time. When Marshall asked how long it might take, in light of the progress made by the other branches of the military, MacArthur replied that he did not think African Americans were yet qualified, and until he thought they were, integration would not happen. When Marshall continued to press MacArthur on that issue, the general had him leave. But MacArthur recognized that Marshall had the support of the president, and he ordered his staff to give their full cooperation to Marshall's investigation.

The first part of Marshall's inquiry focused on the prisoners held in Tokyo. He spent several days traveling to the stockade where they were located and interviewing them one at a time, privately. Each night he wrote up his findings and requested any further information he needed from the inspector general's office. This part of the review process went smoothly, as he had access to everyone he wished, including MacArthur and his immediate staff. Marshall moved carefully, seeking to extract the accurate facts of each of the thirty-four cases he investigated over a three-week period. In addition to the men in the stockades, Marshall also talked with soldiers from their units to gather more information. In the process he learned that evidence important to accurately determining the guilt or innocence of the accused men was left out or ignored by the military.

Even allowing for some exaggeration of the facts from both sides, Marshall was stunned by what he learned. There was little doubt that many of the arrests of the soldiers involved a biased application of army regulations. For example, one soldier charged with dereliction of duty had proof he was in an army hospital during the time he was accused of neglecting his responsibilities. At his trial, despite having written confirmation of his hospital stay from a doctor, the army sentenced him to ten years of hard labor. Part of the trouble Marshall found with many of the cases was that the soldiers faced an all-white court-martial system and defense witnesses were frequently not allowed to testify. Consequently, the process did not allow the accused much opportunity to defend themselves. In one instance, the process was so badly flawed that Marshall wrote directly to Truman asking for dismissal of the death sentence of the soldier who Marshall believed had not received a fair trial. Military medical doctors diagnosed him with mental issues and suffering from acute anxiety, yet the court still found him guilty and sentenced him to death for leaving his post. In fact, Marshall argued, the army had ignored their own procedures when pronouncing sentence. Truman, after reviewing the case, eventually commuted the death sentence to twenty years in prison. It was not the final result Marshall desired, but it saved the soldier's life.

After three weeks of interviews in Tokyo, Marshall felt he needed to travel to Korea and conduct more on-site interviews. He also wanted access to more of the original trial materials and other documents associated with the courts-martial of African-American servicemen on the battlefront. What he found while there convinced him that the army continued to treat African-American soldiers more harshly than their white counterparts. While African-American soldiers made up only about 20 percent of the forces in Korea, the vast majority of the courts-martial cases prosecuted by the army focused on them. Even more disappointing was the execution of the prosecution process. It was clear the military used the slightest excuse to bring charges against black soldiers. Many of the charges Marshall found were in his estimation trumped-up allegations created to bolster the army's claim that African-American soldiers lacked courage and the qualities of character that white soldiers possessed. It was this unsubstantiated and patently false claim that formed the basis for the army's argument against integrating its forces.

This attitude was reflected in the treatment African-American soldiers received from their white officers. When interviewed, African Americans told Marshall many of the white officers openly insulted their troops. They showed little respect for men who were willing to go into battle and possibly die for their country. One white officer was said to have told his troops, "I despise negro troops and I don't want to command you. The regiment is no good and you are lousy. You don't know how to fight" (Tushnet, 2001, p. 135). It was an attitude Marshall found easy to believe after his encounters with General MacArthur. During one of his initial meetings with the general, Marshall noticed MacArthur had no African Americans working on his staff and, more oddly, no African Americans playing in his military band. In each instance he said there were not African Americans qualified enough to hold any of those positions. Marshall thought it strange there were no African Americans in the military good enough to work with the general, let alone skilled enough to play in the band. This bias against the abilities of African-American soldiers flowed from the highest levels of command downward in direct disregard for Truman's orders to desegregate the military. It made for poor frontline morale and distrust between the GIs and their officers.

As he went through the records of the trials, Marshall was shocked by the manner in which the army had conducted them. Men were sometimes pulled from the front lines of battle and brought in for trial on charges they were unaware were pending against them. Due legal process did not seem to hold for these cases. While prosecution witnesses were allowed to testify, defense witnesses did not always receive the same opportunity to share their information. The officers assigned to defend them frequently were not the preferred choice of the accused and rarely had enough time to prepare an adequate defense. In some cases, the attorney might only have met with the accused fifteen minutes or less before they went to trial. The courts-martial themselves operated in a very swift fashion. The military courts sometimes held as many as four trials a day in this manner. Some trials lasted barely fifty minutes and resulted in a guilty verdict for the accused. In Marshall's estimation, the effort to discover the truth was rarely the main concern of the court officials. He believed an African American put on trial in Mississippi had more time to have his case prepared than a soldier in the military. The army process had little respect for the rights of the individual. Moreover, African-American soldiers consistently received far more severe sentences for their alleged crimes than white military men received for similar infractions. During the time he was in Korea, no white soldiers were sentenced to more than five years in prison, while thirty African Americans received longer sentences, and one was sentenced to death (Tushnet, 2001, p. 135).

As black imprisoned soldiers watched the court-martial process unfold, they lost all trust in the military and in the possibility of receiving fair treatment. It seemed that no matter what proof they offered, their guilt was assumed by military tribunals. As one soldier told Marshall during his interview, "We knew when we went to trial that we would be convicted. What could we expect? We knew the score" (Tushnet, 2001, p. 133). When the soldiers found themselves placed on trial, they feared the worst and worried the outcome might be a long sentence or even execution. Despite the unfair treatment directed toward African-American troops, they continued to fight and sacrifice for their country. They did this despite propaganda efforts by the Communists in radio broadcasts and pamphlets reminding them of how their country abused them.

Thurgood Marshall spent five weeks investigating and gathering information related to the military trials of African-American soldiers. Upon his return to the United States, he assembled a report for publication by the NAACP. Before his findings were published, in May 1951, as a *Report on Korea*, Marshall gave several speeches detailing what he discovered. In these presentations, he outlined key critical issues from his vantage point. First among them were the underlying racial tensions between black soldiers and white officers who disparaged them, which he thought resulted in the arbitrary charges and courts-martial. Second, he believed the desire by the army hierarchy to resist desegregation by assailing the fighting resolve of African-American troops motivated many of the arrests. And third, Marshall argued that the persistence of racially discriminatory practices characterized the entire operation of the army and fueled its biased actions. At the heart of these actions stood General Douglas MacArthur, who did nothing to discourage these discriminatory practices and who essentially refused to desegregate the army as ordered by his commander-in-chief, Harry Truman. MacArthur, according to Marshall, "was as biased as any person I've run across" (Tushnet, 2001, p. 452). This bias blinded MacArthur to acknowledging any problems with segregation or trumped-up charges against African-American soldiers who he believed were inferior. After directly observing the impact of this bias, Marshall concluded that as long as there was racial bias in the army, the legal injustices he documented would continue. General MacArthur was a root cause of the problem.

Consequently, Marshall and the NAACP brought growing pressure to bear on the policies of the army under Macarthur. They insisted his racial beliefs undercut the efficiency of the war in Korea. None of the other branches of the military suffered from the same problems Marshall found with the army. And, when black soldiers fought alongside white soldiers as battlefront conditions dictated it, the problems predicted by MacArthur did not appear. Marshall turned to the public to help bring about this change through his speeches and by working with the press. Papers like *The New York Times, The Chicago Defender,* and the *Pittsburg Courier* followed Marshall's lead and called for changes in U.S. Army policy. Truman and others in his administration observed this growing crisis centered around MacArthur. These and other problems of insubordination Truman had with General MacArthur culminated in his replacing the general in April 1951, just four months after Marshall's return from Japan and Korea. MacArthur's replacement, General Matthew Ridgeway, immediately moved forward with integration. He believed segregation was inefficient and improper. His perspective was supported by research done for the army called "Project Clear," which found that "racial segregation limits the effectiveness of the Army" (Shogan, 2013, p. 159). The African-American community hailed this as a victory resulting from the efforts of Marshall and the NAACP.

Besides rallying public opposition to segregation in the army, Marshall also worked on the cases of the black servicemen he investigated who faced long jail sentences or the death penalty. Under Marshall's direction, the NAACP presented their case to the secretary of the army and talked with the judge advocate general about revising the court-martial procedures to ensure greater fairness. Their conversations resulted in the overturning and reduction of the penalties in half of the cases examined by Marshall while in Korea. They also prevented the execution of one soldier. He even eventually gained his freedom. But Marshall was not satisfied and continued to fight for the exoneration of the remaining men.

While the resolution of the Korea cases was important, it was not the end of the injustices faced by African-American soldiers. Prejudice also remained a major challenge back in the United States and resulted in incidents that needed the intervention of the LDF. The goal of the NAACP was to end all forms of racial discrimination and segregation in the military at home and abroad. This involved their participation in cases resulting from the stationing of African-American soldiers on Southern bases. One such issue arose at Fort Benning, Georgia. When fighting occurred between African-American soldiers and the police of nearby Columbus, Georgia, five of the soldiers were arrested. The NAACP had to step in and defend them as well as other black military personnel in other places who found themselves in compromised situations because of their color. But the instances such as the Fort Benning events became less frequent under General Ridgeway. This allowed Marshall to turn his attention more squarely on the task he believed would change the role of segregation throughout the nation.

5

The Bridge to Brown

Many African Americans in the armed services at the conclusion of World War II returned to civilian life seeking a college education and the economic benefits that accompanied a degree. They had access to the GI Bill, which would pay for part of their college expenses, but segregation in higher education made finding a college that would accept them difficult. There were not enough spots to meet the demand, especially in graduate schools. For example, ten times as many people applied to Howard's medical programs than the school could accept. Many Southern states did not provide any graduate programs for African Americans but did provide them for white residents. Marshall said this deprived African Americans of the medical and legal services they needed and deserved. After having risked their lives for their country, veterans did not easily accept this situation and looked to Marshall to make a difference for them as he did when the army mistreated them. Before the war, Marshall had made progress on this front with the case of Lloyd Gaines's efforts to attend the law school at the University of Missouri. The intervention of the war slowed efforts on that front, as other issues took up the resources of the limited LDF staff. Nevertheless, Marshall remained eager to move forward on Charles Houston's plan to attack the concept of separate but equal by way of education.

To that end, Marshall held gatherings of lawyers and legal experts in Atlanta and New York in 1946. In the meetings they discussed what strategies to use going forward to break the back of segregation in education.

What they needed, according to Marshall, was a "unified campaign" to challenge unequal educational opportunities (Memo, 1945). They were going to have to force the South, in particular, to provide equal educational opportunities for African Americans. To do this they agreed to use the concepts undergirding the *Gaines* case and demand truly separate but equal facilities or admission to existing white programs. They also sought to nullify the tactic of Southern schools offering funds to defray the cost of tuition to encourage African-American applicants to attend schools in other states. What they needed were the right candidates and cases to put before the U.S. Supreme Court.

Thurgood identified three cases he felt would fit the bill. One was in Texas and the other two in Oklahoma. In Oklahoma the state NAACP had met and agreed to seek to enroll African-American students in the University of Oklahoma. Marshall attended the meeting and endorsed their plan. The Oklahoma residents had an excellent law school candidate in twenty-one-year-old Ada Lois Sipuel (1924–1995), the daughter of Travis Bruce Sipuel, a widowed minister. The second Oklahoma candidate, G. W. McLaurin, wanted to obtain a doctorate in education and planned to apply to that University of Oklahoma graduate program. The test case involving Ada Sipuel moved forward first. Her family had moved to Norman, Oklahoma, from Tulsa where they lost their home to arson in the 1921 race riots, and their father was put in jail by the militia. A member of the local NAACP board and the editor of the *Black Dispatch*, Roscoe Dunjee, helped organize the test case. The local newspaper, *The Daily Oklahoma*, then wrote a story about their plan. This news prompted the board of regents of the university to issue a directive to the university president to refuse to admit any African-American students in accordance with state law.

Initially, the NAACP plan was to have her brother challenge the law school at the University of Oklahoma, but he entered Howard instead, and Ada Sipuel volunteered to make the application. She was determined and would not disappear the way Lloyd Grimes had if they won the case. Marshall told Houston that Sipuel possessed "the character and commitment" needed to stay with the case (Memo, 1945). An excellent student and graduate of the Colored Agricultural and Normal University at Langston, Oklahoma, Sipuel was a perfect candidate to challenge the segregation policies of the University of Oklahoma Law School. When she brought her application to the president, Dr. George Lynn Cross, in January 1946, he rejected her application. In the process he informed her that her credentials qualified her, but the laws of the state of Oklahoma prohibited blacks and whites from attending school together. Her race and color prevented her acceptance. Had he admitted Sipuel, Cross would face potential fines of one hundred to five hundred dollars per day, and any white students attending classes with her faced fines of up to twenty dollars per day.

Dr. Cross, in an interview years later, noted that Sipuel was an excellent candidate for a test case, given her academic record and her poise. Her application did not come as a surprise to him or others at the school. Dunjee, who accompanied Sipuel, had shared their plan in advance. Dunjee, following steps laid out by Marshall, asked President Cross to put in writing that Sipuel's rejection was due to her race. Cross was sympathetic to their goals and readily agreed. In addition, several thousand white students in support of her application demonstrated near his building for her acceptance. Afterward, a group of white students went to lunch with her. They had to eat at the local YMCA-YWCA because no restaurant in Norman would serve African Americans. They encouraged her not to give up. Marshall took note of this student support and saw it as a positive part of his goal to end segregated education. It took away one more argument used by administrators that students would refuse to attend classes with African-American students or would withdraw from the university (Wattley & Fisher, 2017).

The ultimate goal of Sipuel's application was to bring legal action against the university and have the case wind its way through the court system to the Supreme Court. There, the hope was to obtain a ruling overturning Sipuel's rejection because of her race as well as overturning the 1896 *Plessy v. Ferguson* ruling, which established the separate but equal standard. When the university rejected her application, Sipuel's attorneys quickly filed suit in the county court at the advice of Marshall. From past experience he knew following this path would make it easier to eventually get the case to the U.S. Supreme Court. In their brief, the lawyers argued that by rejecting her solely because of her race, the university was in violation of the Fourteenth Amendment and the court should order the university to admit her. The county judge denied their request.

The case then went to the Supreme Court of Oklahoma in Norman in March 1947. It was at this point that Marshall flew in from New York and became directly involved. Because African Americans were discouraged from staying in Norman after sundown, each night Marshall and the team had to drive to Oklahoma City where they stayed at the homes of local residents (Rowan, 1993, p. 147). The core of Marshall's argument in the case was that Oklahoma had to provide African-American students the same educational opportunity it provided white students. He referenced the *Gaines* case in which the U.S. Supreme Court had decreed as much. Even establishing a separate law school did not qualify unless it provided exactly the same educational opportunities as the white law school. In response, the court took the position that the university did not have to create a separate law school for African Americans until it had sufficient applicants to warrant one. Until then, Ada Sipuel would have to bide her time.

The Oklahoma Supreme Court therefore sustained the lower court ruling. They also agreed with the lower court's point of view that an African-American applicant first had to indicate their willingness to attend a separate segregated school. If that was not available, they could then sue for entrance to the white program. Sipuel had not done those things. Consequently, in the eyes of the court, this invalidated her claim for admission to the university law school. Their ruling did, however, allow Marshall to appeal the case to the U.S. Supreme Court.

The brief presented to the U.S. Supreme Court by Marshall and the LDF focused on several key issues. The first centered on the Oklahoma State Supreme Court ruling, which they interpreted as an error on the part of that court. They believed it should have ordered the University of Oklahoma to admit Sipuel since no other law school existed in Oklahoma for her to attend. Asking her to wait until enough additional African Americans applied to warrant the creation of a segregated law school deprived her of her rights under the Fourteenth Amendment.

Next, they zeroed in on the constitutionality of the *Plessy v. Ferguson* court ruling itself. The logic of that decision, from their perspective, undergirded the rulings of the lower courts in Oklahoma. They argued that it did not apply to this case, as no separate and equal facility existed in Oklahoma

---

NATIONAL COUNCIL OF NEGRO WOMEN

In 1935, women leading twenty-eight African-American women's organizations created the National Council of Negro Women (NCNW). They elected Mary McLeod Bethune, an activist and the founder of Bethune-Cookman College, their first president. Their goal was to fight for improved racial and economic conditions in the United States and around the world with a special focus on topics of importance to African-American women. They lobbied for the desegregation of the military, pressed for more positions for African-American women in the federal government, and joined legal efforts combating voter discrimination. At the grassroots level, they launched voter education and registration drives focused primarily on the South.

As the civil rights movement gained momentum, NCNW under the leadership of its fourth president, Dorothy Height, became an important financial, intellectual, and planning contributor. Height played a key role in the organization of major events, like the 1963 March on Washington. Under Height, the NCNW also created "Wednesdays in Mississippi" in 1964, where teams of interracial women worked together for civil rights in Mississippi. Many NCNW members also were important supporters and contributors to the NAACP.

for Sipuel to use, so she should gain immediate entrance to the program. They took their position a step further by also suggesting that the concept of separate but equal had no social justification and should be repudiated. It hinged on the belief that differences existed between the races that demanded their legal separation from one another. This supposition was illegal and harmful from their point of view. Through the extensive research of social scientists, educators, and other experts, Marshall illustrated the negative impact that the "separate but equal" legal ruling had upon African Americans who were being told they were not as good as their white counterparts. In particular, they cited the influential 1944 work of the noted sociologist and economist Gunnar Myrdal, *An American Dilemma*, in which he contended that the system of segregation in the South was harmful to African Americans and illegal. In addition, they argued that the implementation of the concept over the years showed that separate but equal almost never happened. Invariably, the two facilities were separate and *unequal* in what they provided. The provisions offered African Americans rarely matched that of their white counterparts. This actuality negated the basic premise upon which the idea was based. As a result, the terms "separate" and "equal" were totally inconsistent in their application. Therefore, Marshall argued, the court should no longer allow the concept to stand and should rule it unconstitutional. This was a major strategic shift for the NAACP, as they sought to persuade the court to bring an end to the fifty-year-old landmark *Plessy v. Ferguson* decision. To persuade the court to rule in this fashion would constitute a major victory in the battle against segregation.

Marshall argued the case before the court in January 1948, and within four days the justices provided a ruling. They found unanimously that the university had denied Sipuel admission illegally and that they had to provide her with the same educational opportunity they offered others. The justices sent the case back to the Oklahoma Supreme Court, which directed the university to either admit her to the white law school or open up a separate law school for her to attend. If they did not, they were to suspend operation of the white law school until one was opened for Sipuel. Although the justices avoided the issue of the legitimacy of "separate but equal" as part of their ruling, they did put pressure on the university to provide an equal legal education for Ada Sipuel. Pleased with the victory, the NAACP proclaimed in a press release that the decision brought "educational equality a step nearer" (Press Release).

The Oklahoma Board of Regents quickly voted to create a separate law school for Sipuel. Within two weeks of the Supreme Court decision, they established a new law school as part of Langston University with a budget of fifteen thousand dollars and three faculty members. The new school was set up in Oklahoma City, the state capital, in a space in the library roped off for the African-American law students. The NAACP and Ada Sipuel refused to accept the makeshift operation. When the school officially opened, Sipuel refused to enroll. Instead, on advice from Marshall, she returned to the law school at the University of Oklahoma, which again denied her admission. Faculty and students wearing black armbands staged a massive protest rally on the university campus to express their disapproval of the disingenuous actions of the regents to get around the ruling of the courts. They called the Langston Law School a fraud and a hoax.

Thurgood Marshall immediately filed a motion with the Supreme Court. In it he insisted the board of regents had defied the ruling of the court. However, the justices denied his motion saying the local county court had jurisdiction in the matter, and Marshall would have to carry on the legal battle there. The lower court must decide if the separate law school established by the board of regents met the criteria of separate and equal. The justices also again refused to take on the core issue of the validity of the concept of separate but equal. Marshall led the team who argued the case before the county judge. He brought in professors from Harvard, Columbia, Wisconsin, Yale, and Chicago law schools to testify. They pointed out the shortcomings of the new law school at Langston as compared to other law schools. Marshall further illustrated the discrepancies more explicitly in his pointed cross-examination of the new dean of the Langston Law School. Nevertheless, the judge overseeing the trial ruled against Marshall (Ball, 1998, p. 73). He was not ready to undermine the tradition of segregation. The judge ruled that creating the separate school did not in fact defy the U.S. Supreme Court order, thus removing the basis for any protest on the part of Sipuel or the NAACP.

It was a disappointing setback for everyone seeking her admittance to the University of Oklahoma Law School. Marshall sought to have this ruling heard by the Oklahoma Supreme Court as quickly as possible in order to have it sent to the U.S. Supreme Court for further review. But it was not until January 1949 that the case was scheduled to come before that body, and by then the positive ruling by the Oklahoma Supreme Court on another NAACP challenge to segregated education, *McLaurin v. Oklahoma State Regents*, made pursuing the Sipuel case separately unnecessary.

In June 1949, the dean of admissions for the University of Oklahoma informed Ada Sipuel that she could attend classes there immediately. She started attending classes the next day. However, the stigma of separate but equal continued to plague her. When she went to her first class, there was a chair set aside for her in the back of the room with the sign "colored" affixed near it. Fortunately, her classmates supported her by offering words of encouragement as well as sharing books and notes with her. By the start of her second semester, all of the signs had been taken down, and as she

said, "I just moved down to the first row." Sipuel's attendance and graduation from the law school was an important milestone. Her case helped
open the door for others to get access to an education at the University of
Oklahoma and other schools that had previously refused admittance to
African-American students. As *The Chicago Defender* described, the initial U.S. Supreme Court ruling against the university was a step forward,
but "it did not sound the death knell of Jim Crow higher education in
Dixie'" (Wattley & Fisher, 2017, p. 476). It would take more litigation on the
part of Marshall and his associates to make that happen.

The efforts of George W. McLaurin (1887–1968) to attend the graduate
education program at the University of Oklahoma constituted another
step in the assault on segregation. McLaurin was a sixty-one-year-old professor at Langston University who had a master's degree from the University of Kansas and wished to obtain his doctorate in education. His
application was part of the Oklahoma NAACP's overall effort to desegregate the University of Oklahoma. In January 1948, six African Americans
applied to different graduate programs at the University of Oklahoma.
Once again, the university rejected all the applications, citing the state law
prohibiting black and white students from attending the same schools. Of
the six, Marshall decided to represent McLaurin. Marshall later explained
that they selected McLaurin in part because of his age. McLaurin offered
a rebuttal to charges made by Southern officials that what African

---

MENDEZ ET AL. V. WESTMINSTER

In 1944, when Gonzalo and Felicitas Mendez and other families learned
their children had to attend schools separate from the schools Anglo children
in their school district attended, they decided to file a class-action suit. In it
they challenged the policy in their district and in three other nearby districts.
They based their case on their rights as citizens under the Fourteenth Amendment. After nearly a year of deliberation, the state court judge ruled in their
favor. The school districts appealed to federal court arguing that this was a
local matter and outside the jurisdiction of the Constitution. The federal Ninth
District Court of Appeals upheld the ruling of the state court and the school
districts then dropped their resistance.

The case was the first decision to rule that school segregation itself was
unconstitutional. Previous school segregation cases brought by the NAACP
argued that the inferiority of segregated schools not segregation itself was
unconstitutional. The NAACP wrote a brief in support of the suit. The success
of the Mendez case encouraged the NAACP to more directly confront the
legality of "separate but equal," which became the basis of their position in
Brown v. Board of Education.

Americans truly wanted was social equality and intermarriage. This, they said was one of the key reasons they opposed educational desegregation. According to Marshall they specifically picked McLaurin because "he was sixty-eight years old and we didn't think he was going to marry or intermarry" (Kluger, 1975, p. 266). His case would undermine the social equality argument promoted by white officials.

Marshall focused the McLaurin case as an attack on the state laws in Oklahoma, which forbade integrated education in the state. Because he sought to challenge a state law, Marshall could bypass the local courts and go directly to the federal court system. In the federal district court, he argued that since Langston University did not have a doctorate program in education, the University of Oklahoma was obligated to provide McLaurin access to their program. The state law preventing his attendance, therefore, was unconstitutional, as it denied McLaurin his Fourteenth Amendment rights. The three judges of the federal district court hearing the suit ruled in support of Marshall's argument. They ordered the university to admit McLaurin because it had the legal duty to provide him with access to his desired degree in a state-supported institution. As no separate graduate program for African Americans existed, the university had to enroll him. They specifically noted they were not striking down Oklahoma's segregation laws but enforcing the "separate but equal" concept. It was not all Marshall had hoped to gain, but their decision represented another step toward his ultimate goal.

After the 1949 district court ruling, the Oklahoma state legislature changed the laws to allow African-American students to attend colleges with white students, but with separate facilities. The university subsequently admitted McLaurin but created a segregated environment within the school to educate him. The guidelines they established meant that he sat alone in the back of the classroom in a former broom closet. During the times McLaurin was allowed to eat in the campus lunchroom, all of the white students were barred from using it. In the university library, McLaurin had to work and read in a special section of the building, and there was a segregated toilet designated for his use. The university's goal was clearly to discourage him. Marshall considered the ostracizing of McLaurin humiliating. McLaurin argued that it prevented him from doing his best work, though he did not let it deter him. One bright spot was the sympathetic white students who supported him by tearing down "Reserved for Colored" signs created by the university to designate spaces set aside for McLaurin. When interviewed by the local paper, most students thought the actions of the school "were pointless and he should go to school like everyone else" (Hubbell, 1973, p. 189). What the students could not change was the strong racist attitude of the "sundown town" of Norman.

McLaurin had to schedule his classes so they ended before evening so he could safely leave the city.

Marshall went back to the federal courts to insist the university had undercut the intent of the U.S. Supreme Court ruling. The segregated restrictions placed on McLaurin did not allow him to interact with his fellow students, which Marshall argued provided an important part of the educational process. The lower-level federal courts rejected his reasoning with the response that separate but equal accommodations were acceptable. Marshall then appealed his objections to the U.S. Supreme Court. While McLaurin and Marshall waited to appear before the court, the university made some adjustments in their treatment of McLaurin. They now allowed him to use a table on the main floor of the library instead of sitting behind a book cart. But only he could use it; no white students could join him. The school allowed him to use the cafeteria at the same time as other students, but again, he had to sit at a table by himself. During classes he was moved into the main school room, but he still had to sit in a special row reserved only for "colored" students.

Marshall's appeal reached the U.S. Supreme Court, accompanied by amicus briefs from President Truman's Justice Department—yet another indication of Truman's commitment to fairer treatment of African Americans. After hearing all arguments, the court ruled unanimously in favor of Marshall, but in a decision of very narrow scope. Without addressing the issue of separate but equal, the justices examined only "whether a state may, after admitting a student to graduate instruction in its state university, afford him different treatment from other students solely because of his race." Within this narrow scope, they ruled against the state and the university, agreeing with Marshall that the conditions created by the university impaired McLaurin's ability to learn through regular interaction with other students. It made his education unequal. This the court found unacceptable, ruling that all students must receive the same treatment to ensure an equitable education. The university had to remove the impediments they had placed on McLaurin.

The court ruling in *McLaurin v. Oklahoma State Regents* further complicated other challenges faced by the University of Oklahoma. Earlier rulings had forced the university to accept African-American applicants in other graduate programs not offered at Langston University. The school opened up several courses that they decided would be segregated and available at different times from comparable white classes. What they didn't expect was for several dozen African Americans to enroll in these new classes. This unexpected demand forced them to scramble for additional instructors and increased state funding to underwrite the enforcement of a segregated system of classroom instruction. Things became even more complicated when in the fall of 1949, Julius Caesar Hill, an African-American student from Tulsa, demanded a dormitory room. To the dismay of school officials, he had acceptance papers and a receipt verifying his payment for a dorm room. He expected to have a place to stay. In response, the regents immediately instructed President Cross to locate separate dormitories for at least fifty African-American students. It was a wake-up call for the regents as to the expenses connected with maintaining a "separate but equal" education system. They had to somehow modify this strategy or go bankrupt in the process. This new challenge made clearer to them the larger goals of Marshall and the NAACP, who sought to disable segregation financially and cause its dissolution. The state and university had to either allocate more funds to operate a truly separate but equal system or accept desegregation. They also had the problem of the social complications of integration. African-American students wanted to attend football games, go to school dances, and participate in other campus social activities. Solving these issues became a complicated balancing act, especially as other white students criticized segregation on campus and threatened to breach the rules on numerous occasions. This was another set of challenges facing the university and the state as Marshall brought his appeal to the court in 1950. In some ways, the ruling of the court helped ease the problems facing the university by declaring the system the school had in place unconstitutional.

While working on the McLaurin case, Marshall also battled segregation in higher education on another front in Texas. As was the case in Oklahoma, the goal in Texas was to reject acceptance of segregated facilities and insist upon access to the programs at the major white institutions in the state. Going back to his work in Texas against the white primary in the *Smith v. Allwright* litigation, Marshall had developed strong connections with the Texas African-American community. When the NAACP decided to aggressively litigate against segregation in higher education, Marshall's Texas connections proved valuable. He convinced the Texas State Conference of the NAACP to publicly push for integration of the graduate program at the University of Texas, the largest university in the state. As they planned how to approach the legal battle, the Texas NAACP leadership invited Marshall to come and help them strategize. As a result of that summer of 1945 meeting, Marshall agreed to lead the legal attack with the financial support of the Texans.

Crucial to their strategy was identification of the right plaintiff. In general, for this kind of effort Marshall said, "It is more important to have the proper type of plaintiff than anything else in these cases, other than the community support" (Long, 2011, p. 217). Finding the right person was not a simple matter because potential candidates knew that this case would be psychologically, physically, and financially stressful. And even if they won the case, what would follow as they took classes might generate even greater strains. It was not a decision to be taken lightly. After several months of searching, Marshall and the team had almost given up hope they would find a suitable candidate. Finally, at a church meeting in Houston, a local NAACP leader made an inspiring presentation about the case and the search for a volunteer. After she finished, a volunteer stepped forward. He was Herman Marion Sweatt (1912–1982), a thirty-two-year-old mail carrier.

Sweatt later said it was an impulsive decision, as he had not gone to the meeting intending to volunteer. It surprised others in attendance as well, though Sweatt was active in the local community. He had participated in voter registration drives, raised funds to challenge the white primary in Texas, and served as the local secretary of the National Alliance of Postal Employees. In that role, he supported the alliance's charges of employment discrimination in the post office. They argued the postal service excluded blacks from supervisory positions. Working with lawyers on this project encouraged his interest in the legal profession. But in accepting the role as the plaintiff in an NAACP suit against the University of Texas Law School, he risked a great deal. He was married, had a federal job, and a comfortable life. This might all disappear because of his decision that night.

After the meeting, Sweatt talked with his wife, Cynthia, to ensure her support. As a public schoolteacher, Cynthia worried about losing her job. She also recognized that the litigation would take place in the state capital of Austin, often leaving her alone and vulnerable in Houston. Retaliation against Herman or Cynthia or other members of the Sweatt family was a real possibility. To calm the financial worries of the couple, the Texas NAACP promised to cover the costs associated with the litigation and the costs of graduate school if they won the case. He received these assurances, in part, because he fit many of the attributes described by Hastie as necessary for a strong plaintiff. Sweatt came from a long-standing and respected family in Houston. Herman Sweatt attended Wiley College in Marshall, Texas. It was the first college for African Americans in the west to gain an A rating from the Southern Association of Colleges and Schools. This was significant concerning his submission to the University of Texas Law School because many graduate programs did not accept applications from graduates of unaccredited colleges.

After graduation, Herman Sweatt worked as a principal for a couple of years and then went to graduate school at the University of Michigan. While at the university, he met another African-American grad student, Lloyd Gaines, who was there while awaiting a decision on his case before the U.S. Supreme Court against the University of Missouri. He was not impressed by Gaines's sense of his own importance. Sweatt thought Gaines had an overblown ego. He was struck, though, by Gaines's willingness to serve as the defendant in such an important civil rights lawsuit. This impression undoubtedly stuck with him and may have influenced his decision to take a similar step in Texas.

With the support of his family, Herman Sweatt moved forward with the plan to apply to the University of Texas Law School. To ensure that the only reason the University of Texas could reject his application was because of Sweatt's race, the NAACP carefully went over his academic credentials. Marshall played an important role in making sure they moved forward carefully and got the outcome they needed. The requirements to gain entrance to the law school only demanded the applicant have a bachelor's degree from an accredited college, have good moral character, and be over the age of nineteen. There was some concern on the part of Marshall that Herman Sweatt's alma mater, Wiley College, only gained accreditation the last two years he attended, but he decided to proceed, given Sweatt's strong qualifications.

On February 26, 1946, Herman Marion Sweatt, accompanied by a delegation of distinguished Texas African Americans, met on the University of Texas campus with the interim president, Theophilus Painter (1889–1969), and selected members of his staff. President Painter greeted the delegation and then heard a statement read by delegation member R. A. Hester, president of the Progressive Voters League in Dallas, Texas, stating Texas was not accepting its legal responsibilities per the *Gaines* case by denying African Americans the same educational opportunities it offered to whites. In particular, he wanted to know what Painter had done to push forward his public declaration to create a committee to study how to provide higher educational opportunities at the university for African Americans. Hester especially wanted more opportunities for returning African-American veterans and their children who needed a good education to compete for jobs in the state. President Painter responded by stating that the committee was not yet functioning, but the state offered out-of-state scholarships for African Americans. He also dismissed efforts by the state to provide more funds to upgrade one of its African-American state colleges, Prairie View A&M. Hester viewed that idea as a long-term plan that did not solve the immediate graduate school educational needs of African Americans.

After more discussion, Sweatt came forward and declared his wish to become a lawyer and his right to comparable legal training provided for other Texas law school students. He wanted to obtain that education in the state of Texas and not through an out-of-state scholarship. It did not matter if that training occurred at an equivalent African-American law school in Texas or at the university; he wished to obtain it in his home state. What he knew for sure was that he could not wait and wanted to begin studying the law immediately. Sweatt then provided President Painter with the appropriate paperwork for application to attend the University of Texas Law School. Painter had expected to receive an application that day and accepted Sweatt's material. After accepting the material, Painter told the delegation he was not accepting Sweatt's submission but intended to correspond with the Texas attorney general about the appropriate response by the university. The meeting ended at that point. The next day Marshall received a letter letting him know the process was underway. He was pleased to learn of the successful launch of the effort (Lavergne, 2010, p. 104). The question was how they would respond.

One worry of President Painter and the regents of the university was how the state legislature might respond to the graduate school demands of Texas African Americans. The Constitution of Texas had set up a permanent endowment, the Permanent University Fund, in 1876 to support the operation of the University of Texas system. In 1946 it provided nearly one million dollars to the university. The regents feared that the creation of a reputable law school for African Americans would draw a portion of those funds permanently away from the university. This was a part of the concern Painter had when he wrote to the attorney general for guidance. In the letter he made it plain that Sweatt was a qualified applicant except for the fact he was African-American. If the attorney general instructed him to deny admission to Sweatt, race was the crucial factor, and a court battle certainly would follow. It was exactly the type of letter and evidence Marshall needed as the centerpiece of any litigation he might bring forward. President Painter left it to the politicians to decide what should happen next. For their part, the law school students appeared unbothered by Sweatt's desire to join them, as an unofficial poll of the students indicated they saw nothing wrong with having him as a classmate.

The Texas attorney general, Grover Sellers, responded in a public ruling that Texas did not need to immediately provide for the law school education of Sweatt. They needed time to respond to his request, which they had begun to do prior to Sweatt's request for admission by elevating Prairie View A&M to university status and allowing it to teach any professional or graduate-level courses offered to white UT students. To accommodate Sweatt, the state, Sellers noted in his response to president Painter, would establish an appropriate law course for him at Prairie View University within forty-eight hours. Painter subsequently sent a letter of refusal to Sweatt.

To support Sellers's ruling, the Texas governor started the machinery to create a place to provide the graduate professional school level of education African Americans like Herman Sweatt had requested for many years. He hoped that his efforts to create a segregated graduate program of any type and quality would satisfy their demands. He was wrong. The court cases led by Thurgood Marshall in Oklahoma and Missouri, which the

U.S. Supreme Court ruled on prior to the conclusion of the Sweatt set of trials, had changed the legal landscape and what was now considered separate but equal.

As part of Sweatt's legal team, Marshall participated in the crafting of the brief brought before the district court in Austin. In a letter, he advised Sweatt to make himself familiar with its contents. The ruling of the district judge to this brief would help set the ground rules for the legal battles that followed. After hearing the arguments for each side in June 1946, the judge ruled for Sweatt in the sense that he believed Sweatt's right of equal protection under the law was violated because Texas had denied him the opportunity to obtain a legal education. However, Texas could rectify this oversight by establishing the necessary courses. The judge gave Texas six months to create the needed training opportunity for Sweatt and other interested African Americans. This outcome was expected but still disappointing to Thurgood Marshall. He hadn't expected the judge to force the university to admit Sweatt. Usually at that level of the courts, they supported local custom. Unfortunately, it meant he could do nothing for six months but observe the efforts of the state to accommodate the mandate set forth by the judge. He knew Texas would fall short of his goals but had to allow things to run their course.

To attempt to meet the judge's ruling, a committee set up by the state made two recommendations. The first was to elevate the status and funding of Prairie View A&M, and the second, to establish a "university of the first class for Negroes" (Lavergne, 2010, p. 131). The location suggested for the new university was Houston. While the state explored these plans, the law school at UT had six months to provide separate law training for Sweatt or have the judge force them to accept his application. In response, they created the law school of Prairie View located in Houston. As faculty, they identified "qualified" African-American lawyers. They also designated fifty thousand dollars for salaries and for the purchase of office space and a law library. To this end, the state acquired four rooms located in an office building in Houston. The rooms were renovated with new furniture and office equipment. Four hundred law books were assembled to get the law library off the ground. The state hoped that these steps would satisfy the judge and perhaps Sweatt and the NAACP. Anticipation of how the judge would perceive these efforts ran high on both sides.

Thurgood Marshall argued the case for Sweatt in district court after the six-month waiting period previously set by the judge had passed. He took the position that the cobbling together of a segregated law school in Houston did not meet the standard of equal education. The Prairie View Law School was not as good as the one at UT, and Sweatt should receive admittance there instead. The judge disagreed, as expected, and ruled the new segregated law school met the spirit of his previous judgment and the

Constitution. After the ruling, Marshall talked with reporters and let them know his efforts had just begun on behalf of Sweatt. He predicted they would take the case all the way to the U.S. Supreme Court if necessary. They planned to appeal the recent ruling immediately. At a later gathering attended by Marshall, Herman Sweatt echoed that same outlook, indicating he was ready to stay the course all the way to the Supreme Court.

While Marshall was optimistic about getting the *Sweatt* case to the U.S. Supreme Court, he was not as pleased with opposition he faced within the Texas African-American community. It was not a new issue, but a particularly bothersome one, as he faced white officials in Texas eager to find an alternative solution to the desegregation of the graduate programs. The challenge before the Texas African-American community was the best tactic to follow: one focused on desegregation or one which embraced the extra resources offered by the state for a segregated program. There were forceful arguments and voices on both sides of the issue.

A particularly influential voice on the side of pragmatic segregation and equalization in Texas was Charles Wesley, the publisher of the African-American newspaper the *Houston Informer.* As part of their response to the *Sweatt* ruling, the state floated the idea of creating a new university for African Americans in Houston. Houston had a large African-American population; a hospital and medical personnel for African Americans; a sizeable professional community; and a moderate educational institution, the Houston College for Negroes. Wesley felt this was a unique opportunity for Texas African Americans, and they should take advantage of it. He was not as optimistic as Marshall about overturning segregation. For Wesley, enhanced segregated educational facilities that would provide more jobs and educational opportunities for African Americans offered a viable alternative to idealistically pushing for desegregation of the University of Texas. Texas officials had strongly resisted fair treatment of African Americans for years, and there was no reason to expect it would change. In fact, Marshall's legal action might anger Texas officials and result in retaliation by reducing the resources directed toward African-American education. This would mean fewer jobs for that community. Wesley thought Marshall and the NAACP were "cuckoo" for fighting only for desegregation (Rowan, 1993, p. 151). There were sizeable new resources available for African-American education for the first time in Texas, and black Texans should leverage it to their advantage. Equalization of the resources put into African-American institutions by the state seemed a pragmatic alternative to Wesley.

Wesley echoed concerns that troubled many in the local African-American community. They worried about the impact of fighting for and even attaining desegregation. Retaliation for disrupting racial tradition by bringing legal suits was often the issue faced by the individuals brave enough to step forward. And successful efforts at desegregation often resulted in the loss of jobs for African Americans when their positions disappeared with the desegregation of schools or teaching positions. Winning a court case did not end racism and unfair treatment of African-American workers. Wesley felt the reality was that African Americans lived in a world separate from their white counterparts and "that inasmuch as we are separated, we should demand our right to equality" (ibid., p. 115). His point of view was supported by a poll taken of African-American Texans that indicated that about 60 percent of them favored the creation of a university for negroes instead of the integration of the University of Texas (ibid., p. 139).

This concern about the chances for success versus the drawbacks in pursuing a strategy of integration was not new to Thurgood Marshall. The NAACP staff had quarreled over similar issues when Charles Houston headed the legal division and Marshall worked for him. W.E.B. Du Bois, the editor of the NAACP publication *The Crisis*, took a public stand in opposition to integration as the best strategy to follow. He suggested, instead, a focus on economic segregation in which African Americans leveraged institutions they controlled for the forward progress of the race. If this meant accepting segregation in the short run, he saw that as more useful than focusing on integration. This was not a policy Houston or the other leaders of the NAACP would endorse. Their goal was to attack Jim Crow laws and shape new legal interpretations that supported integration. It stood as the guiding principle for many of the cases they sought to get before the U.S. Supreme Court.

The attack by Charles Wesley on Marshall and his legal strategy echoed similar concerns Marshall faced in the past. It was not unusual for Marshall to be approached by African Americans who told him how much they resented segregation in one breath but, in the next, wondered if it might make more sense to not to rock the boat and avoid putting their homes and jobs in jeopardy. When he had pushed for desegregation of schools in South Carolina, he created an uproar among African-American teachers worried about their jobs, even as he pushed for equal pay for them. Marshall recognized the fallout associated with his legal efforts but firmly believed things would not change for African Americans if they did not bring pressure to bear on the nation. The slow route of politely requesting equal treatment and relying upon the generosity of white officials often resulted in great disappointment and no progress.

In Texas, Thurgood knew white officials sought an excuse to avoid desegregating the law school at UT. He worried that Wesley's attacks in his newspaper would give those officials more ammunition to use against Sweatt's case. Marshall also worried that Wesley's editorials might drive a wedge within the African-American community that state officials could exploit. He knew, in particular, the newly elected attorney general, Price Daniel, wanted to paint Marshall as an outsider, a man who did not understand what Texas African Americans really wanted: "equal educational opportunities in the best separate schools that can be built" (Lavergne, 2010, p. 140). Daniel threatened that not accepting the separate school would be a serious political blunder for that community. Marshall felt he had to take a strong public stand to remind African Americans what was at stake and that progress was possible following his lead.

He made his position clear after reading another Wesley editorial severely criticizing Marshall and his integration strategy. He traveled to Texas in September 1947 for the state NAACP conference where he offered a forceful rebuttal of Wesley. He began by asserting that without equality of education, no American citizen has complete equality, and a dual system of education segregating the races prevents equal education, which was why the NAACP firmly opposed that possibility. For Marshall, separate educational institutions were unconstitutional, unlawful, and immoral. In a criticism of Wesley and others who were willing to embrace segregated schools, he pointed out that equality in separate schools was easy to obtain, as the staunchest segregationist agreed with that idea. That is why the Texas legislature offered to put money into a "Jim Crow University" that kept the races separate. Marshall also said he was not surprised there were individuals in the African-American community who would accept this option in order to get a job, a contract to help build the school, or any other thing that might result in their personal gain. He was not surprised that those individuals and their allies would attack him and the NAACP to attain their goals. These accusations did not deter Marshall's resolve as he declared a full-fledged battle against segregation in the public schools of Texas.

Marshall then went on to call out Wesley directly by accusing him of being an opportunist, seeking the easy solution to the education problems of Texas, which would not work. He pointed out that for many decades African Americans had fought for equality in separate schools with no success. For him, there was no easy answer to segregation and discrimination. The only approach that made sense was to attack segregation directly. It would not be an easy struggle. In fact, it was going to be a very difficult process, a long-drawn-out fight. But the struggle was well worth the effort. It was how they won the white primary battle in Texas not so long ago. There, success had come because everyone pulled together for the same goal. Following that same pattern in the school segregation battle gave them a better chance of success. Cooperation was the key.

Marshall concluded with the words, "We are convinced that it is impossible to have equality in a segregated system, no matter how elaborate we build the Jim Crow citadel and no matter whether we label it the 'Black

University of Texas,' 'the Negro University of Texas' . . . or a more fitting title, 'An Apology to Negroes for denying them their constitutional rights to attend the University of Texas'" (Rowan, 1993, pp. 151–153). Marshall could not have made his ideas on the topic any plainer or his resolve to continue on that path clearer. He had no doubt that by attacking the legal foundation of segregation, African Americans in Texas and elsewhere would benefit in the long run. Marshall intended to prove Wesley wrong through his work on the Sweatt litigation. To emphasize his unwillingness to accept segregation in his appeal of Sweatt's case, for the first time, he attacked segregation head-on, suggesting that "there can be no separate equality" (Lavergne, 2010, p. 143). In the process, he signaled to the state legislature that the separate university they were building in Houston with its Austin law school did not meet his criteria for the resolution of the Sweatt litigation. Acquiring the support of parts of the African-American community for the state project would not slow or end Marshall's legal battle either.

Consequently, when UT sent Herman Sweatt a letter of acceptance to the hastily created segregated law school in Austin, Marshall counseled him not to accept. The new school was not equivalent to the one at UT, despite the claims of state officials. Marshall also worked with local leaders to discourage other African Americans from applying to and attending the college. Only admission to the law school at UT would suffice. Not a single student applied. The forthright stand against segregation now embraced by Sweatt, Marshall, and the legal team elevated it to the forefront of the NAACP's legal cases. Its claim that segregation in itself violated the Fourteenth Amendment pushed the NAACP further away from the Margold plan, which had pursued an indirect assault on segregation. They now forthrightly condemned separate but equal and demanded an end to the reign of *Plessy v. Ferguson* (Long, 2011, pp. 213–214). As Marshall noted in a 1947 letter to the *Dallas News*, he would only stop when segregation stopped (ibid., p. 214).

This focus on the inherent inequality of separate law schools dominated the *Sweatt*'s sessions in the district court. Marshall tirelessly pushed to illustrate that the new Austin law school did not measure up in any way to the UT law school. He did not expect a favorable ruling from the judge but sought to create a trial record for use in his appeal to the U.S. Supreme Court. One of the steps he took was to introduce a sociological perspective into the proceedings by having noted law and anthropological scholars, such as Dr. Robert Redfield of the University of Chicago, speak to the detrimental impact of segregation. It was an early instance of a tactic Marshall would employ in later cases to add to the power of his condemnation of segregation. It was not an approach everyone on the team initially thought was appropriate. They worried the evidence was not scientific hard data from a laboratory and that judges might disregard it or use it to undermine the NAACP case. But Marshall felt it offered another pathway to illustrating the irrationality of segregation and its impact on the people who suffered under it. He saw it as an important argument to make. People attending the trial said Marshall was impressive in his questioning of witnesses and in the way he carried himself throughout the process of arguing his case. Many people attended just to see him in action. Despite his efforts, however, the judge ruled in favor of the state and against Marshall in June 1947.

As Sweatt's case worked its way to the U.S. Supreme Court in the months that followed, Herman Sweatt proved a much more stalwart client than had Leonard Grimes of Missouri. He did not seek special treatment and patiently went back to his job as a mail carrier. During this time, Marshall remained in contact with him and encouraged his resolve to see the process through to the end. He also sought to support Sweatt, as he experienced harassment from local whites. Opponents sent him harassing letters, vandals broke his windows with rocks that had threatening notes attached, while others defaced his home. Sweatt even experienced physical problems caused in large part by the pressures of the case. But he understood the significance of his lawsuit and remained committed to seeing it through to conclusion despite all the harassment.

The U.S. Supreme Court finally agreed to hear Sweatt's case in November 1949. When Texas attorney general Price Daniel learned of the court's decision, he appealed to all Southern attorney generals to write briefs in support of his case. They believed, as Harry McMullan, the North Carolina attorney general, put it, "This was the most important Supreme Court case to come out of the south since the Civil War" (ibid., p. 241). The key perspective the Southern group put forward in their defense was that in researching the writing of the Fourteenth Amendment, no link was evident that Congress made any connection between school desegregation and the intent of that amendment. Congress, in their view, had not considered school desegregation an issue that might emerge. They accepted segregation as a normal aspect of society and believed the court should view it in the same manner.

Marshall remained firmly against "separate but equal" as a principle and sought to have it overturned. He received briefs of support from a wide variety of organizations, including an unprecedented amicus brief from the American Council of Churches of Christ; a brief signed by over two hundred law professors and deans of prestigious colleges; and one from the solicitor general of the United States, provided at the direction of President Harry Truman. The brief of the solicitor general was important, as it was one of the first times the federal government took a position in opposition to segregation, saying it ran counter to the democratic ideals of the nation. The brief also significantly called for the overturning of *Plessy v. Ferguson*.

Marshall's brief to the U.S. Supreme Court echoed this sentiment, as it described segregation as unconstitutional and called for reversing *Plessy v. Ferguson*. Marshall had assembled a formidable array of support to reinforce the issues he sought to emphasize in the case. On April 1, 1950, the day preceding his appearance before the court, Marshall held his customary mock run-through at Howard to prepare him for his presentation. As he practiced, Marshall hoped he had a chance to make history the next day and bring an end once and for all to the fallacious concept of separate but equal.

Legal presentations by the attorneys for *McLaurin v. Oklahoma* and *Henderson v. United States* joined the *Sweatt* case at the direction of the U.S. Supreme Court. The justices saw parallels in the cases and desired to consider them together. The *Sweatt* and *McLaurin* cases challenged school segregation while the *Henderson* case challenged segregation on railroad dining cars. Marshall and the NAACP were not the litigants in the *Henderson* case. Thurgood had his colleague and assistant, Robert Carter, present the *McLaurin* case while Marshall took the lead for the *Sweatt* case. With Herman Sweatt and his wife Connie in the audience, Marshall argued his eighth case before the U.S. Supreme Court. The central point of his presentation was that separate but equal was impossible, especially in this instance. The law school for African Americans assembled by the University of Texas in Houston did not compare in any way with the UT law school. And even if the facilities were comparable, the long history and influence of the UT law school gave its graduates an advantage unavailable to students at the African-American school. The UT alumni network—including members in the state house of representatives, the state senate, and even on the U.S. Supreme Court, Justice Tom Campbell Clark—gave them access to contacts unavailable to African Americans attending the Houston law school. Marshall argued further that even if Sweatt's presence made some students or faculty uncomfortable, his access to an education should not be determined by the concerns of other citizens. After the lawyers representing Texas made their presentation, everyone adjourned to await the decision of the justices.

As he waited to hear from the court, Marshall received heartbreaking news. His mentor and friend Charles Hamilton Houston had suffered a second severe heart attack while hospitalized at Freedman's Hospital at Howard University. In April 1950, three weeks after Marshall's presentation before the U.S. Supreme Court, Houston died from acute coronary thrombosis. It was a devastating blow to Marshall. The man who trained him and instilled in him the drive to use the legal system to fight discrimination and injustice was gone. Houston had provided advice on the *Sweatt* case just as he had for Marshall in other earlier cases, but as the *Sweatt* case came to a decision, he would not be there to learn of the ruling or offer advice in the future. Marshall served as a pallbearer at Houston's funeral. He did not make any public statements about his loss at the time, but years later, Marshall paid tribute to his "idol," as he described Houston in this manner: "I don't know of anything I did in the practice of law that wasn't the result of what Charles Houston banged into my head" (Long, 2011, p. 276). To Marshall, "He was a great man. No, he wasn't a great Negro. He was a great American" (Tushnet, 2001, p. 275).

In June 1950, the U.S. Supreme Court issued its decision in favor of Herman Sweatt. In their unanimous ruling, written by Chief Justice Fred M. Vinson, the court did not address the issue of the constitutionality of *Plessy v. Ferguson*. Once again, they narrowly focused their verdict on the right of states to distinguish between students of different races in professional and graduate education at a state university. The question was how to interpret the Fourteenth Amendment in relation to this specific issue. To make their ruling, the court reviewed the objective measures of the quality of the education provided between segregated educational facilities at that level. They also looked at the subjective advantages that accompany a school with a long-standing and influential body of alumni. The latter they found extremely important and impossible to duplicate, as reputation, standing in the community, and tradition emerged over time. As such, neither the University of Texas in the *Sweatt* case nor the University of Oklahoma in the *McLaurin* case could equally replicate the education provided by their law schools in separate segregated schools for African Americans. Consequently, regarding Sweatt specifically, the court held: "The legal education offered petitioner is not substantially equal to that which he would receive if admitted to the University of Texas Law School; and the Equal Protection Clause of the Fourteenth Amendment requires that he be admitted to the University of Texas Law School" (p. 635 of ruling).

While the court did not explicitly rule against separate but equal, it had done so implicitly by highlighting the intangible things that made separate but equal difficult, if not impossible, to provide for all parties. While the specifics of the ruling focused on professional and graduate education, the principles it endorsed had applications for future cases. Robert L. Carter, who argued the McLaurin case for the NAACP, said he believed the *Sweatt* ruling made *Plessy v. Ferguson* moribund and no longer applicable. In his and Marshall's eyes, legal segregation was on its deathbed. They could not have been more optimistic or excited about the future (Carter, 2005, p. 92).

Part of their enthusiasm had to do with their sense that the U.S. Supreme Court, for the first time, was open to reevaluating the legal appropriateness of the *Plessy* case of 1896. More importantly, the court appeared open to nullifying it as the law of the land. Finally, the many previous cases brought by Marshall and the NAACP were bearing fruit in their assault upon segregation. The U.S. Supreme Court justices named by Roosevelt and Truman appeared ready to embrace new ways of looking at the issue of racial discrimination. The court decision gave the NAACP "the tools to destroy all governmentally imposed racial segregation" (Williams, 1998, p 185).

The verdict of the court meant that Herman Sweatt could attend the UT law school. Marshall officially informed Sweatt of this in a letter he sent to him, thanking Sweatt for his courage and resolve as well as for the crucial role he played in the court victory. Herman Sweatt formally reapplied to the law school and was accepted that July. In celebration of the court victory, Marshall traveled to Dallas to attend a Sweatt victory rally at the local YMCA. There he announced the intention of the NAACP to continue their battle against segregation in the courts. That September, Herman Sweatt, along with five other African-American students, began classes at the law school. After four years of court battles, he finally had the opportunity to pursue a law degree at the University of Texas.

The court decision also increased the reputation of Thurgood Marshall. In many ways, the death of Charles Houston represented the unofficial transfer of the legal leadership of civil rights litigation efforts to Marshall. His victory in the *Sweatt* and *McLaurin* cases reinforced that role. Consequently, Marshall's reputation grew, as he was featured in a variety of pieces in both African-American and white media. There was even talk of an appointment to a federal judgeship. While Thurgood Marshall did not actively seek the position, the rumor concerned one prominent NAACP member enough to write a letter to the board voicing his concern that the talk of the judgeship was distracting Marshall's focus on his legal work. The board responded in defense of Marshall by pointing out he was deserving of such a position but that he was not lobbying for it nor was he distracted from the job at hand. More important than the issue of talk about a possible judgeship for Marshall was how he was to reckon with the legacy left to him by Houston, which was to find a way to bring segregation to its knees once and for all. It was a goal shared by Marshall, and one he was closer to than ever before. The dilemma he faced was how to take the next steps toward achieving that objective. Publicly, Thurgood took a very bold position, predicting the end of forced segregation was near at hand. Marshall told one reporter he had a plan to end "all phases of segregation in education from professional school to kindergarten" (Williams, 1998, p. 195). It would take hard work and dedication, but the walls of segregation were crumbling. The challenge lay in devising an effective strategy that would not undermine the progress already made and would carry the court and the nation to the desired goal. To think this through, Marshall convened a meeting in New York of attorneys from around the country to discuss and devise the next steps in their litigation.

6

The Cases That Ended Legislative School Segregation

The issue faced by Marshall as he called together an interracial group of some of the best legal minds from around the country was whether they thought the U.S. Supreme Court was ready to confront the precedent created by *Plessy v. Ferguson* more than fifty years before. More important, if forced to rule on it, would the court overturn the concept of separate but equal as valid? Perhaps, it would it be safer to follow the slower path of letting Southern officials expend money toward making segregated facilities more equal and improving African Americans' access to better opportunities in a gradual fashion. While Marshall felt that attacking segregation directly was the just thing to do, he was not positive it was the wisest course to follow at this time. If a frontal attack on segregation failed, it might set back all the gains made in the fight thus far. This was the central issue for discussion at the major policy meeting Thurgood Marshall called at NAACP headquarters in New York in the summer of 1950.

Marshall's usual strategy in major meetings like this one was to allow the people he brought together to make an argument for the legal course they felt the NAACP Legal Defense Fund (LDF) should take. His associate, Robert Carter, described the sessions as a series of no-holds-barred conversations in which every idea put forward received close scrutiny and, at times, an unforgiving attack (Carter, 2005, p. 98). The theory was that if the idea could not hold up in the group, it would not hold up before the

U.S. Supreme Court justices. This also allowed Marshall to hear the pros and cons of each point of view before reaching a decision on what he wanted to do. He did not vary from that approach during the summer of 1950 meeting since so much was at stake for the organization and for the entire African-American community.

One faction did not want to undermine the progress already in motion as a result of the *McLaurin* and *Sweatt* cases. They saw changes now occurring in ways that had not happened before for African Americans and worried that taking the position that segregation in any form was unacceptable would cut short that progress. The new school buildings, the equalization of pay for African-American teachers, and other improvements might all come to a halt. Moreover, if segregated facilities were closed, they knew from past experience that African Americans would lose their positions, as whites would not allow African Americans to have authority over their children. They also worried that the chief justice of the Supreme Court, Fred M. Vinson, from West Virginia, was not disposed to overturn the *Plessy* case. Without him, it would be difficult to get a majority of justices to support such a decision. In particular, some of the representatives from the local NAACP branches as well as Professor Thomas Powell of Harvard believed Marshall should protect the gains made to that point.

Among the advocates for an alternative point of view were Spotswood Robinson (1916–1998) from Richmond and Virginia and James Nabrit (1900–1997) from Howard University. They believed a direct attack on segregation was the best strategy to adopt. They felt the time had come for boldness, and there was little jeopardy in pushing the court to rule on the issue. If the court did not find *Plessy* unconstitutional, they could then return to using it as the lever to continue improving educational opportunities for African Americans. For them, there was little to lose by forcing the court to rule on *Plessy*.

After hearing these different points of view, Marshall decided to move forward in actively attacking segregation but do it without putting the gains already achieved under separate but equal in jeopardy. The NAACP board of directors endorsed Marshall's decision when they passed a litigation policy "aimed at obtaining education on a non-segregated basis and that no relief other than that will be acceptable" (Kluger, 2004, p. 294). It was a bold public policy that did not reveal the concerns Thurgood still had about launching this attack on education below the graduate level. He understood the risks and wanted to move cautiously so as not to lose past gains in the process. The key was to locate cases he believed gave him the best chance for success before the Supreme Court.

The other strategy that emerged from the meeting involved increased use of sociological data, highlighting the effects of segregation, as a key part of the litigation. Robert Carter introduced the idea in the session. He

Rosa Parks

The decision by forty-two-year-old Rosa Parks to refuse to give up her bus seat in Montgomery, Alabama, in 1955 helped spark the onset of the modern civil rights movement. Parks was not new to activism. Years earlier, she had trained at the Highlander School in Tennessee, which advocated civil disobedience. At the time of her arrest, she was the secretary of the local NAACP. When Montgomery African-American leaders learned of her arrest, they decided to use it as a test case challenging local segregation practices. In addition, a call went out for a one-day boycott of the buses on the day of her court hearing. The one-day boycott turned into a yearlong refusal to use the buses. A new minister to Montgomery, Martin Luther King Jr. became a spokesperson for the movement.

In the end, the Supreme Court ruled against the segregation policies in Montgomery, which brought the boycott to an end. While Parks lost her job as a seamstress in a local department store, her bravery made her a national hero. Her actions inspired others to resist segregation in other areas of the country and catapulted Martin Luther King Jr. into national prominence as a civil rights activist.

had learned of the work of the psychologist Kenneth Clark (1914–2005) and his wife Mamie (1917–1983). In their work, the Clarks tested African-American children to observe the impact segregation had upon their self-image. What the Clarks found was that when asking African-American children to choose their preference between black and white dolls, the children preferred the white dolls, which they perceived as prettier and smarter than the black dolls. The Clarks connected this phenomenon to the treatment of African Americans as second-class citizens. They also saw segregation as an important contributing factor. Carter believed the inclusion of their work would make the NAACP case against segregation even stronger when presented to the court.

Others in the group, and especially Spotswood Robinson, belittled the idea. They felt that judges would find the use of this kind of data inappropriate in a court case and would weaken their argument. While Marshall had used the testimony of social scientists in the past, making the work of the Clarks an essential aspect of his legal argument raised the use of sociological input to a new level. This they believed was not a good option. But Carter persisted with his idea and eventually won Marshall over to his point of view. Thurgood felt he should use whatever options were available to enable the judges to better understand the negative impact of segregation. His analogy was "If you had an automobile accident, and you are 'injured,' you have to prove your injuries—you had to put on a doctor, and the doctor will explain what your injuries are and how you are damaged . . . [T]hese negro kids are damaged, we will have to prove it" (Tushnet, 2001, pp. 461–462). The work of the Clarks consequently became an important aspect of the cases he sought to initiate against *Plessy* and segregation. But the challenge would be to find parents willing to have their children become the focus of lawsuits attacking segregated schools in their towns. Marshall understood the repercussions parents might face by agreeing to sue. They could lose their job or confront threatening visits from the local Ku Klux Klan. These risks would naturally make parents hesitant to volunteer. For example, in New Orleans, the local NAACP lawyer wrote Marshall telling him that he was unable to find any family willing to initiate a suit against the all-white public schools after several weeks of talking to African-American residents.

Fortunately for Marshall, some parents in other cities were so frustrated with the educational conditions handicapping their children that they stepped forward to serve as litigants. The suit brought by twenty parents against the school system in Clarendon County, South Carolina, offered Marshall the first opportunity to launch his new campaign. A report issued to Marshall by a Howard University professor highlighted the poor educational facilities for African Americans in the county. White schools had a student-teacher ratio about half that of African-American schools. Some African-American schools had no running water, electricity, indoor plumbing, or desks. In general, expenditures for African Americans, who were a sizeable majority of the students in the county, were much less than the funds spent on white education. These conditions offered Marshall an ideal opportunity to show the harm done by segregation.

To provide sociological data specifically from Clarendon County, Marshall sent Kenneth Clark to South Carolina with his dolls to test the children there. After two days of psychological testing, Clark observed consistent low self-esteem among the children with whom he worked. According to Clark, "The majority of black children tended to reject themselves and their color and accept whites as desirable" (Williams, 1998, p. 202). This was very useful news for Marshall who traveled by train to Charleston, South Carolina, to personally handle the case. What he hoped to do was assemble enough evidence to mount an overwhelming case illustrating the inequities inherent in segregation that would sway the South Carolina court.

The trial in South Carolina did not go totally as planned. The lawyers for the state, to the surprise of Marshall, began by admitting the school systems in South Carolina were not separate and equal and that they were committed to equalizing them. But they said that would take time. They asked the court to give them the opportunity to make improvements. This tactic, the attorneys hoped, based on previous court decisions, would convince the judges to rule in their favor. Marshall, in turn, took the position that equalizing the separate school systems was not enough. It would not end the injury to the self-esteem of African-American children that his key witness, Kenneth Clark, had found in his tests. As long as segregation persisted, their self-image would suffer, and Marshall sought to end the system of school segregation in the county and the state. It was an injustice the court should end immediately. The state attorneys countered by arguing that equalization should suffice and that attempting to end segregated schools would result in violence. Unfortunately, for Marshall, two of the three judges overseeing the case agreed with South Carolina. They saw the *Plessy* ruling holding sway, and the effort of South Carolina to equalize schools as sufficient. They also disagreed with the use of sociological data as a reason to overturn separate but equal. They instructed the state to report their progress to the court in six months to determine if they were in fact moving to equalize the segregated systems. It was a defeat for the inclusion of sociological information and for Marshall's endeavor to define segregation in any form as unacceptable.

This 1951 *Briggs v. Elliott* ruling disappointed Marshall and his team but did not surprise them. They quickly began working on an appeal they hoped would get them before the U.S. Supreme Court. They still believed that arguing against maintaining segregation was the best course to follow. Not all African Americans agreed with them. Led by the words of a lawyer and columnist for the *Pittsburgh Courier*, Marjorie McKenzie, a number of influential individuals questioned the tactic. They felt continuing on the path of forcing white officials to equalize educational facilities offered the route of least resistance and greater ongoing success. They did not believe the courts at any level were inclined to declare *Plessy v. Ferguson* unconstitutional and that Marshall was wasting resources and perhaps risking past gains on a fruitless strategy. In response, Marshall argued that the South would never voluntarily equalize schools or any other institution. He firmly believed that if they did not pressure Southern officials and challenge segregated schools, things would not change. Instead, African Americans would get what they had always gotten before: "separate but never equal" facilities. He also pointed to the encouragement he received from people on the local level suffering from segregated schools who told him, "We want our rights now, not a century hence" (Kluger, 2004, p 524). Marshall was determined to stay the course.

Another case taking place in the state of Kansas offered further opportunity to argue against separate but equal. The schools in the city of Topeka became the focus of the litigation there. Topeka embraced legal segregation, especially at the elementary-school level. The legislation in Kansas gave each local school district the power to decide if they wished to maintain segregation within their jurisdiction. The Topeka school board had

THE MURDER OF EMMETT TILL

In the summer of 1952, Emmett Till, a teenager from Chicago, traveled to Mississippi to stay with relatives. While there, he allegedly insulted the wife of a white store owner by whistling at her. Her husband and his friends later kidnapped Emmett from the home of his relatives to teach him a lesson. Several days later his battered body was found in a nearby river. The local authorities sought to quickly bury him and ignore Till's death. His mother, Mamie Till, blocked them by insisting she return her son's body to Chicago for burial.

In Chicago, she held an open casket funeral attended by thousands of people. She was determined to let the world see what had happened to her son and shine a light on the brutality directed toward African Americans in the South. Till's death sparked national and international outrage, which increased with the acquittal in Mississippi of the men accused of his death. Till's murder along with the actions of Rosa Parks were catalysts for the civil rights movement, which emerged after their experiences.

decided to maintain a segregated school system. When the Topeka NAACP wrote Walter White in August 1950, saying they were prepared to go to court to overturn laws that supported segregated schools, it culminated two years of presenting petitions and demands by parents that the local school board ignored. In response, Marshall assigned Robert Carter to help them prepare a case.

Lucinda Todd, the secretary of the Topeka NAACP, and Oliver Brown, a veteran and a welder, headed the list of eight families who agreed to participate. They were unhappy that their children could not attend schools designated for white children located much closer to their homes than the African American–designated schools their children were forced to attend. They filed their case in February 1951 as *Brown v. Board of Education of Topeka, Kansas.* The trial began in June, just a month after the Clarendon County, South Carolina, case presentation. Robert Carter told Marshall he believed their odds of winning in Kansas were better than in South Carolina. They hoped that because Kansas was a border state, it would offer a different examination of segregated schools, as segregation was optional, not required by statute as it was in the South. Marshall did not have the time to handle the Topeka case personally and assigned it to Carter, now a six-year veteran member of the LDF team. Since the schools above elementary-school level were mixed, and the segregated elementary schools were not substantially different in operation, the focus for Carter was the NAACP position that segregation was detrimental to African-American children, no matter how equal the facilities. He made his case before three judges in the U.S. District Court and a room filled with

African-American onlookers. Kenneth Clark did not testify, but Carter brought in other expert witnesses, including Professor Louisa Holt, from the University of Kansas. She described the psychological impact of segregation on both African-American and white children. She believed that for white children like hers, segregation limited their exposure to other people and would handicap them later in life when they had to function in a more diverse work world.

A key part of Carter's case was the testimony of Oliver Brown. During his testimony, Brown described his seven-year-old daughter Linda's daily travel to Monroe, her segregated school, which was about a mile's distance from her home. Each day Linda left at 7:40 a.m. to get to school by 9:00 a.m. To catch her school bus by 8:00 a.m., Linda walked a dozen blocks between railroad tracks to the bus stop. Brown pointed out that the bus often came late, which forced her to stand in the rain or snow until it arrived. After a thirty-minute ride, she arrived at the school, where she stood outside as long as thirty minutes waiting for the building to open. In contrast, Sumner, the white school, was only about seven blocks from the Browns' home, with a much shorter and less dangerous route to travel. But when he sought to enroll Linda at Sumner, the principal denied his request, prompting Brown to join in the suit.

The trial lasted for three days, with the lawyers for the school system taking the position that the African-American schools were not inferior and, as such, did not violate separate but equal. They also argued that public opinion in their community supported the maintenance of segregated schools, and it was not the duty of the schools to go against community preferences. After five weeks of deliberation, the district court judges handed down their decision. They found in favor of the Topeka school board. In their judgment, earlier U.S. Supreme Court decisions, such as the McLaurin case, pertained only to graduate and professional schools. The *Plessy* decision still ruled, and the actions of the school board met the requirements set out by it. At the same time, the judges gave hope to Carter and the NAACP through an attachment to their ruling containing nine "Findings of Fact" related to the case. In five of the facts they gave credence to the psychological argument offered by the NAACP. The last sentence in that finding indicated that the judges accepted the detrimental impact of separate systems: "Segregation with the sanction of law, therefore, has a tendency to retard the educational and mental development of Negro children and to deprive them of some of the benefits they would receive in a racially integrated school system" (Kluger, 2004, p. 424). Marshall and the NAACP saw this statement as a small moral victory. They felt the 1951 ruling of the Kansas judges would place pressure on the U.S. Supreme Court to provide their view on whether *Plessy v. Ferguson* should stand. Marshall quickly had the appeal of the case sent forward to the U.S. Supreme Court.

Meanwhile, in South Carolina, officials filed the six-month report required by the district judges. In it they pointed to progress in providing funding for equalizing school buildings, the purchase of new equipment, upgrades to the curricula at African-American schools, as well as the equalization of teacher salaries. They asserted their commitment to seeing these actions through to completion and asked only for additional time to make them happen. In light of this report, the U.S. Supreme Court, to whom the NAACP had appealed the original decision, directed the lower court to issue a final judgment. It again found in favor of South Carolina. Marshall immediately appealed their decision to the U.S. Supreme Court, asserting that only an end to segregation would meet the immediate needs of their clients.

Also moving toward consideration by the U.S. Supreme Court were three additional cases shepherded by the NAACP from Virginia, Delaware, and the District of Columbia. The Virginia case began as a result of a walkout by high school students in Prince Edward County, Virginia. As was the case throughout the South, educational access for African Americans in the county was segregated and inferior. There was only one overcrowded and poorly maintained high school, Robert Moton, for African Americans. It did not have a cafeteria, school lockers, lab equipment, or adequate toilet facilities. In addition, there were not enough buses to bring students to the high school from all over the county at the same time. Consequently, some students repeatedly arrived after the start of classes. African-American parents regularly requested the white school board to build a new "colored" high school, but to no avail.

Frustrated by their educational conditions, high school students, led by sixteen-year-old Barbara Johns, hatched a plan to stage a walkout. She told her coconspirators they could do something that "would broadcast Prince Edward County all over the world" (ibid., p. 467). In April 1951, her group led the rest of the student body out of the school and vowed to remain out until white officials responded positively to their demands. They believed the only way to equal educational opportunity was to attend school with white students. Based on past history, they knew segregated facilities for African-American students never would receive the resources they needed.

To support their efforts, the students contacted the southeastern regional lawyers for the NAACP in Richmond, Virginia. Spottswood Robinson and Oliver Hill (1907–2007) responded to the student's request and agreed to represent them. The focus of the lawsuit was to end segregation in the schools altogether, reflecting the strategy of the NACCP in other similar cases at the time. Reverend L. Francis Griffin, the local NAACP leader, who backed the students' actions, rallied the parents to enthusiastically support the students and the lawsuit for desegregation. At a key meeting, he declared that anyone who would not back the students was not a man (Kluger, 2004, p. 478). With the support of the community, a month after the start of the student strike in Farmville, the NAACP brought suit in support of the 117 Robert Moton High School students. Their goal was the end of segregated schools in Virginia. The case, *Davis v. County School Board of Prince Edward County*, featured the name of Dorothy E. Davis, a ninth grader whose name appeared first on the list of litigants.

It took more than six months for the case to come to trial. During that time, the school board fired Boyd Jones, the principal of Moton, claiming he aided the student uprising. The board also applied for and received money to begin building the new school that had been long requested by African-American parents. For her safety, Barbara Johns, the student leader, relocated to Montgomery, Alabama, to finish high school. She lived there with her uncle, Vernon Johns, the pastor of Dexter Avenue Baptist Church. Johns later was followed as pastor at Dexter by the young minster Martin Luther King Jr.

When the case finally went to trial, the Virginia attorneys mounted a vigorous assault against the NAACP position that segregation in itself was discriminatory and therefore illegal. They were determined to differ from attorneys in other state cases and directly contested the sociological issues raised by the NAACP. They argued that the NAACP position was not based on sound scientific fact and aggressively attacked the testimony of Kenneth Clark and other expert witnesses presented by the NAACP team. They also brought their own star expert witness, a Columbia University psychologist, Henry Garrett. Garrett testified that separate schools did not produce any stigma for the individuals involved. He also discounted Clark's findings and abilities as a researcher. The Virginia lawyers further took the position that segregation was within the legal and moral rights of Virginia to codify in order to protect the rights of white citizens. It was a part of the state constitution and the ability to make any changes belonged to the legislature and not to the courts. They further intimated that if forced to desegregate, Virginia might close down its schools rather than accept mixed education.

The judges offered their decision within a week of the close of the trial and rejected the position of the NAACP. They believed prejudice was not the foundation for racial separation of schools in Virginia. Social mores valued by the people of Virginia for generations were what powered the system. The judges believed that separate facilities had provided African Americans greater opportunities than they might have had without the system. They saw no harm to either race as the result of a segregated system. They subsequently ordered the Prince Edward board to move diligently toward the equalization of the facilities for African Americans but did not set a timetable for the completion of the work. Disappointed by the decision but not surprised, the NAACP included this case among the ones appealed to the U.S. Supreme Court for review.

More encouraging for Marshall and the NAACP was the outcome of litigation brought against the Delaware State Board of Education. That lawsuit included two separate cases, one focused on school segregation in Wilmington and the other in the small town of Hockessin, Delaware. In each instance African-American students had to attend subpar schools while their white counterparts attended much newer, more modern facilities. For example, in the Wilmington case, the combined grade school and high school available to white students sat in a fourteen-acre setting with well-maintained playing fields and landscaping. In contrast, African-American students attended school in a deteriorating building in downtown Wilmington. It did not offer the same curriculum as the white school, and it suffered from severe overcrowding. What's more, African-American students living near the newer school had to travel fifty minutes by bus to attend the segregated high school. Eight parents petitioned to have their children attend the white school and were denied by the state board. Only one resolute parent in Hockessin took up the fight with the state board. She began with the simple request to have a bus take her daughter to the segregated school and, when denied, chose to contest the larger issue of the segregated school policy of the state. Marshall sent his colleague Jack Greenberg to work with the local lawyer, Louis Redding, on the suit.

The *Bulah v. Gebhart* case relied more heavily on the social and psychological harm done by segregation than any of the other cases executed by the NAACP. Along with the testimony of Kenneth Clark and other psychologists, they also enlisted the testimony of an eminent clinical psychiatrist, Federic Wertham, to report his findings after working with a group of thirteen white and African-American children from Delaware. Wertham found negative impacts of segregation on both groups of students. He believed segregation interfered with the educational process, hurting the ability of the children to take full advantage of what education had to offer. African-American children felt they were being punished because of their color (Kluger, 2004, p. 444). The state countered by arguing that money had been allocated to improve conditions of the African-American schools. They asked for the patience of the court as the refurbishment process moved forward.

Delaware State Court of Chancery judge Collins Seitz presided over the case and took the unusual step of inspecting the schools in question personally. His visit to the respective facilities verified the disparity between them described in the courtroom. It had a significant impact on the decision he rendered five months later in April 1953. He began by criticizing the state for supporting segregation and the psychological impact it had on children. He believed that segregation resulted in inequality, which he could not condone. However, as the concept of separate but equal remained constitutional, he could not overturn the segregated school system because of its negative emotional impact. It was up to the U.S. Supreme Court to decide that question.

What Judge Seitz did find was great disparity between the schools set up for white and black children. He also found the time needed to bridge that gap requested by the state unacceptable. African-American children should not have to wait months or years for equal educational opportunity. Unlike the judges' decision in South Carolina, he refused to accept the state's request to accommodate continued segregation while they worked to change conditions. Because the schools for African Americans were *not* equal as required under *Plessy*, Seitz ruled the state should immediately allow for the desegregation of the schools. Seitz used a strict interpretation of *Plessy* to force the integration of public schools in Delaware. It was the first time the court had ordered white public schools to accept African-American students. As Thurgood Marshall described the decision: "This is the first real victory in our campaign to destroy segregation of American pupils in elementary and high school" (ibid., p. 449). It was not exactly the total victory they aspired to attain, but it was an important step along the way. Hoping for a more favorable decision, the lawyers for Delaware and the NAACP appealed the case to the U.S. Supreme Court.

The outcome of another case, closely watched by Marshall, did not turn out as well as the verdict in Delaware. This case in the District of Columbia emerged under the guidance of Charles Houston as part of his private practice. The issue in the nation's capital was that a U.S. Congress strongly influenced by Southern politicians controlled funding for education in the city. They had little interest in providing funds for African-American education and underfunded their schools. Consequently, schools in African-American neighborhoods were overcrowded, did not offer kindergarten classes, and lacked the equipment provided to white schools. After African-American parents staged a strike in protest, Houston agreed to file briefs demanding educational equivalency for their children. He also pushed for desegregation of recreational facilities as well as conversion of a white high school to one for African-American students. Houston did not make the sociological argument in this instance, instead arguing that segregation deprived the students of their rights under the Fourteenth Amendment. Specific congressional actions in the past had made it clear the Fourteenth Amendment did not apply in the district. Houston instead demanded strict application of separate but equal.

When the case, *Carr v. Corning*, came before the Court of Appeals of the District of Columbia in 1950, the judges ruled 2–1 against the parents. The majority ruling was that *Plessy v. Ferguson* remained the law of the land and, as such, separate but equal education was legal. In their eyes, there was not enough ongoing educational disparity in the city to warrant decreeing changes in policy. They adopted the position that the treatment accorded African-American students was roughly equivalent to the treatment of white students; therefore, the school system was not in violation of their rights. But before he could file an appeal, Charles Houston died of a heart attack. While in the hospital, Houston directed the leader of the parents, Gardner Bishop, to meet with a law professor at Howard University.

The professor, James Madison Nabrit Jr., consented to handle their case, but only if the parents agreed not to continue focusing on educational equalization. He wanted them to directly challenge segregation. Gardner Bishop agreed, and when Nabrit filed papers for a new case in the U.S. District Court, *Bolling v. Sharpe*, he advanced the position that race should not restrict one's admission to a school. He used the Fifth Amendment instead of the Fourteenth Amendment to argue that the school system was punishing the children without a trial as guaranteed in the Fifth Amendment. As such, the actions of the school board were unconstitutional. It was a very creative legal attack on school segregation. Unfortunately, the district judges rejected this approach and ruled against Nabrit and the parents. Appealing the case to the U.S. Supreme Court followed.

Prior to Nabrit's appeal of the *Bolling* case, the Supreme Court had agreed to review the decisions for the three cases from South Carolina, Kansas, and Virginia. Once Nabrit appealed his case for the District of Columbia and the attorney general for Delaware filed his case for review, the court scheduled all five cases for presentations the same day, December 9, 1952. Marshall spent the weeks leading up to the hearings meeting with all the lawyers involved and crafting a coordinated strategy.

The choice of John Davis to defend South Carolina worried Marshall. One of the most accomplished constitutional lawyers of that time, Davis had argued more cases before the U.S. Supreme Court than any other lawyer. While in law school Thurgood became an admirer of Davis and went to the U.S. Supreme Court to watch him presenting cases. Because of the importance of the case, Davis took it on at the request of the governor of South Carolina. Davis believed the Constitution supported segregation and that the only way to outlaw it was through an act of Congress or by amending the Constitution. In his view, the courts did not have the desire or the authority to rule against it. Precedent was on their side. He also gave little credence to the sociological arguments offered by the LDF. As a senior partner at a major New York law firm, he had access to all its lawyers and resources to help prepare what he saw as an easily winnable case.

Having John Davis as one of his opponents gave Marshall even more reason to prepare the best possible brief to present to the justices. He drew upon both the LDF lawyers and respected attorneys outside that group, including Judge William Hastie and William Coleman, a magna cum laude graduate of Harvard Law School and a former law clerk to sitting justice

Felix Frankfurter. He also enlisted the expertise of an impressive group of scholars to provide historical and sociological evidence to support his brief. Marshall's goal in these preparatory discussions was to determine if they should directly seek to have the court overturn *Plessy v. Ferguson* and whether they should continue to include sociological testimony as a key aspect of their presentation. He decided not to make a direct assault on *Plessy* but to encourage the court to seriously consider whether it still had relevance in the light of recent decisions handed down by the courts in Oklahoma and Texas.

Marshall's team was not in as much agreement over the continued usefulness of sociological evidence as part of the brief. In the past, that evidence had not persuaded enough judges to have them rule in favor of the NAACP. Many in the group felt that the U.S. Supreme Court justices would have the same reaction to what one team member, John B. Weinstein, described as dubious psychological material (Kluger, 2004, p. 555). Robert Carter, who stood as the chief defender of the use of social scientific evidence, asked Kenneth Clark and a group of his colleagues to prepare a report for possible inclusion with the brief. He hoped it would convince others of the usefulness of this evidence. Their essay made a strong case for the negative impact of segregation on the psyche of both African-American and white children. In part, they argued, that "it created feelings of inferiority that in time gave way to self-hatred" (Davis & Clark, 1992, p. 158). Segregation also created "moral cynicism" in a nation allegedly based on the ideal of all men created equal (Davis & Clark, 1992, p. 158). Marshall was impressed enough by the report to include it as an appendix to his brief with the title "The Effects of Segregation and the Consequences of Desegregation: A Social Science Statement" (Ball, 1998, p. 120). He was determined to use every type of evidence available to make his case.

Thurgood also sought support from other organizations who agreed with his efforts. He obtained "friend of the court" briefs from nineteen different organizations. They represented an impressive diversity of organizations, including the American Federation of Teachers, the Congress of Industrial Organizations, and the American Veterans Committee. Most importantly, the Truman administration also offered a supporting document. In light of the upcoming presidential election, the document offered only measured support. It described compulsory racial segregation as unconstitutional and only rarely was separate but equal truly the case. It did not, however, ask the court to overrule *Plessy v. Ferguson* because Attorney General James P. McGranery did not think the courts were willing to take such a big step. They were only willing to go so far with their friendly support of the NAACP. The government only asked that the court set a timetable to have schools move toward integration at some point in the future. While the government's brief did not go as far as Marshall had hoped, he was happy to have even lukewarm support from the attorney general and the president.

The process of assembling supportive data, debating the issues, crafting the brief, gathering support from outside organizations, and reviewing the printer proofs of the brief for submission to the U.S. Supreme Court took its toll on Marshall. During the months leading up to the presentation, he put on weight, became more irritable, and smoked too many cigarettes. Vivian Marshall noticed the change in her husband's disposition as he became less calm and more nervous. LDF lawyer and friend, Constance Baker Motley, could tell how important the case was to Marshall because of his out-of-character flare-ups. He would at times yell at the office secretaries, which was not at all normal for him. She believed the possibility of losing the case haunted him. As a nationally recognized African-American leader, he did not want to be responsible for a major setback in the battle against segregation. She did not think he could have survived defeat, so he considered every possibility in preparing for his day in court (Motley, 1998, p. 86). Marshall himself called it the most important case of his life (Rowan, 1993, p. 189).

Once the group finished preparation of the brief and submitted it to the court, their attention shifted to crafting the presentations for each of the five cases. Marshall assigned lawyers to speak for each of the cases and assumed personal responsibility for presenting the case for the South Carolina parents. As was the case before previous U.S. Supreme Court appearances, Marshall held mock trials at Howard University before a supportive but critical group of attorneys and scholars. They sought to anticipate any question they thought the justices might raise. In particular, they worried about Justice Frankfurter, who regularly asked piercing questions and who they knew was against the idea of the U.S. Supreme Court breaking precedents such as *Plessy*. Frankfurter believed in judicial restraint, not judicial activism. Along with Justice Robert Jackson, Frankfurter preferred not to take on the issue and would rather have the court avoid the question altogether. The challenge for Marshall and the NAACP was whether they could persuade the court that the time had come to act. This time, Thurgood did not participate directly in the dry run at Howard as he usually did in the past. Instead, he remained apart, asking questions and coaching the lawyers speaking for the different cases. He wanted to ensure they were all as well prepared as possible for any question they might get from the justices.

The presentations for the cases began at the U.S. Supreme Court building on December 9, 1952. A long line of people assembled early to get the limited seats available to the public. Vivian Marshall drove down from New York with Kenneth Clark to watch the trial. Everyone recognized the importance of the proceedings and wanted to see how the justices would react to the presentations. Robert Carter spoke first for the NAACP team on behalf of the African-American parents in the *Brown v. the Board of Education* case. After the lawyer for Kansas offered his response to Carter, Marshall stepped to the front to address the South Carolina case.

As he addressed the court and responded to their questions, Marshall offered a masterful presentation. In the process, he made several key points. Marshall highlighted the terrible repercussions to children caused by segregation, as described by well-respected social scientists. He reminded the court how that body had ruled against racial discrimination in the past, meaning a ruling in the school cases would not take them onto totally new ground. He also argued that just because a discriminatory practice had a long-held tradition, it was not reason enough to allow discrimination to continue. In Marshall's mind, the path to equality for African-American schoolchildren did not include segregation since separate but equal implied inferiority. He believed it was the responsibility of the court to allow all children access to equal educational opportunity despite any resistance local communities might offer. To deny them this equality ran counter to the intent of the Fourteenth Amendment. Marshall told the court he truly believed that if the justices ordered an end to segregation, local communities would eventually comply.

In response, John Davis for South Carolina reminded the court how often it and the lower courts had upheld segregation. They had not seen the Fourteenth Amendment as an obstacle in those instances nor should they now. He contended that the framers of the Constitution did not explicitly end segregation, and the court should not look to do so either. Segregation was an important policy in many local communities, which the court should respect and demur to the preferences of local governments. South Carolina had followed the orders of the court and begun to equalize educational opportunities for African-American children. Consequently, they were in legal compliance even as they maintained the tradition of segregation, which was their right as a local government. Davis also attacked the sociological arguments put forth by Marshall as unreliable, and the self-fulfilling prophecy of a researcher looking to find fault with segregation. Furthermore, not all social scientists agreed with these findings, which Davis saw as of little importance to the issues at hand.

Following up Davis's presentation, Marshall reminded the court that Davis had not offered a rebuttal to the main point of his argument. Davis had not answered the question of why "Negroes" were excluded from the rights enjoyed by other citizens. In Marshall's view, segregation had only to do with color and a supposition on the part of segregationists that African Americans were somehow different and inferior. From this supposition, segregationists crafted traditions that stymied the opportunities available to African Americans. Even though whites might represent the majority, under the Constitution, the rights of the minority may not be placed at the mercy of the majority. Consequently, it was not local governments, which often did not include minority members, who should determine individual rights, but the justices of the court who must balance the rights of the minority against the preferences of the majority.

Arguments for the Virginia, District of Columbia, and Delaware cases followed the presentations on South Carolina. After three days of proceedings and numerous questions directed to both sides, the court session came to a close on the afternoon of December 11. John Davis believed his side had won over the judges. He thought the vote would be 5–4 or 6–3 in his favor. Thurgood Marshall was worried. The judges had posed very tough questions to him and his colleagues and frequently offered negative comments related to NAACP positions. Returning to New York, Thurgood was not optimistic that he had enough votes to win. In contrast, Walter White publicly declared the trial went well. He issued a statement in which he noted the importance of the legal proceedings and the accomplishments of the NAACP team. For him, the performances of his legal staff were magnificent.

The court did not offer a response to the proceedings for several months, waiting until the last day of their session to provide news. During that time, a new president, Dwight D. Eisenhower, entered office. Marshall did not hold him in high regard because of Eisenhower's military career. He believed Eisenhower was not much better than General MacArthur when it came to integrating the military and treating African-American soldiers fairly. In his view, both McArthur and Eisenhower thought "that their role is to thwart change—especially racial change" (Rowan, 1993, p. 210). He feared he had lost an important supporter in the White House with the departure of Truman.

The response of the court to the cases brought before them in December did not make Marshall any happier. In June 1953, the court still did not have a decision but instead asked the legal teams to provide responses to five questions they had concerning the cases. They wanted the litigants to explore whether Congress intended to abolish segregation when creating the Fourteenth Amendment, or if they anticipated that succeeding Congresses or the courts might abolish segregation in the future. They also wanted the opinion of the lawyers on whether the court had the power to abolish school segregation, and if they did, what form the implementation of their decree might take.

Marshall had not lost, but he had not yet won. His biggest worry, as he took up this new task, was Chief Justice Fred Vinson. Thurgood had a bad feeling about Vincent. In Marshall's view, Vinson was his enemy and likely a major roadblock to any chance of victory (ibid., p. 205). Nevertheless,

Marshall brought together a team to provide responses to the questions posed by the court. They had six months before the next session of the court to perform the necessary research and provide new briefs. They were guardedly optimistic, given the tenor of the questions, that the justices were seriously considering the possibility of ruling for them. But they had no real idea of what the court would finally decide.

In the process of pulling in legal experts, scholars, and researchers, Marshall assembled a group of more than two hundred interracial supporters. They were divided into research teams to explore different aspects of the issues posed by the court. It was tiring and demanding work to accomplish in a relatively short period of time. And Marshall stood in the middle of it questioning and pushing the group in their work. His response to the work of one researcher was emblematic of Marshall's approach to the effort. He told the man, "Whatever you do, please do not let up but keep digging until we are sure that we have everything that will do us any good" (Kluger, 2004, p. 636). What they presented to the court the second time around, Marshall knew, might make history and had to be beyond reproach.

As the research moved forward, a major shock altered the makeup of the court. Chief Justice Vinson took ill and died from a heart attack in September, before the reconvening of the court. Now the new worry was whom Eisenhower might select to succeed Vinson as chief justice. When Eisenhower chose Earl Warren, Marshall was originally concerned. As governor of California during World War II, Warren had overseen the relocation of Japanese Americans into internment camps. But Marshall's worries abated to a degree as he inquired about Warren with associates in California who spoke positively about him. Those reports increased Thurgood's optimism about the outcome of the case. If Warren stood on the issues the way Marshall's friends anticipated, Thurgood believed he had a 5–4 majority supporting his case.

By November, Marshall's team produced a 256-page brief in response to the issues raised by the court. The document took the position that the Fourteenth Amendment prohibited state efforts to discriminate on the basis of race or color in the area of civil rights. The court's own past rulings supported this fact when they found it illegal to deprive African Americans of rights they could have enjoyed if they were white. Moreover, the only way the court could condone segregation of African Americans in public schools was if they presumed they were inferior to their white counterparts. Marshall argued they were not inferior and consequently segregation in education in any form was unconstitutional. Separate but equal facilities created psychological and emotional issues for the individuals impacted by it. The court, therefore, should declare separate but equal unconstitutional and, at last, overturn *Plessy v. Ferguson*.

On the other side, the team led by John Davis provided a document that examined the historical record regarding the Fourteenth Amendment. His research demonstrated that Congress did not intend to end school segregation in crafting the Fourteenth Amendment. They were more focused on other matters concerning the challenges faced by newly emancipated slaves. Consequently, maintaining segregated schools did not violate the Constitution, and *Plessy v. Ferguson* should stand.

A third brief requested by the court from the federal government took a middle position. Marshall doubted that Eisenhower's Justice Department would provide a document favorable to the NAACP's interpretation of the issues. He was not quite correct in his prediction. The Justice Department felt the record showed Congress inconclusive with regard to its perspective on school segregation, which was different from the NAACP position. But they also took the position that forced segregation of students violated the equal protection principles as described in the amendment. Because of the complex racial and social issues connected to the case, the Justice Department advised giving the South a one-year period to make the transition to end segregated-school facilities. It was not the full-fledged document of support Marshall preferred, but he was pleased to gain any support from the Eisenhower administration.

With all the briefs submitted, oral arguments took place from December 7–9, 1953. The audience observing the proceedings were just as large as during the previous appearance before the justices. This time, Marshall's mother, Norma, along with Carl Murphy, the president of the *Baltimore Afro-American*, joined Vivian to observe the presentations. Marshall and Spotswood Robinson presented for the NAACP, while John W. Davis was joined by two of Virginia's most respected lawyers to present for the opposition. Marshall's first appearance before the justices did not go as well as he wanted, as the justices aggressively questioned him on a number of issues. And his answers were not satisfactory. But he recovered in rebuttal, as he highlighted the inconsistency of the Southern rationale for school segregation.

Marshall's opponent ended his presentation with a plea that the court should acknowledge the right of states to determine what is best for them. It is not racism to separate the races, he argued, but what the South believed benefited both races. Why jeopardize years of tradition and the more recent efforts of South Carolina to equalize the separate systems for what he saw as a deluded grasp for "racial prestige"? Marshall countered this argument with his own view of the absurdity of segregation. He asked, why should the same children who played together outside of school have to be separated in school? The world did not fall apart outside the building; why would it fall apart as the South claimed if they sat together in school? From his perspective, the segregation laws were arbitrarily created to keep formerly enslaved people "as near that stage as possible," which Marshall argued was not the intention of the Constitution. The Constitution said all men were equal, not that some were more equal than others, and he believed the court should make that clear in its ruling (Kluger, 2004, p. 674). One of the opposing lawyers later said Marshall's rebuttal was "the most forceful argument I have ever heard in any appellate court" (Williams, 1998, p. 224).

One of the surprises of the proceedings was the presentation of Assistant Attorney General J. Lee Rankin. As in the government brief, he argued that once a state offered public education, it had to do that equally—a position that the historical record around the Fourteenth Amendment supported. But he took the government position beyond the words of the brief when asked directly by the court if Jim Crow schools were illegal. For the first time, the government took the position "that segregation in public schools cannot be maintained under the Fourteenth Amendment." With regard to implementation of desegregation, the government advised giving the school districts a year to implement the changes and that they move forward "with deliberate speed" (ibid., p. 657). It was the first time the Eisenhower Justice Department took a public stand against separate but equal.

At the completion of the proceedings, it was still a mystery as to how the court would rule. The Davis group believed they had the majority in a split decision. Marshall was not sure what to expect. He hoped several of the justices—Hugo Black, William O. Douglas, Harold H. Burton, Sherman Minton, Tom C. Clark, and Felix Frankfurter—might support him. He was less sure of the views of Robert H. Jackson, Stanley F. Reed, and Chief Justice Earl Warren. The only thing Thurgood felt sure of was "that Justice Reed will vote against us and . . . as many as four other justices" (Rowan, 1993, p. 214). As it turned out, both Davis and Marshall misread the final decision of the court. It did not vote in the way he anticipated. The skills of the new chief justice, Earl Warren, heavily influenced the final decision of the body. As a former politician, he understood how to broker compromise among competing viewpoints and used this ability when working with his fellow justices. He believed it was time to overturn *Plessy* but did not want a split decision from the court. He needed a unanimous vote to give their ruling the force that such a controversial decision would need when put into effect. During the discussions of the justices over the months that followed, Warren skillfully crafted a decision that all could support. That verdict called for the overturning of separate but equal as the law of the land. The court finally made its decision known on May 17, 1954. Chief Justice Warren read the opinion, which included the all-important point "that in the field of public education the doctrine of 'separate but equal' has no place. Separate educational facilities are inherently unequal." With that pronouncement, Marshall was vindicated in his decision to include sociological data as part of his argument. The court, in its written decision, had acknowledged the negative sociological impact of segregation, and this acknowledgment had impacted their final ruling. Marshall had the decision he had worked so many years to attain.

Marshall and his colleagues were stunned. They had never expected a unanimous decision, much less one in their favor. "I was so happy I was numb" was the reaction Marshall later said he had (Ball, 1998, p. 134). His words probably reflected the reaction of African Americans around the country. It was the greatest court victory in the history of the NAACP and a watershed moment for African Americans across the nation. They were proud of the accomplishments of Thurgood Marshall and of the NAACP, but they were cautious and reserved in their response. Based on past disappointments that followed promises of change, there was a skeptical wait-and-see-what-will-happen-next attitude.

Thurgood also knew the battle was far from over. In fact, he told associates the fight had only just begun. What the court did not decide that day was how to implement this monumental decision. To advise the court about devising a plan of implementation, Marshall worked to create a brief for the following fall, outlining the NAACP's ideas for executing the desegregation process. Marshall knew full well that segregationists disagreed with the court and would not willingly desegregate their schools without resistance. Senator James Eastland of Mississippi captured that sentiment when he declared the South "will not abide by or obey this legislative decision by a political court" (Kluger, 2004, pp. 710–711). At a meeting of seventeen Southern NAACP state presidents in May, Marshall worked with the group to craft the "Atlanta Declaration," which highlighted the plan moving forward. It, in essence, emphasized the resolve of the organization to push onward with desegregation and to work with law-abiding citizens who supported them. They further wanted federal funds denied to school districts, which defied the court order. Marshall also used the meeting to begin data gathering for the brief he planned to provide the court during its next session (Wilkins, 1955).

As they assembled the brief, Marshall was undecided about the best strategy to follow. On one hand, they could demand a shorter period of time for the implementation of the court order. A year seemed sufficient if school officials acted promptly. Or the NAACP could champion a more modest approach, which allotted more time for the school districts to act. He thought the justices would respond more favorably to the latter gradualist approach. It might also make it easier for Southern schools to accept and implement the court order if it was not forced on them all at once. However, Marshall was not sure that represented the best interests of African-American schoolchildren.

When the lawyers met with the court in April 1955, each group offered different suggestions for a plan of implementation. Southern states primarily expressed unhappiness with the decision and advocated delays or a gradual approach to implementation as the best course. This would give white citizens more opportunity to adjust to the idea of mixed schools, which represented a significant change in cultural mores. The lawyers for the Justice Department maintained the position they presented during the trial in their brief. They suggested flexibility on the part of the court in setting any timetable for change. The justices should send oversight responsibilities back to the district courts, which better understood local issues and challenges. But at the same time, segregation must come to an end, and resistance should not be tolerated. They said there is no local option with regard to that reality.

In the brief Thurgood Marshall submitted to the court, he decided to adopt a compromise approach. He did not want to allow the South as much time as they wished to move forward with desegregation. He worried that if they felt they had any discretion, they would find numerous reasons to delay implementation for as long as possible. Moreover, sociological studies cited by his academic experts showed that gradualism made the process more difficult than immediate desegregation, which forced people to adjust quickly and not debate it. Instead, his brief took the position that desegregation should happen as quickly as possible, taking into account administrative and facilities adjustments school officials had to make. A deadline was critical to hold the districts accountable. The LDF felt one year was sufficient to get any needed apparatus in place. Desegregation plans should be in place by the upcoming school year in the fall of 1955 and complete integration achieved by the fall of 1956. Any delays beyond that point should face penalties, including the withholding of federal funds.

After reviewing the different perspectives, the court chose a response in May, which most closely followed the suggestions of the Department of Justice. It was a path of gradualism with flexibility. They recognized that different locals faced different challenges in implementing the orders of the court. But, while allowing for local issues, the U.S. Supreme Court expected the district courts to require a prompt and reasonable start toward desegregation. Any delay must be part of a good faith standard as determined by the district court. In the end, the federal government's expectation was that the district courts would push plans and actions for desegregation forward "with all deliberate speed."

The decision of the court disappointed Marshall. The decree contained no specific deadlines against which to hold school districts accountable. Measuring "all deliberate speed" was subjective and dependent upon the judgment of local district judges each of whom might measure it differently. A more specific set of deadlines was Marshall's preference. But, he decided to offer a positive spin in his public statements. He called the decision a good one in which the court again declared segregation as unconstitutional. The court also indicated it expected compliance with its decision. It meant that desegregation would occur throughout the nation. He urged every parent and child to take advantage of the new opportunities available to them and that the NAACP stood ready to assist them in their efforts. Marshall was hopeful that the nation would get behind the desegregation program and not mount major resistance to its implementation.

As Marshall navigated the highs and lows of the *Brown* decision, he also had to navigate troubling issues in his personal life. His wife, Vivian Marshall, faced a life-threatening illness. She was not feeling well during the original arguments of the *Brown* trial, and she did not improve in the months that followed. She had trouble breathing and, at times, became bedridden. Chest X-rays finally revealed that she had cancer. She had hidden the severity of her sickness throughout Marshall's work on the trial, but after a verdict was reached, she revealed the full measure of her illness.

Marshall was devastated and dropped everything he was working on to be at home with her. He spent several weeks by her bedside keeping her company and caring for her. During that time, she slowly succumbed to the disease. It was a sad period for Marshall. As he described it, the hardest part was "just to watch her lie there dying" (Rowan, 1993, p. 225). Vivian died the night of February 11, 1955. She was forty-four years old. According to friends, Marshall took it hard. They had been married twenty-six years and gone through a great deal together. During law school and through all his travels and work schedules, she had been there for him. There had been difficult times during the marriage, including the inability to have children, but they were devoted to one another. After the funeral, Marshall took a long vacation for the first time in years. He traveled to Mexico. But while away, he received news that Walter White too had died.

His colleagues worried about Thurgood, as he lost weight and seemed depressed. Marshall's solution was to turn to his work. There was plenty to keep him occupied, as the scheduled April presentation before the U.S. Supreme Court concerning how to implement their groundbreaking decision was imminent.

7

A Time of Turmoil

How the South might react to the Supreme Court's implementation decision for the *Brown* case was of great concern to Thurgood Marshall and his staff. They hoped that respect for the court and its decisions would guide local and state officials and cause them to move forward with the desegregation of their schools. As lawyers, they firmly believed in the power of the courts and the law. As a result, they hoped that as the interpretations of the law by the justices shifted more in support of African-American rights, the majority of Americans, North and South, would accept the change and abide by it. At the same time, after years of struggle, they knew challenges still lay ahead before they could reach their ultimate goal "to go out of business with a realization that race is no longer a problem" (Davis & Clark, 1992, p. 180).

If Marshall had any doubts that work still remained, the response of numerous Southern officials quickly set him straight. Before the court made its final pronouncement about how to implement the *Brown* decision, several Southern congressmen indicated their opposition to the end of separate but equal. John C. Stennis, U.S. senator from Mississippi, took the position that the majority of people in the South did not want integrated schools and would oppose efforts to desegregate. They feared it would lead to interracial marriage, which many Southern states prohibited. Interracial marriage, in Stennis's eyes, would destroy each race and must be prevented. Marshall found Stennis's rationale against desegregation ridiculous and saw no connection between schooling and interracial marriage. It was an issue often brought up as an excuse any time African Americans pushed for equal treatment. Even if it was a possibility, Marshall pointed out, to prevent it from occurring, all the white person had to do was say no (ibid., p. 184).

But Stennis's words, unfortunately, offered a foreshadowing of the feelings of other Southern congressmen. In March 1956, eighty-two Southern members of the House and nineteen senators unveiled what they called the *Southern Manifesto*. The document protested the decision of the U.S. Supreme Court regarding the *Brown* case. The congressmen believed the justices had overstepped their power and ignored the established law of the land, disregarding states' sovereign rights in the process. In its place the court substituted their personal, social, and political beliefs improperly. The congressmen urged local Southern officials to use every lawful means they could to resist the court's decision and to work to have it reversed. In their view, school desegregation was contrary to the Constitution and would result in chaos.

While the congressmen took a very public position of opposition, a secret meeting occurred in Virginia of governors and officials of a dozen Southern states who gathered to map out plans to undercut the court's decision (Tushnet, 2001, p. 477). Led by Virginia, a plan of massive resistance emerged. The plan took the form of the passage of laws and actions initiated by state and local officials to blunt desegregation efforts. Some places ended compulsory attendance of school, others set aside funds to pay for private schools, while others passed legislation that withheld funds from any school district that decided to desegregate. Virginia closed the schools in places such as Norfolk, Charlottesville, and Prince Edwards County, where the students had walked out. White parents then established private schools to educate their children while African-American children languished or relocated.

In places where school system leadership sought to create plans for phased desegregation, they faced resistance from politicians who saw the issue as a rallying point for their political careers. This was the case in Little Rock, Arkansas, where school officials put in place a phased plan beginning with the high school and slowly moving to lower grades over the next several years. The local NAACP opposed the plan, with Marshall's support, but the district court ruled the plan met the "all deliberate speed" criteria. Despite this modest proposal, the governor of the state, Orval Faubus, who was running for a third term, chose to oppose the plan. He sent National Guardsmen to the school to turn away the nine students attempting to enter it. One student walked through a hostile crowd to Central High School only to have the guardsmen turn her away to walk back through the mob. In spite of Faubus's actions, the students and their parents remained determined to attend the school, and Thurgood Marshall promised to do all he could to help them. He went before a federal judge who then ordered Faubus to remove the National Guard. When the mob outside the school remained, President Eisenhower reluctantly ordered the 101st Airborne Division of the U.S. Army to the city to protect the students. They remained there for the remainder of the school year. During that time, the students suffered taunts and bullying while many teachers ignored their difficulties. Marshall had great admiration for the children and the adults who supported them in light of the constant threats they received. He was impressed when the father of one of the children refused a bodyguard by saying, "I am just not afraid" (Ball, 1998, p. 162). Marshall said he wasn't sure he could have done what they did.

Unfortunately, the departure of the troops the next year allowed racial tensions and potential violence to rise once again. The fear of violence prompted the school board to ask for a delay of the segregation plan. Marshall appealed the case to the U.S. Supreme Court, which ordered the plan to move forward without delay. In response, Faubus cut off funding for integrated schools and had them closed for the upcoming school year. This time Marshall took Faubus to court to stop his actions. Again, the U.S. Supreme Court ruled against efforts to delay desegregation and ordered that the school reopen and allow the African-American children to attend.

RUBY BRIDGES

In New Orleans in 1960, six-year-old Ruby Bridges was the first African-American child to desegregate a Southern elementary school. To qualify to attend this school, she took and passed a test that allowed her to go to the white school closer to her house instead of the "colored" school much farther away. Her first day, her mother and U.S. Marshals accompanied her to protect her from the hostile crowd gathered outside the school. At the school, teachers and students refused to interact with Ruby. Only one teacher agreed to instruct her. They became a two-person class, as white parents refused to have their children in the same classroom. She also faced threats that resulted in her only eating food brought from home and having a U.S. Marshal walk with her to the restroom.

Ruby's bravery impressed one Marshal who noted "she never cried or whimpered, but just marched along like a little soldier" (Donaldson, 2009, p. 23). But Ruby had nightmares and needed sessions with a child psychologist to help her manage. Even so, she successfully graduated from that school and later graduated from a desegregated high school. Born in 1954, the year of the *Brown v. Board* decision, Bridges embodied the bravery necessary for the children who made desegregation a reality.

Actions to prevent desegregation efforts were not only directed toward schoolchildren. Parents and other individuals who signed petitions or took other steps to initiate desegregation also found themselves under attack. In Mississippi, the White Citizens Council took the position that any African American professing support of equality will not keep their job, get credit, or exist comfortably in their community. Similar organizations sprang up in other Southern states. In their eyes, the NAACP was the cause behind all these problems, and anyone associated with that organization came under attack. This especially was the case for local office holders or activists such as Reverend L. Frances Griffin in Prince Edwards County, Virginia. As the NAACP county coordinator, Griffin led the call for the NAACP to file a lawsuit on behalf of the high school students who walked out. While his role as the minister of a black church protected his salary, local white leaders found other ways to punish him. They denied him credit at local businesses and demanded immediate repayment of any credit purchases, including immediately repossessing his car. They refused to sell him fuel to heat his home. These tactics made it increasingly difficult for him to provide the basic necessities for his family. While Reverend. Frances ultimately survived this economic attack, it took great determination to get through it.

The threats faced by activists were not only economic. They also took a more physical and psychological form. Pro-segregationists called them with death threats in the middle of the night. The state office of the IRS audited them. The names of people who signed a petition were published in the local newspaper in order to harass them. Some people were even killed for daring to fight for equality. When Medgar Evers accepted the position of NAACP field secretary for the state of Mississippi in 1954, it was described as a "suicide mission" because of the constant threats to his life. During the years he served, eight civil rights workers were killed in Mississippi, and no one was ever charged. Evers himself was murdered in his driveway after attending an NAACP meeting in 1963. The difficulty for the NAACP, Marshall pointed out, was that they had to play by the rules even when others did not. It was a painful reality for Marshall and the NAACP to have to accept.

Another threat faced by the NAACP was attacks in state courts. In 1956, Southern legislatures in Virginia, Texas, Louisiana, and Alabama passed laws banning or undermining the NAACP. These state courts brought lawsuits seeking to undermine the tax status of the NAACP and to access local NAACP records, including their membership lists. With access to the membership lists, local officials could identify and further intimidate current associates and frighten others from taking out memberships. In June 1956, the state court in Alabama ruled in favor of state officials and insisted on the release of NAACP members' names in that state. When the NAACP refused, the court fined them one hundred thousand dollars, which they immediately appealed. It took eight years of litigation before the NAACP finally won the case.

During the litigation, opinions within the NAACP differed over whether or not to give the membership lists to Alabama or other states requesting them. Marshall believed that if the U.S. Supreme Court supported the Alabama courts, he was duty bound to release the membership lists. He also felt the time spent battling this case took valuable resources away from litigating more important desegregation cases. Other associates of the LDF and the NAACP did not agree. They felt duty bound to protect their members no matter how the justices ruled on the matter. They saw this position as a matter of principle and vital to the long-term survival of the organization. They worried that Marshall knew only one way to function in the legal system and that it blinded him to the possibility of defying a court order and fine. Robert Carter opposed Marshall's viewpoint and lobbied to have the NAACP defy the courts if necessary. When they voted, the NAACP board sided with Carter and decided to defy the court if it ruled against them. This certainly was not the outcome Marshall wanted. His concerns about the expenditure of resources proved right, as it took eight years of litigation to finally resolve the case in favor of the NAACP. In the process, a great deal of time and energy was redirected toward it. But, the NAACP ultimately did win the case without surrendering membership lists as Marshall's critics wished.

Another of the criticisms directed toward Marshall was the belief that his legal approach too easily allowed him to make accommodations to the

MARCH ON WASHINGTON, DC, 1963

A. Phillip Randolph and Bayard Rustin joined with Martin Luther King Jr. to sponsor a march on Washington, DC, in the summer of 1963. Their goal was to demand passage of a civil rights bill and fairer treatment of African Americans. They titled it a march for "Jobs and Freedom." The group hoped to convince hundreds of thousands of people to join them. President Kennedy and congressional leaders tried to dissuade them, fearing violence might result. Unconvinced, the organizers held the march, and more than 250,000 people traveled from across the country to attend the event.

The demonstration was very peaceful as people marched and gathered before the Lincoln Memorial to listen to performers and speakers. The most impactful presentation was the "I Have a Dream" speech given by King in which he described the kind of future society he hoped lay ahead for the nation. The day was a resounding success and left all involved with a spirit of optimism about the future and the passage of a civil rights bill. It was one of the most positive moments in a very momentous and, at times, heartbreaking year.

court system. These critics believed Marshall should adopt a more aggressive strategy as he attacked segregation. This view emerged most openly at the 1956 NAACP National Convention, when delegates there wanted more militancy in his actions and language regarding segregation. They also wanted him to broaden the scope of the litigation he pursued beyond school segregation cases to issues concerning housing restrictions and segregation in public places. They wanted segregation under attack on multiple fronts. The delegates consequently brought pressure on Roy Wilkins, the NAACP executive director, to press Marshall to broaden his strategy. Marshall did not like the idea of the delegates trying to dictate where he should deploy the limited resources of the LDF and said so.

As a solution to the ongoing debates around membership lists and the tax status, to outside efforts to direct the work of the LDF, and to the philosophical clashes between him and Robert Carter, Marshall sought to split the LDF officially from the NAACP. This step would give him his own personally selected board, allow him to fund-raise, which the NAACP as a lobby group could not do legally, and relocate Robert Carter into another office. Using growing IRS pressure about the tax status of the NAACP, in 1956, Marshall convinced Wilkins to allow for the separation of the LDF from the NAACP. Marshall then resigned as special counsel for the NAACP to take full control of the LDF. He had Carter named as the lawyer for the NAACP and removed as a member of the LDF team. When enacted, the new organizational scheme gave Marshall full control over the day-to-day operations and case litigation choices of the LDF. It was exactly what he wanted, as he believed that he knew the most effective path to follow in attacking segregation. Marshall still worked in coordination with the NAACP and Carter, but Wilkins and the NAACP board no longer controlled his work.

For Marshall, a systematic controlled approach offered the surest pathway to success. This methodology was not flashy and could at times be tedious, but it had a proven track record. It entailed following the proper legal procedures, litigating cases at the state and federal district court venues, and eventually appealing them to the U.S. Supreme Court for review. It was the method he and Charles Houston used in cases prior to and leading up to the *Brown* decision. Marshall believed this method remained the surest strategy moving forward. He described it as "working out integration problem by problem until it is finally achieved" (Davis & Clark, 1992, p. 182). This, he firmly believed, must be achieved without the use of violence or illegal acts. This "gradualism" approach, as he called it, worked for him in Little Rock when Faubus sought to undercut desegregation there, and it worked for him in other cases under his direction. Between the time of the *Brown* decision and the end of the 1950s, Thurgood Marshall argued and won seven cases before the U.S. Supreme Court. The cases resulted from resistance on the part of state and local officials to desegregation of their schools. The Little Rock cases garnered most of the headlines, but school cases from Virginia and other states also were decided in favor of the LDF.

Marshall understood the symbolic importance of the *Brown* case and other school desegregation lawsuits he fought. They led the way not only for integration of public schools but also for similar efforts to integrate other aspects of public life. Marshall viewed the importance of the *Brown* decision as a wake-up call for African Americans. For him, the decision "did more than anything else to awaken the Negro from his apathy to demanding his right to equality" (ibid., p. 179). After *Brown*, actions by African Americans to gain equal access to buses, department stores, restaurants, and other public places grew in number and intensity. They were spurred, in part, by the belief that the courts were at last willing to support their efforts, as Marshall had demonstrated through his use of the law. The new challenge for Marshall was that as these demands for civil rights escalated, they did not always retain the same respect for obeying the law that Marshall advocated. This proved a difficult transition for Marshall to make as his role and that of the LDF as a protector of civil rights altered.

In the turmoil of the numerous lawsuits Marshall coordinated in the aftermath of the *Brown* decision, he did manage to find some much-needed happiness. In the fall of 1955, he made a surprise announcement. He intended to marry Cecelia Suyat, one of the secretaries in the NAACP office. Suyat came to the NAACP headquarters in 1947, after a referral from an employment agency. Born and raised in Hawaii, her parents were from the Philippines. Her ethnicity did create some complications. Because she was not African-American, there was concern about how the outside world might react to "Mr. Civil Rights" marrying someone of a different culture. Years earlier, when Walter White divorced his first wife to marry a white socialite, it caused major reverberations in the civil rights community and nearly cost him his position as executive director. The organization did not want to experience that kind of disruption again with Marshall. Suyat shared those concerns, and Marshall said he asked her several times to marry him before she finally agreed.

The announcement of their intentions so soon after the death of Vivian Marshall also worried the organization. Vivian died in February, and Thurgood married eleven months later. A friend who knew the couple well pointed out that Thurgood was a man who needed to be married. He needed someone to organize his personal life and provide him with a place of refuge from the grind of traveling around the country and coordinating the work of the LDF. In Cecelia he found a kind, beautiful woman who understood the all-consuming nature of his work. She also filled an important emotional need for Marshall after the loss of Vivian. Her goal was to provide the support he needed in the key aspects of his life. Eventually, she also provided something Vivian could not, which Thurgood badly wanted: children.

The couple married in December 1955 and then made a public announcement of their nuptials. The NAACP described Cecelia as a member of the family and "just about black," even though she was of Asian descent. Marshall's response to the muted criticism the marriage received was "I've had two wives and both of them are colored" (Williams, 1998, p. 244). The couple escaped for a two-week honeymoon in the Caribbean, which was one of the few vacations taken by Marshall. It was an opportunity to leave behind the turmoil of the office as well as the many issues coming to the surface in the wake of the *Brown v. Board of Education* verdict. In August 1956, their son Thurgood Marshall Jr. was born, at last giving Marshall the child he had desired for so many years.

The couple's trip to the Caribbean provided only a brief escape from the challenges facing Marshall. When he returned, the nature of the civil rights struggle was shifting and put him in a position quite different from what he had occupied in the past. In the same month of his wedding, a momentous event took place in Montgomery, Alabama. On December 1, 1955, an NAACP member and secretary of the local chapter, Rosa Parks (1913–2005) made the decision to refuse to give up her seat on a segregated bus. Her action spurred a bus boycott in Montgomery, which ultimately lasted 381 days. It also propelled to national notoriety the pastor of the Dexter Avenue Baptist Church, Martin Luther King Jr. (1929–1968). The initial demands of the Montgomery Improvement Association (MIA), led by King, did not include changing the segregation laws but only asked for more courteous treatment, the hiring of African-American bus drivers, and a different system of allocating segregated seating. When city officials ignored the requests of MIA, they decided to sue for the integration of the bus system.

E. D. Nixon, a past president of the Montgomery branch of the NAACP, contacted Marshall about what they were doing. Marshall put Robert Carter in charge of advising the MIA on legal matters. It was Carter, on behalf of the NAACP, who persuaded the MIA legal team to expand their suit and push for an end to segregation. While King's rise to prominence surprised Marshall, as he had not heard much about him before, he was committed to helping the effort. The lawsuit of *Browder v. Gayle* eventually reached the U.S. Supreme Court, which in 1956 ruled against the bus company and the city, declaring bus segregation unconstitutional. While King captured the national headlines, Marshall felt his legal team did the critical work. He thought the boycott and the impassioned speeches given by King made great publicity but were not the real actions that created success. What made the boycott successful was the victory won through the courts as a result of the diligence of the LDF team.

King's idea of employing the tactic of nonviolent protest, as used by Mahatma Gandhi, concerned Marshall. Gandhi believed in social change through nonviolence. The goal was achieved not by inflicting suffering on the opponent, but on oneself. In his use of this nonviolence philosophy, King sought to confront and expose those forces that supported segregation. As he noted in his famous 1963 "Letter from a Birmingham Jail," King wanted to dramatize the issue of discrimination so it couldn't remain hidden or ignored any longer. These confrontations he believed would open the door to negotiations and change. Reverend King wanted to generate a "creative tension" in society that would allow it to "rise from the dark depths of prejudice and racism to the majestic heights of understanding and brotherhood" (Stanford, 1963, p. 4). This approach King believed would foster change more rapidly than had occurred in the past. It offered an alternative means of transforming American society to the systematic but slow method of working through the court system, which often took months and years to bring to a conclusion.

Thurgood worried about how well these ideas would work in American society. Too often, he had witnessed the violent white backlash frequently associated with the protest activities of African Americans. During the course of his work for the NAACP, he had learned of lynchings and white mob violence directed toward African Americans who the mob felt did not know "their place." He worried that nonviolent protesters were vulnerable and possibly setting themselves up for greater harm. Marshall also disliked the idea that the protesters many times broke local laws, which they felt were unjust. He wanted people to obey the laws and the courts. But, in the eyes of nonviolent protesters such as King, there existed just laws and unjust laws. Unjust or immoral laws degraded human dignity and required opposition. In offering opposition, protesters must stand ready to accept the consequences of their actions, but it was their obligation to resist. For Marshall, change occurred best when working through the legal system. Breaking existing laws while protesting, Marshall felt, would set back the progress made to date.

The change in momentum on the civil rights front also made Marshall uneasy. For decades, the NAACP and the LDF were the front-runners with regard to strategy and organized resistance to segregation. With the Montgomery bus boycott, that no longer was the case. The African-American residents of that city set the direction and goals for that movement. Martin Luther King Jr. served as the spokesperson and the leader in a movement that gained nationwide attention. The Montgomery bus boycott was a grassroots movement born from the frustration felt by African Americans after years of discriminatory treatment. The original idea was to conduct a one-day boycott in support of Rosa Parks, who was arrested for breaking the local segregation laws. But it blossomed from that original concept into a full-fledged yearlong demonstration. The decision of so many people to walk or find alternative methods to get to work rather than ride the buses characterized the essence of the movement. While King stood as the spokesperson, the heart of the movement was "the nameless cooks and maids who walked endless miles for a year to bring about the breach in the walls of segregation" (Burks, 1990). Consequently, the NAACP played more of a supporting role to the actions of local residents and legal representatives. In fact, the NAACP did not officially support the boycott, as it technically broke the law. Local Montgomery NAACP members participated as private individuals, not as NAACP representatives. Now it was no longer Thurgood Marshall whom everyone looked to for guidance and assurance; it was the charismatic, young preacher Martin Luther King Jr. The newspapers and television outlets interviewed King, not Marshall, about events in Montgomery. The legal work of the LDF did not receive the same attention directed toward King and others in Montgomery. As a result, the final success of the movement, in the eyes of the public, did not stem from the legal work of Marshall and the positive court decision but from the effectiveness of the boycott and its leadership. It was an oversight that bothered Marshall. In his eyes, the public put the emphasis in the wrong place. It was the legal team that made the real difference, from his perspective. In Marshall's assessment, "All that walking for nothing. They might as well have waited for the court decision" (Zelden, 2013, p. 118).

King's philosophy of nonviolent protest consequently began to challenge the legal methods traditionally employed by Marshall in the mind of the public. It was not an issue that people had questioned during Marshall's career up to this point. But, at the 1956 NAACP San Francisco convention, attended by the young minister, when asked if nonviolence would be effective against school segregation, King replied in the affirmative. Marshall saw this as a critique of his legal methods and caused him to respond to reporters that King was commenting on issues he did not fully understand. He was in over his head when talking about things other than the bus boycott.

The clash of perspectives did not disappear after Montgomery, as King built upon the boycott's success by organizing the Southern Christian Leadership Conference (SCLC) in 1957. Its goal was to use nonviolent action to create change in the United States. The group intended to support and help coordinate the efforts of local groups throughout the South. SCLC played important roles in mass protest campaigns and voter registration drives in many Southern cities. They intended to make change happen more quickly than occurred with lawsuits and doing it the NAACP and Marshall way.

GREENSBORO, NORTH CAROLINA, SIT-INS

On February 1, 1960, four students from North Carolina Agricultural and Technical College initiated one the earliest and most publicized student sit-ins. After contacting a reporter to ensure publicity, the men walked to the local Woolworth's store where they bought items and then sat at the segregated lunch counter where they requested service. When the manager refused to serve them, they remained seated until closing when they left. They returned the next day with thirty students. The protest consequently increased in size and spread to other stores in the city and across the state. Throughout their actions, protestors remained nonviolent even though they were spat upon, pelted with eggs, harassed, and arrested. Within a month, lunch counters across North Carolina began desegregating. But the movement did not end in North Carolina, as similar protests emerged in other locations in the country as sit-in protests became a popular and effective tool used by civil rights activists. The Greensboro protests also led to the formation of the Student Nonviolent Coordinating Committee, which became an important civil rights organization of young people.

The desire for "Freedom Now!" assumed even greater momentum with the formation of the student group SNCC, the Student Nonviolent Coordinating Committee, in April 1960. The SNCC were even less willing to have change come slowly, but instead used nonviolent confrontations and direct action to bring attention to racial inequalities and put pressure on lawmakers. They were, in part, inspired by the student sit-in movement that began in February 1960 in Greensboro, North Carolina. There, four college students ordered food at the Woolworth store's segregated lunch counter and refused to leave when they were denied service and told to leave. Over the next several days, three hundred additional students joined their effort. The media coverage spurred similar activity in other locations in the country, fueled primarily by college students. They saw the NAACP and Marshall as representing the old way of operating, which in their eyes was conservative, ponderous, and accommodationist. They felt putting themselves in harm's way to force change was well worth the danger they might face. They did not want to wait months for change to happen, and sit-ins often brought change much quicker than lawsuits. Within six months of the sit-in, the Woolworth's in Greensboro integrated its lunch counter.

It was not a method for creating change that Marshall could embrace. In a moment of anger, he told his staff he would not represent students who violated the property rights of white folks by going in their stores or lunch counters and refusing to leave when ordered to do so (ibid., p. 120). They were breaking the law, and the point of much of his legal career had been to force whites to obey the law when it was altered legally. If he condoned breaking the law by the students, it was more difficult to argue that whites should respect it. This was not a point of view that would endear him to the students. At best, they might view him as John Lewis, a leader of SNCC, did. He believed Marshall only sought to protect the students from danger. Marshall, according to Lewis, was saying the students did not need to have people spitting on them, pulling them off lunch counter stools, and putting lighted cigarettes in their hair. He could fix it through the courts instead (Davis & Clark, 1992, p. 198). But others saw Marshall as out of step with the times and resistant to the change in strategy their methods promoted.

Eventually, Thurgood had a change of heart and told the students he would support them by providing bail and legal representation when they were arrested. But he still found himself regularly at odds with the students. When arrested, they sometimes refused bail. The students did not want to go through the long process of litigation to get segregation laws changed. They wanted more immediate action from local lawmakers and were willing to stay in jail to make their point. Theirs was a protest aimed at pressuring elected officials to act. In their eyes, accepting bail was tantamount to supporting injustice and immoral practices. They were not willing to follow the traditional path so important to Marshall. Their revolt, according to John Lewis, was not just against racial segregation and discrimination, but against the nation's traditional black leadership structure (Zelden, 2013, p. 122).

Marshall found this view of the students disconcerting. Without clients who pleaded guilty, his staff could not move cases forward through the courts and ultimately get a decision that supported the goals of the protesters. When protesters did relent and accept bail, they were not as much interested in generating lawsuits as they were in continuing their protests. As a result, the help provided by the LDF moved in the direction of supplying bail money for arrested protesters or representing them in court so they could get out of jail. They helped several thousand people in this way, including the Freedom Riders, who sought to desegregate Southern bus facilities. These students rode buses into the South and looked to integrate bus station facilities along the way. They were attacked by white mobs on several occasions and severely injured. Others were arrested and put in prison. Marshall still did not agree with their tactics but was committed to helping them.

This new phase of the civil rights movement demanded a different role from Marshall and the LDF. Marshall and his team were no longer conducting the measured and carefully planned lawsuits that won the day in the *Brown* case. Instead, their new function was a reactive one in which the actions of younger activists shaped how the LDF could best serve the movement. Whole new legal approaches were needed to help clients who knowingly and willfully broke the law. This took the organization and Marshall out of their comfort zone and demanded an entirely new way of operating. It was an adjustment Thurgood Marshall had difficulty embracing. The control he once had over the litigation process no longer existed. It made Marshall wonder if his long-held principles concerning how best to attack segregation still had relevance. Certainly, his conversations with the student activists didn't make him comfortable. In many ways, he no longer was the leader of the movement but rather a past leader trying to catch-up with its new direction (Dudziak, 2008, p. 14).

As Marshall contemplated his role as a civil rights lawyer and leader, an unexpected opportunity presented itself. One of the leaders of the movement in Kenya to gain freedom from Great Britain, Tom Mboya, traveled to the United States in 1959 on a speaking tour to raise money. During that time, he met a number of African Americans, including Thurgood Marshall. The next year when Kenyan nationalists began talks with the British government about creating a new constitution, Mboya and others thought Marshall was the person to help them create this new document. It represented an initial step toward independence from Britain, giving the African majority greater representation in Kenya's government. Marshall took a leave of absence from the NAACP to travel to Kenya and later to London.

In Kenya, while meeting with black African elected officials, Marshall received a firsthand look at race relations under the white-controlled colonial government. He was surprised at the extent of the restrictions faced by native Kenyans. The colonial government, for example, banned political parties and reserved the best land in the nation for whites. It even refused to allow Marshall to attend the meeting in Kenya by revoking his permission to attend after he arrived. What he saw and experienced strengthened Thurgood's belief that independence for Kenya was due. In his eyes, Kenya was at a critical juncture, and if steps toward greater representation and independence did not take place, more violence was on the horizon (ibid., pp. 45–46; Tushnet, 2001, p. 444). He hoped his work on the constitution might prevent that from happening.

From Kenya, Thurgood traveled to London in January 1960 for the constitutional conference where the British were not quite sure how to respond to his presence but welcomed him as an advisor. His task there was "to write a tricky constitution that will give the Africans in Kenya complete political power on the basis of democratically elected government by universal franchise, while protecting the rights of the white minorities . . . outnumbered about 100 to one" (ibid., p. 46). It was a difficult assignment for which Marshall had little prior experience. What everyone hoped was that his extensive knowledge of the law and belief in universal human rights would enable him to craft a document acceptable to all parties.

To guide his work, Marshall reviewed the constitutions of nations worldwide as well as the Universal Declaration of Human Rights created by the United Nations in 1948. But in the end, he decided that the soundest model to follow was the Constitution of the United States. Thurgood said it was the best he had ever seen. One of the key features of the final document he submitted was a Bill of Rights for Kenya. For him, they were "to protect the rights of every individual in Kenya, rather than the rights of any particular minority group" (ibid., pp. 74–75). He also included in his proposal the creation of an independent court system that would interpret and protect the rights delineated in the bill. Marshall submitted his document in the hopes it might bridge the differences between the competing interests at the conference, which included native Kenyans, a mixed-race group of moderates, Asian-Indian Kenyan residents, and the conservative white United Party. He did not solve all the issues dividing them but did help move discussions forward in a positive direction. Marshall saw a link between the battle against school segregation in the United States and the fight for independence by African peoples. They were part of the same struggle for freedom. As for his work in London, Marshall declared, "I'm damn proud of the constitution I wrote" (Williams, 1998, p. 286).

Marshall could not stay through to the end of the London meeting, as he was needed back in the United States. The nonviolent civil rights movement continued to gain momentum and increasingly drew upon the legal support of the NAACP. Upon his return, while working with the legal staff, Thurgood spent much of his time raising money for bail and other legal expenses needed for the activists. His goal, he told donors, was to ensure that protesters "will have adequate legal representation in the courts if they are arrested" (Dudziak, 2008, p. 85). But even as he raised money and mapped strategy, Marshall continued to wonder if it was time to move on. As he later described it, "I thought I'd kind of outlived my usefulness, in original ideas, in the NAACP hierarchy" (Tushnet, 2001, p. 444). Perhaps it was time to turn the fight over to a new generation.

But before Marshall made that decision, there was one more presentation to make before the U.S. Supreme Court, which in many ways captured the transition taking place in Marshall's life. It was the case of a Howard law student traveling by bus from Washington, DC, to his home in Alabama for Christmas vacation. When the bus stopped in Virginia for food, Bruce Boynton found the colored section filled and took a seat in the white section. The waitress refused to serve him, and he refused to move. He was arrested for trespassing. The local court convicted him of breaking state law and fined him ten dollars. Boynton appealed the conviction in collaboration with the NAACP. When the case reached the U.S. Supreme Court, Thurgood Marshall made the presentation in October 1960.

First, Marshall took the position that the restaurant acted in violation of the Interstate Commerce Act, which banned discrimination in interstate commerce activities. Second, Thurgood argued the actions of the restaurant violated the Fourteenth Amendment when the police made the arrest. This interpretation of the law was a new approach developed earlier in a national meeting of lawyers sponsored by Marshall. The concept reasoned that if racial prejudice at a local establishment was enforced by the state police and courts, it no longer was a private matter and became a violation of due process as well as equal protection and therefore unconstitutional. The idea was a variation on the reasoning used in previous graduate school desegregation cases. This argument became one later regularly employed to represent other sit-in protestors (Goldman & Gallen, 1992, p. 135).

The U.S. Supreme Court ruled in favor of Boynton. Their verdict, however, only focused on the interstate commerce aspect of the case. They took the position that when an interstate bus carrier made its terminal facilities available to its passengers, they must do it without discrimination. While the court did not address the Fourteenth Amendment portion of Marshall's presentation, the occasion allowed for the introduction of the concept that the NAACP would employ more successfully in the future. For Marshall and the LDF, the case also highlighted the shift in the emphasis of the civil rights movement and the role they would play moving forward. This realization for Thurgood Marshall further heightened his sense that a new direction in his life might also be at hand.

8

Transition to Federal Life

Thurgood Marshall did not have a high opinion of Dwight D. Eisenhower in the realm of protecting civil rights. In Marshall's view, Eisenhower fell short on these issues, especially in comparison to his predecessor Harry Truman, who took a strong public stand supporting human rights. When the *Brown v. Board* decision occurred, Eisenhower privately opposed it and publicly resisted making strong statements in support of the U.S. Supreme Court. Chief Justice Earl Warren reported that before the decision Eisenhower attempted to influence Warren to have the court rule in favor of continuing school segregation. His comment, following the decision, was hardly an enthusiastic endorsement of the ruling: "The Supreme Court has spoken and I am sworn to uphold the constitutional processes in this country; and I will obey." Supreme Court justice William O. Douglas believed that Eisenhower's refusal to publicly support the decision of the court only encouraged Southern resistance. If instead he had stood before the nation and actively encouraged support, Douglas believed, the desegregation process would have proceeded much more smoothly. Marshall shared that opinion.

The end of Eisenhower's presidency and the election of a new president presented an opportunity for a more aggressive stance on civil rights in the White House. The two nominees running for the office, Republican Richard Nixon and Democrat John F. Kennedy adopted differing positions regarding the civil rights movement. Nixon, who served as Eisenhower's vice president, worried about offending white voters and embraced a low-key public stance on civil rights. When Martin Luther King Jr. was arrested and sent to prison in Georgia for participating in a sit-in and violating his parole for a parking violation, Nixon did little on behalf of King, even though Georgia officials sentenced King to four months of hard labor at Reidsville State Prison. Officials there were noted for their harsh treatment of African-American prisoners. Coretta King, his wife, feared for the life of Reverend. King if he remained there very long. When she and other civil rights leaders sent requests to the White House to protect King, Eisenhower and Nixon, as the Republican running to replace Eisenhower, were slow to act. Nixon did ask the Justice Department to check on him.

John F. Kennedy responded more aggressively to African-American concerns in this instance, as he had throughout his campaign. When first contemplating seeking the Democratic nomination, Senator Kennedy talked with Marshall about civil rights and his thoughts about Kennedy seeking the nomination for president. While Marshall had a positive impression of Kennedy, he advised the senator not to run. Marshall felt his Catholic religious beliefs and support of civil rights would prevent him from getting the support needed, especially among Southern Democrats. Despite Marshall's advice, Kennedy ran anyway and won the nomination. During his presidential campaign, he frequently spoke to issues of concern to African Americans and promised, if elected, to address issues of importance to them. The jeopardy facing King while in prison allowed Kennedy to put his words into action. He contacted Mrs. King to let her know he would try to get Reverend King out of prison as quickly as possible. He then had his brother, Robert, who served as his campaign manager, contact the Georgia judge who had sentenced King and persuade him to have King released from prison. When released, King offered high praise for Kennedy's humanitarian spirit and willingness to act in support of civil rights activists.

The King episode benefited Kennedy's reputation among African-American voters and helped him win a very close election in November 1960. Sixty-eight percent of the African-American vote went for Kennedy. These voters anticipated that as president, Kennedy would take a more active role in the area of civil rights than Eisenhower. One of the campaign statements made by Kennedy was "to give segregation its death blow through the stroke of a pen" (Davis & Clark, 1992, p. 231). Once in office, Kennedy did not in fact end segregation with "a stroke of a pen," but he did make efforts on other fronts. One area in which he focused was voting rights. Kennedy believed that if African Americans could gain the vote in the Southern states where they were prevented from doing so, they could have a major impact on who was elected and the laws limiting their rights. Through his brother, Attorney General Robert Kennedy, President

Kennedy actively used the Justice Department to initiate numerous court cases to ensure the enforcement of voting rights for African Americans. Under Robert Kennedy, the Justice Department also more aggressively sought to enforce court decisions regarding school desegregation instead of leaving it to the NAACP, as was the case under Eisenhower. Along with these efforts, Kennedy's administration looked to nominate and appoint judges who supported protecting the rights of all Americans. When Kennedy took office, only one African American, William Hastie, held a position as high as a federal appeals court judge.

Thurgood Marshall was among the individuals many anticipated to receive an offer of a judicial position. He was by far the best-known lawyer in the African-American community and highly regarded for his efforts on behalf of civil rights. Carl Murphy, the owner of the *Baltimore African American,* wrote an editorial promoting the elevation of Marshall to one of those positions. He noted that other African Americans had received jobs in the Kennedy administration and Marshall would be "a wise and able federal judge" (Williams, 1998, p. 28). Murphy knew Marshall had reached a point where he was open to leaving the LDF for such a position. Thurgood had said as much in an earlier interview where the fifty-two-year-old admitted that elevation to a federal judiciary position appealed to him. Murphy also may have been aware of Marshall's growing sense of displacement with the shift in the direction of civil rights activism. The role of the LDF was changing, and Marshall was not sure the new direction suited him. Marshall, in a later interview, noted, "I thought I'd kind of out-lived my usefulness, in original ideas, in the NAACP hierarchy" (Ball, 1998, p. 174). The time was at hand to investigate other possible opportunities, either with a law firm or with a federal judiciary position. After years of sacrificing monetarily to lead the legal efforts of the NAACP, Thurgood looked to make a comfortable salary and provide for his wife and two sons.

As Kennedy considered the possibility of appointing Marshall as a federal judge, Thurgood did not make the process an easy one. He had an early meeting after the election with the new attorney general to discuss the civil rights movement. The meeting went poorly. Marshall did not like the fact that Robert Kennedy spent the session trying to tell Marshall what to do. Later when Robert Kennedy invited him to another meeting to discuss a possible judicial position, it did not go well either. People advising Kennedy had hesitations about Marshall's ability as a lawyer and as a judge. They claimed he did not have the breadth of experience needed by a judge. He mainly had represented civil rights cases, which they thought limited his ability to judge other kinds of issues. They said this despite the fact the American Bar Association gave him their highest recommendation for a nominee for a judicial position. This mixed information presented to him prompted Robert Kennedy to offer Marshall a position as a federal district court judge, a level below a court of appeals position. Marshall turned him down. Thurgood believed he was not suited for that role, as he had a short temper, which he thought would not serve him well there. He did tell Kennedy he would accept a position on the court of appeals, which better suited his temperament. Kennedy replied that position was not available for Marshall, and the only choice was to accept a district judge position or nothing. He expected Marshall to accept the district judge position faced with that reality. But Marshall did not settle. Instead he told Kennedy, "All I've had in my life is nothing. Its not new to me, so goodbye" (Tushnet, 2001, p. 484). Then he walked out of the meeting.

When Marshall said his temperament was not right for the district judge position, he meant that in two ways. One was that his "short fuse" would get him into trouble and result in reversal of his decisions by a higher court. The other aspect was his belief that at that stage of his career, and in light of his national fame, he deserved a higher-level appointment. His nomination to a judicial position would carry symbolic significance with it and would boost President Kennedy's standing in the African-American community. A U.S. Supreme Court position would have been ideal, but short of that, a judicial position one level below the U.S. Supreme Court carried the appropriate prestige. Marshall would accept an appeals court position and nothing less. Robert Kennedy needed to understand how essential this was to Marshall, and that was why Thurgood walked out when only offered a district-level judge's position. Marshall had other options and refused to allow Kennedy to force him to settle.

After Marshall turned down the district-level position, Robert Kennedy faced pressure to give Marshall the judicial position he desired. Louis Martin, vice president and editorial director of the African-American newspaper *The Chicago Defender* and deputy chairman of the Democratic National Committee, led the cause to have Mr. Civil Rights receive a judicial nomination. In the process, he gathered letters of support from prominent white lawyers and even from director of the Federal Bureau of Investigation J. Edgar Hoover. Faced with this support for Marshall and the need to make a high-profile African-American judicial appointment, Kennedy changed his mind. President Kennedy nominated Marshall to serve on the U.S. Court of Appeals for the Second Circuit in September 1961. It had jurisdiction over New York, Connecticut, and Vermont, which made it second in importance only to the Court of Appeals for the District of Columbia. In his memo of nomination of Marshall, Robert Kennedy noted Marshall's high recommendation from the American Bar Association, excellent reputation, and his judicial temperament, which made him "worthy of appointment as a United States Circuit Judge."

Marshall accepted the nomination, but it was not a straightforward choice. Some of his friends wondered if he could have the same impact on the court as he had heading the LDF. The nomination represented a token appointment on one level, which had symbolic importance but not the same broad impact as his legal work. He wondered the same thing himself. "I had to fight it out with myself. But then I knew I had built up a staff—a damned good staff—an excellent board, and the backing that would let them go ahead. And when one had the opportunity to serve his government, he should think twice before passing it up" (Rowan, 1993, p. 235). What's more, it was time for new ideas and strategies to lead the organization. The best thing he could do for the LDF and the African-American community was to accept an influential position on the court of appeals.

The question then arose of who might succeed Marshall at the LDF. For years, many saw Robert Carter as the natural choice, given the important role he played on many of the legal cases of the organization after his arrival in 1949. But, the split between the LDF and the NAACP for tax reasons in 1957, placed Carter in charge of the legal activities of the NAACP as general counsel and no longer affiliated with the LDF. It also caused a strain in the relationship between Marshall and Carter, as Carter perceived his reassignment out of the LDF as a demotion engineered by Marshall. Carter's departure left two senior members of the team as logical choices for the role of director council: Jack Greenberg and Constance Baker Motley, who was slightly junior in service at the LDF to Greenberg. Motley felt that Marshall had difficulty with the idea of a woman in charge

---

BLACK POWER MOVEMENT

Activist Stokely Carmichael brought the concept of "black power" to national prominence during a speech he gave at a mass rally in Mississippi. The concept promoted the importance of racial pride and self-respect. It also rejected the idea of integration and the use of nonviolence as promoted by many civil rights leaders. Instead, black power advocates encouraged African Americans to defend themselves and to strengthen their own institutions and communities without the help of whites. As the idea grew in popularity, it also promoted the importance of African and African-American history and culture. The phrase "black is beautiful" came to epitomize the core value of the movement.

Martin Luther King Jr. and other civil rights leaders objected to the rejection of their ideals. They believed alliances with other groups was central to their belief system and ultimately reaching their goals. The different perspective of black power advocates came, in part, from the violence and resistance they had faced as nonviolent civil rights activists. They sought an alternative strategy that made them less vulnerable and less dependent upon the larger society to improve the lives of African Americans.

of the LDF in what he saw as a male world. She also had no supporters willing to speak up on her behalf other than civil rights lawyer and women's rights activist Bella Abzug and Medgar Evers, the NAACP field secretary in Mississippi. When Marshall informed her that Jack Greenberg was his choice, Motley was not surprised.

Marshall planned and executed his preference to have Jack Greenberg replace him. He had to move carefully, for the idea of a white man leading the LDF was unexpected in many quarters, and a disappointment to many. Since the days of Charles Houston, African Americans had led the legal efforts of the NAACP. Houston groomed Marshall, who was his student at Howard, and many expected Marshall to follow the same path when he left. African Americans were proud that they led the fight against segregation, which impacted them more than any other group in society. To have someone other than an African American lead the charge was, according to Motley, "one of the more stunning developments in the civil rights community" (Motley, 1998, p. 152). But, Marshall was determined to turn the reins over to Greenberg, a Jewish graduate of Columbia Law School and a member of the LDF since 1949.

To cement his decision, Marshall garnered support from key individuals. He gained the backing of Roy Wilkins, the executive director of the NAACP, to prevent any opposition to Greenberg from that organization. Thurgood also talked with key financial supporters of the LDF, who were white, and secured their support. Finally, he talked with the members of the LDF board and convinced them to support the elevation of his candidate. Some opposition to Marshall's choice arose from the rank and file of the NAACP, but it was not strong enough to prevent the change Marshall desired. Plus, the only argument for excluding Greenberg would have been because he was not African American, as his credentials as a lawyer and important member of the LDF team were beyond reproach. This was not a position the NAACP could take in good conscience. As Marshall put it, "As those who are fighting against discrimination, we cannot afford to practice it" (*Black Worker*, 1961). After Marshall left, Jack Greenberg would serve as director counsel for the LDF for the next seventeen years.

Marshall's transition to the U.S. Court of Appeals did not move forward smoothly. When President Kennedy made the announcement, the reaction of the press varied considerably. The African-American press hailed the nomination while Southern papers like the *Richmond Times-Dispatch* called the nomination controversial and risky. The president knew that the nomination would face opposition, which was one of the factors that caused him to move slowly on the nomination. A tactic he used with Marshall's nomination to get it moving forward was to submit it shortly before the Senate went into recess. With the Senate away and unable to schedule a hearing for the Marshall nomination, Kennedy gave Marshall a recess appointment. The Constitution allowed the president to appoint judges temporarily until the Senate returned from their recess and could schedule hearings. This presidential power enabled Thurgood Marshall to take the oath of office of a circuit judge the October following his nomination.

The ceremony took place in Manhattan before a large crowd of well-wishers. His wife, Cissy; his two sons; Judge William Hastie; Senator Jacob Javits; and Roy Wilkins were among the people who came to witness the occasion. The chief judge of the Second Circuit administered the oath of office and complimented the wealth of experience Thurgood brought to his new position. The appointment represented the fulfillment of a lifelong dream of Marshall. Back in Baltimore, when he first began practicing law, his aspiration was to one day become a local judge in that city. Now he was a judge at the federal level and the first African-American judge for the Second Circuit. Both he and the Kennedys hoped this ceremony would blunt Southern opposition. They hoped the pronouncement of *Time* magazine that "Southern senators who disagree with Marshall . . . are expected to make only a token fight against his confirmation" was an accurate prediction (Ball, 1998, p. 181). They also hoped that having Marshall perform the job before the return of the Senate would make it even harder for them to oppose his nomination.

Unfortunately, Southern opposition to Marshall's nomination proved even more entrenched than expected. This resistance even included deception on the part of Southern senate leaders. Early in the discussions about the Marshall nomination, the White House held discussions with the chair of the Senate Judiciary Committee, James O. Eastland of Mississippi. Eastland saw the NAACP as a communist-backed organization and proudly talked of using his influence to prevent votes on numerous pieces of civil rights legislation. The attorney general was then surprised when he discussed Marshall's possible nomination and Eastland indicated he was open to a deal. He wanted the president to nominate his college roommate, Harold Cox, to a Southern district judgeship. Then he would have a judge in place who opposed the civil rights activism taking part in that region. In exchange, he promised to allow the nomination of Marshall to go forward out of the subcommittee hearings for a full vote. Believing he had cleared the way for Marshall, President Kennedy made Cox one of his first nominees for a federal judgeship. Eastland did not keep his part of the bargain and put in motion actions to delay and perhaps prevent the final appointment of Marshall.

The first step taken by Eastland in opposition to his promise was the selection of the membership of the Subcommittee on Nominations, who initially would examine Marshall's qualifications to determine if he was fit to be a federal judge. All three men—Olin Johnson of South Carolina, Roman Hruska of Iowa, and John McClellan of Arkansas—showed no eagerness to move the nomination forward quickly. Johnson and McClel-lan supported segregation, and Hruska was not an enthusiastic supporter of civil rights. In addition, Johnson faced a tight reelection campaign in South Carolina where any support of the Marshall nomination would work against him. When the Senate officially received Marshall's nomination after its return from recess, they moved slowly on holding hearings. Olin Johnson, the chair of the committee, twice scheduled hearings to question Marshall but canceled both sessions. Marshall traveled from New York to Washington to attend one of the hearings only to have it called off. The first official meeting to review Marshall did not take place until April 1962, seven months after his nomination by President Kennedy. Only one com-mittee member, Roman Hruska, showed up for that session, which began fifteen minutes late and lasted only twenty minutes.

Review of Marshall's qualifications did not seriously get underway until the summer of 1962. Then five hearings took place in July and August. They were not friendly in tone. It quickly became clear the objective was to bring to the surface any information the committee might use to disqual-ify Marshall. The lawyer for the subcommittee, L. P. B. Lipscomb, led the assault upon Marshall. He presented a series of charges against Marshall that represented a desperate attempt to twist any information they could against him. Lipscomb began by raising issues about Marshall's efforts as the head of the LDF. He implied Marshall broke the law by actively seeking cases to bring lawsuits against segregation. At the time it was illegal for lawyers to solicit business. Clients had to come to them on their own.

The subcommittee questioned the tax-exempt status of the LDF. They attacked Marshall for his past association with the National Lawyers Guild, which included members sympathetic to the Communist party. In response, Marshall put in the record the letter of resignation from the Guild he had written years before when he realized the communist pres-ence in the organization (Tushnet, 2001, p. 486). In addition, the commit-tee argued there was a strong communist influence within the NAACP to which Marshall could point to his very active efforts to keep communist influences out of the organization. Lipscomb even sought to charge Mar-shall with practicing law without a license. He noted Marshall only was licensed to practice law in Maryland but did work in New York where he was not certified. To this, Marshall made it clear that he did not bring cases himself outside of Maryland but worked with and advised lawyers certified in those locations. Thurgood also pointed out that he was certi-fied to practice before the U.S. Supreme Court.

Maybe the strangest charge brought by the subcommittee painted Mar-shall as a racist. In support of this accusation, they took a quote from an article written by a historian who had worked with Marshall. In the essay, he described one of the meetings concerning the *Brown* case in which a group discussed the debate in Congress regarding the passage of the Four-teenth Amendment. At one point, Marshall made the remark that "when us colored folk take over, every time a white man draws a breath, he'll have to pay a fine." The committee even made the scholar, Al Kelly, travel to Washington from Detroit to explain what he had written. Kelly arrived, angered by the twisting of his essay by the subcommittee. He called their accusations in this instance absurd, grotesque, and a bizarre distortion of reality. He added with respect to Marshall's views on communism that Marshall had told him that it was not good for African Americans and "must be avoided like the plague" (Davis & Clark, 1992, p. 239). His was the last testimony given to the subcommittee as they brought their review of Marshall to a conclusion.

The goal of Johnson's committee to delay the vote on Marshall's nomi-nation as long as they could quickly became obvious to outside observers. They did not have substantial accusations they could bring against Mar-shall but hoped he might make a mistake in the course of their question-ing. This was pointed out by the members of the Senate working to push through the nomination. As Senator Kenneth Keating of New York pointed out, the "opponents of civil rights were maneuvering to delay the confir-mation, [their] opposition centered not on the man but on the results he has achieved" (Ball, 1998, p. 182). He was, in part, correct, but there was another factor fueling their opposition.

Many Southern politicians, and they were not alone in this view, believed that an African American, no matter who he was, did not have the intelligence or ability to hold an important judicial position. In the mind of those individuals, Marshall only understood civil rights law and would fail in navigating the wide variety of cases faced by the circuit courts. Others believed it had been the support of his staff and others, mostly white, which fueled his successes that led to the breakthrough in the *Brown* case. To them, Marshall did not possess that strong a legal mind. Among these critics was U.S. Supreme Court justice Felix Frankfurter, who told people that Marshall was not qualified for the court. He thought the praise heaped upon Marshall's nomination was absurd and that Marshall had not made a deep impression on the justices when he made his presentations. It was rumblings like these that the judiciary subcommittee probably hoped might gain enough momentum to derail Marshall's nomination.

However, their delaying tactics had the opposite effect. As time passed, pressure increased to have the subcommittee move the nomination for-ward with their recommendation. Outside of the judiciary subcommittee, many observers accepted Marshall's consistent testimony defending the integrity of the NAACP and its legal activities. Marshall's supporters in the Senate consequently threatened to take the process away from the sub-committee if it did not act. Faced with this threat, the subcommittee ended its hearings and eventually voted 2–1 against confirming Marshall. But before having that vote, Chairman Johnson sought to delay moving the nomination before the full Senate until after their upcoming recess. His thought was that while they were away, Marshall's temporary appointment would have to be renewed, but by law, he could not get paid until he was officially confirmed. Johnson and others hoped this would create a financial hardship for Marshall and force him to resign to find other work to support his family (Tushnet, 2001, pp. 485–486; Williams, 1998, p. 301).

But colleagues in the Senate pressed to get the process resolved before they recessed. The full judiciary committee took over the process and voted to confirm Marshall. When sent to the full Senate for the final vote, both Eastland and Johnson held up the process for five hours debating the nomination. However, in the end, the Senate voted to confirm Marshall nearly a year after Kennedy sent them the nomination. Only four Southern Democrats voted against his confirmation. The conclusion of the hearings greatly relieved Marshall. The approaching one-year deadline, after which he would not get paid, worried him. He brought this up to President Kennedy at a White House function. The president advised him not to worry, as hearings took time, and implied that if the judiciary committee passed the deadline, arrangements were in place to protect Marshall financially. Thurgood finally was confirmed for the position in which he had been working for the past year.

After the swearing-in ceremony in October 1961, before the senate confirmation hearings, Marshall began the task of mastering the complexities of a court of appeals judge. The Second Circuit Court was one of the most prestigious of the appellate courts because of the complexity of the lawsuits it reviewed. Its judges listened to cases ranging from civil rights issues to security and exchange questions to labor disputes to maritime matters. Marshall faced a steep learning curve to get up to speed on the laws governing these kinds of cases. But he faced this task with the same determination he mustered when pursuing segregation lawsuits. He was honored to join the ranks of federal judges and did not intend to disappoint the many people who took pride in his elevation to the court. It was the burden many African Americans carried when they were one of the firsts to occupy a position. "I will do my level best to live up to their expectations" (Williams, 1998, p. 303). These were the words he used after his senate confirmation. He would not disappoint the many people who took pride in the success of one of their own.

Thurgood Marshall was, in fact, a first for the Second Circuit Court. When Marshall arrived, not many African Americans worked in the building. The elevator operators were the only African-American employees besides Marshall. An incident described by Marshall conveyed how groundbreaking his presence as a judge there was. The chief judge

J. Edward Lumbard arranged to have a picture taken of the nine judges of the court. As the photographer set up the equipment for the session before the arrival of the judges, he blew a fuse. He had a secretary call for an electrician. Thurgood arrived shortly thereafter, and the secretary mistook him for the electrician. When he identified himself as the new judge, she quickly apologized, much to Marshall's amusement. He later joked to his clerk when telling the story that the secretary must have been crazy if she thought an African-American man could become an electrician in New York City (ibid., p. 304).

Marshall increased the number of African Americans employed at the court by hiring the first circuit court African-American secretary, Ruth Alice Stovall, whom he brought with him from the NAACP. She attracted quite a bit of attention as other secretaries wandered past the office to peek at her as well as Marshall. Stovall said she tried to get Marshall to take on more of the formalities of a federal judge, but he refused to do it. Unlike other judges, he would not close the doors to his chambers unless he was in conversation with another judge. In his defense he would ask, "What have I got to be locked up about?" (Ball, 1998, p. 185). The law clerks saw Marshall's open door as a reason to visit with him. Marshall was a marvelous storyteller and shared with the law clerks many of the experiences he had while working for the NAACP. It exposed them to situations they had not imagined and provided a stronger sense of the challenges facing African Americans.

But what occupied most of Marshall's time were his duties as a member of the court. As the newest member of the team, he was asked to write opinions for the more technical and less interesting cases to the other judges. Many of these cases focused on areas outside of Marshall's expertise, such as security fraud or tax suits. These frequently were cases his colleagues could not judge because of their own financial holdings, which created potential conflicts of interest for them. As he increased his expertise in these areas, it did not always go smoothly. Marshall recalled how it pained him when one lawyer wrote about how during Marshall's early days on the court, he seemed to know little about tax laws and corporations. But Marshall readily sought help when he felt unsure of his knowledge. One of the other judges, J. Henry Friendly, an expert in corporate law, became an important advisor to Marshall. Thurgood also only hired law clerks from the best law schools to help him decipher the nuances of the laws connected to the cases for which he wrote opinions. With them, and on his own, Marshall dedicated long hours studying the laws and sharpening his knowledge in those areas he felt deficient. Unfortunately, since few African Americans matriculated from places like Harvard and Yale, where Marshall mostly selected his clerks, it meant he never had an African-American law clerk while sitting on the circuit court.

During the four years Marshall spent on the court, he grew in confidence and expertise. Through hard work he developed into a skilled appellate judge who held his own with his colleagues. While on the court, Marshall wrote 118 opinions; 98 were majority opinions, 8 constituted concurring opinions, and 12 dissented from the majority. His record of success before the U.S. Supreme Court was unblemished, as none of his opinions was reversed when appealed to that body.

One of his opinions for the majority anticipated a change in the view of the U.S. Supreme Court with regard to the issue of double jeopardy at the state level. In the case *U.S. ex rel. Hetenyi v. Wilkins*, the state of New York tried a defendant, George Hetenyi, three separate times for the murder of his wife. Hetenyi argued that the state had violated his Fourteenth Amendment rights to due process. Marshall and the court agreed, saying the state was limited by the Constitution from doing this. The ruling was the first to make this connection to state actions. The U.S. Supreme Court later reinforced this concept in its ruling in *Benton v. Maryland*. A dissent by Marshall in which he argued that an accused hospitalized person had the right to counsel when questioned by the police was also a view later adopted by the U.S. Supreme Court. These and other opinions rendered by Marshall reflected, as Irving Kaufman, one of Marshall's fellow judges noted, Thurgood's ability to see the human side of issues born out of his civil rights career. This was a perspective his colleagues lacked, given their legal experiences, and added another dimension to the considerations of the group. The Bill of Rights and the Fourteenth Amendment, understandably, were important to him, and he looked to ensure they were respected in the cases brought before him and his colleagues. Marshall consistently looked to protect the rights of the individual from unfair application of the laws. But, he did not condone the breaking of the law. As he often said, "Rules is rules," and when one breaks them, there are penalties that ensue.

As Marshall adjusted to learning new laws and regulations as a circuit judge, he also had to adjust to life away from the NAACP offices. For years, every day at the LDF brought new issues and challenges to confront. There was a constant stream of telephone calls, correspondences, meetings, and travels that filled his days. Now he was the judge considering cases, as opposed to the litigator in a hostile courtroom seeking to dismantle segregation or to save the life of an African-American defendant. Life as a judge was much tamer. His focus was on the cases brought before the court, which meant limiting the interaction he had with others. Preserving his objectivity and avoiding any perception of impropriety was crucial. As a result, he had to carefully control his interactions with lawyers when outside the courtroom, including many of his previous colleagues connected to the LDF or the NAACP. At first, Marshall occasionally traveled back to the NAACP offices to reconnect with the people who had been his professional family for years. But as he became more deeply involved with cases before the circuit court, he had to decrease and finally stop those visits. Probably the interaction he missed most was with Roy Wilkins. His wife, Cissy, described the close relationship they had as like brothers. In fact, Roy was closer to Thurgood than Thurgood's own brother, Aubrey.

While Marshall was honored to have his new position, it was a change he did not always enjoy. One of his early law clerks believed that Marshall was bored in his role as a judge. He often would walk to the window and just stare out when things slowed down. He missed the camaraderie and excitement of his old life. He also missed the notoriety that accompanied his work with the LDF. As director counsel of the LDF, Thurgood became "Mr. Civil Rights," the best known African-American lawyer in the country. People recognized him as he walked down the street and thanked him for his contributions. Now as a circuit court judge, that high public profile went away. The work he did was important, but hardly contributions that commanded headlines. That life was behind him, as were the old professional relationships. Consequently, his law clerks became his new professional family. Marshall expected a lot from them but also spent time with them sharing stories and his life experiences. These were things Alice Stovall believed he thought they needed to hear and understand (Williams, 1998, p. 228). He invited them to his home for meals and introduced them to his friends. For many of them, it was probably their first introduction to the world of African Americans, with all of its joys and challenges.

His new position allowed Marshall to provide a new home for his family. As a federal judge, Marshall's salary rose from the eighteen thousand dollars he received with the LDF to twenty-five thousand dollars. With that increase, he moved Cissy and the boys into a seventeenth floor apartment in Morningside Gardens, a cooperative housing unit near Columbia University. Built in 1957, the cooperative sought to house a racially diverse group of residents. It was one of the few locations in New York at the time that actively promoted an integrated clientele. Cissy Marshall said they enjoyed their time there. They had a young family, so many of their friends, who also lived in the complex, would come to their place to visit. They would cook, play cards, exchange stories, and enjoy one another's company. The higher salary also allowed Thurgood to buy a white Cadillac. He had long wanted one, and it was a thrill to finally own his dream car. He drove it around Harlem with great pride with the letters USJ stamped on it. They stood for his role as a U.S. judge.

Thurgood's new status also prompted the Kennedy administration to call upon him to advise them about civil rights issues and to represent them at high-profile public events. Marshall provided advice on the desegregation crises at the Universities of Alabama and Mississippi. They also sought his guidance after the assassination of Medgar Evers in 1963.

Marshall knew Evers well from his days at the NAACP and thought highly of him. Marshall believed Evers "had more courage than anybody I've ever run across" (Tushnet, 2001, p. 510). Evers's death was a major loss to the NAACP and the movement in Marshall's view.

Besides serving as an advisor, Marshall also had the opportunity to represent the State Department on a goodwill tour in Africa in July 1963. It was not long after the news coverage of civil rights demonstrators under attack by police dogs and fire hosed in Birmingham, Alabama, emerged around the world. Particularly in Africa, the Kennedy administration wanted to assure its leaders of their support for civil rights reform. The fear of communism on the African continent made maintaining good relations there important to the government. They sponsored Marshall's travel back to Kenya to allow him to talk with the friends he had made there previously. The State Department hoped he and his traveling companion, Berl Bernhard of the U.S. Civil Rights Commission, would facilitate an open discussion about the rule of law and the challenges inherent to solving racial challenges in the United States. The State Department believed the success attained by Marshall offered a powerful example of civil rights progress. While more changes needed to take place, Marshall said during his trip, he agreed with the government position that it would take time to achieve all the changes needed. He pointed this out when he noted that in the United States "it is just a matter of time before practice is brought into conformity with the law and that should occur within the next few years" (Dudziak, 2008, p. 112).

While Thurgood supported the objectives of the State Department, he had an additional reason for accepting the trip. He had helped formulate the Constitution for Kenya and wished to see how it worked in application. He hoped the Bill of Rights he crafted to protect minorities had guaranteed a positive future for all of Kenya's inhabitants. Unfortunately, as it turned out, that was not the case. When he arrived, conversations with Asian residents highlighted the troubles they faced trying to survive economically. Boycotts of their businesses made it difficult to remain open. They faced troubling pressures in other areas as well. When Marshall met with Jomo Kenyatta, the prime minster of Kenya, Thurgood aggressively pressed him to provide more protection for the rights of Asian residents. Kenyatta, in turn, grilled Marshall about the racial issues of the United States. But despite their areas of disagreement, they had great respect for one another. Marshall wished Kenyatta would do more to protect the rights of minorities in the nation, but he also understood how fragile the nation-building process was in Kenya. Marshall believed it was the political savvy of Kenyatta that prevented his country from suffering a bloodbath similar to what happened in other African nations. Nation building sometimes required compromises. As a result, Marshall only pressed Kenyatta so far about changes in his policies during his visit.

Marshall talked with a number of other groups during his visit as well. He was a hit nearly everywhere he went. His State Department companion, Berl Bernhard, found that the Kenyans loved Marshall. When they initially flew into Nairobi, arriving about four in the morning, a red carpet and an official welcome awaited Marshall as he descended from the plane. The royal treatment continued throughout the time he was there. Even though disappointed by the discrimination faced by Asians, Marshall was very proud of the progress made by the country. The role he played in helping it begin the process of moving toward independence also pleased him. His admiration for the Kenyans and their appreciation of Marshall made the trip a success.

Two major events riveted the attention of the nation and the world after Marshall's return. The first focused on a decision by civil rights leaders to organize a major march on Washington, DC, to mark the centennial of the issuing of the Emancipation Proclamation in March 1863. In recognition of the aspirations created by that document not yet achieved, march leaders felt they needed to place more pressure on the government. They wanted more legislation passed that positively impacted the rights of African Americans. To impress upon Congress their demands for freedom and jobs, they took out permits to bring massive numbers of protestors to the nation's capital. Congress and President Kennedy feared bringing so many people to the capital would lead to violence as well as hurt chances for the passage of a civil rights bill. Thurgood Marshall shared the concerns of the politicians. He was not a fan of the protest marches organized in the past and did not see what this march would accomplish. When the event took place in August, most of the leaders of major civil rights organizations attended and contributed. Thurgood Marshall did not travel to Washington to participate in what became a historic event. He watched the march on TV but had no comment about it when asked.

Marshall did have a reaction three months later in November 1963, when President John F. Kennedy was assassinated in Dallas, Texas. Marshall appreciated what the president had done for him and was saddened by his death. He described Kennedy as "terrific" and mourned his loss. Like others around the nation, Marshall must have wondered what would follow as Vice President Lyndon B. Johnson from Texas succeeded Kennedy. What would Johnson, a Southerner, do in the realm of civil rights? This issue also was one of interest to African nations like Kenya, which Marshall and Cissy visited the next month. They traveled there primarily to attend the celebration of Kenya's independence from Great Britain. Marshall also went there with members of the State Department to carry reassurances from President Johnson that the foreign policy of the United States would not change nor would its commitment toward civil rights. Johnson reinforced his intentions when he expressed during his first State of the Union Address that he wanted "this session of Congress . . . [to be] known as the session which did more for civil rights than the last hundred sessions combined."

Over the next two years, President Johnson made civil rights–related initiatives a priority. Under his prodding and leadership, despite strong Southern opposition, he pushed through two major laws. The first one, the Civil Rights Act of 1964 made discrimination in public places illegal and banned employment discrimination. The following year he sent a Voting Rights Act to Congress with the goal of banning efforts to prevent African Americans from exercising their right to register and vote. In 1966, he named Robert Weaver secretary of the Department of Housing and Urban Development, the first African American to hold a cabinet-level position. Johnson also nominated eight African Americans for federal judgeships between 1964 and 1967. Among the appointees were former colleagues of Thurgood Marshall, Spotswood Robinson and Constance Baker Motley. Motley's appointment came as a surprise to her, as she was asked to come to the White House to have a conversation with the president. When she arrived, he informed her that he had appointed her to the federal bench for the Southern District of New York. She became the first African-American woman appointed to a federal judiciary position.

As Johnson moved forward with his civil rights agenda, Thurgood Marshall was part of his future plans. After his trip to Kenya for its independence celebration, Thurgood settled back into the routine of a circuit court judge. He had come to accept the benefits and the changes in lifestyle that came with the position. While he no longer was in the spotlight as "Mr. Civil Rights," his life was more orderly as he kept regular hours, had time to spend with his family, and to watch his young sons grow. His position as a federal judge gave him tenure for life and a salary that allowed him to live comfortably. By all accounts, he was respected by his colleagues and produced thoughtful opinions. But this all changed in July 1965, when a bailiff interrupted his lunch with the news that the president was on the telephone and wanted to talk to him. Surprised, Marshall asked: "The president of what?" The bailiff replied, "The president of the United States." Thurgood Marshall's career was about to change once again.

9

Solicitor General

When Thurgood Marshall took the telephone call from President Johnson in 1965, he had to wonder what the president wanted. He did not know Johnson well. They had met once in Texas in the 1940s and had crossed paths in Washington a few times after Johnson became a senator. After they talked for a few minutes, the president told Marshall he wanted to make him the solicitor general. This was an important position, as the task of that individual is to oversee and litigate government cases before the U.S. Supreme Court. The solicitor general, by statute, is required to be "learned in law" and to assist the attorney general in executing his duties. He has offices both in the offices of the attorney general and in the U.S. Supreme Court. The position is involved in the majority of lawsuits that come to the court. The solicitor general normally makes the government's argument to the justices, although he can assign that task to other lawyers under his control. The position is the third highest post in the Justice Department, just below the attorney general and his deputy. If he accepted the position, Marshall would be the first African American to hold that office. Thurgood understood the significance of this decision by the president. He told Johnson he needed time to consider the offer. There were factors he had to weigh, including what Cissy might have to say.

President Johnson agreed to give Marshall time to ponder the issue but swore him to secrecy about the proposal. When Marshall went home that evening, he had a family meeting to discuss the advantages and disadvantages of the offer. The prestige that came with it made it tempting. It gave Marshall the opportunity to become one of the highest-ranking African-American government officials. It would also represent another first in Marshall's career. But accepting the position meant Marshall must give up a lifetime tenure appointment as a federal judge, his retirement pension, and accept a forty-five-hundred-dollar salary reduction. Thurgood said he told Cissy that if he took the job, they would have to cut back on their spending. She and the boys might have to forgo buying new clothes and other treats they took for granted. In addition, the new position lacked the security of the judgeship, as Johnson could fire him at any time. If Marshall said or did anything that angered Johnson, he could find himself without a job. The solicitor job also entailed possibly having to move to Washington, DC, or Marshall commuting between New York and Washington, DC. Cissy did not see that as an issue and encouraged him to accept Johnson's offer.

Determined to move forward quickly with the nomination, Johnson called the next day to get an answer from Thurgood. The president listened to the worries Marshall had about accepting the job but was not prepared to take no for an answer. He had Marshall travel to Washington for a face-to-face meeting. As they talked, Johnson reminded Marshall of the symbolic importance of his occupying that position. Johnson wanted people, and especially black and white children, to come to the U.S. Supreme Court and see an African-American solicitor general standing before the justices representing the federal government. In the end, Marshall agreed to take the offer. He too wanted the country to see that image. As he told *The New York Times*, "It is impossible to consider the appointment . . . apart from its symbolic aspects" (Zelden, 2013, p. 136). The president also informed Marshall that the job offer was not a stepping stone to a higher position, such as on the U.S. Supreme Court. He wanted Marshall to focus on the job of solicitor general and to perform the duties of that office. Marshall said he understood and agreed to leave his position on the Second Circuit Court. He was ready to serve both his race and his country in this instance. "I believe that in this time especially, we do what our government requests of us. Negroes have made great advancements in government, and I think that it is time they started making some sacrifices" (ibid.).

When Johnson told Thurgood that his new position was not a stepping stone, his objective was to keep Marshall in the dark about his true plans. His aide, Jack Valenti, later revealed that Johnson, early in his presidency, decided to appoint an African American to the U.S. Supreme Court. The Kennedys had considered doing it but had not made it happen. Johnson intended to succeed and had a plan in mind to accomplish his goal. The first criteria in his plan was to select an individual who could survive the challenging and, at times, bruising process of hearings and congressional investigations. He wanted the person he sent forward to have credentials that made it difficult to block his approval. As a politically savvy former senator, he understood the intricacies of the nomination process and what was needed to successfully navigate it. The person he had in mind for the position was Thurgood Marshall. According to Valenti, Johnson admired Marshall. He saw Marshall as an excellent courtroom lawyer and a judge of great ability. He also believed Marshall a patriotic American of integrity with deep convictions. Selecting Marshall as solicitor general served to make him a stronger candidate for the next job Johnson had in mind for him. As Johnson told Valenti, by having Marshall serve in the solicitor general position, later when he faced senate hearings, if someone tried to say he didn't have a lot of experience with the U.S. Supreme Court, Johnson could respond that Marshall had "prosecuted more cases before the Supreme Court than any lawyer in America" (Rowan, 1993, pp. 287–288).

Ramsey Clark, deputy attorney general, under Johnson, agreed that Johnson had a plan to eventually elevate Marshall. He had a conversation early in 1965 in which Marshall's name came up in another context. During that conversation, Johnson expressed his admiration for Thurgood. He also shared his plan to make him solicitor general and then nominate him for the U.S. Supreme Court. He believed that as solicitor general, Marshall could prove his abilities to handle the responsibilities of an associate U.S. Supreme Court justice. Lady Bird Johnson noted the same sentiments of her husband about Marshall in her diary, weeks before he appointed Marshall as solicitor general. She wrote about her husband's admiration for Marshall and that appointing him solicitor general was a first step. If Marshall proved himself there, "perhaps when a vacancy on the Supreme Court opened up, he might nominate him as a justice—the first of his race" (Williams, 1998, p. 315).

President Johnson announced Thurgood Marshall as his new solicitor general on July 13, 1965. At the press conference, he highlighted Marshall's

---

ROBERT WEAVER APPOINTMENT AS SECRETARY OF HUD

When President Lyndon Johnson created the new cabinet position of Housing and Urban Development, he appointed Robert C. Weaver as its leader. This represented the first ever appointment of an African American to head a federal cabinet-level post. Weaver was eminently qualified. He had three degrees from Harvard University, including a doctorate in economics. He previously worked in the Department of the Interior during the New Deal, was an expert in economics and housing discrimination, and served as director of the Housing and Home Finance Agency under President Kennedy. At that time, his appointment made Weaver the first African American to hold such a high level of responsibility.

qualities and his admiration for him as a lawyer. Media reaction was as expected, positive in the African-American press and, at best, skeptical in Southern newspapers. The concerns expressed in the latter were issues that might come up in the confirmation process in the Senate, but Johnson had taken that into account when deciding to nominate Marshall. He did not want a repeat of the prolonged hearings that characterized Marshall's confirmation for the circuit court. He used his power as the president to convince the committee to act efficiently. When individual senators proved resistant, he threatened to withhold funding for federal projects in their states or to close military bases important to them. As a result, when hearings began two weeks later, they did not last very long. Of the sixteen members of the committee, only two of them had questions for Marshall, intended to promote his approval rather than hinder it. The hearing took only half an hour, after which the committee voted 11–5 for confirmation. There were no Southern senators on the committee. The following day, the full Senate, without debate, also approved Marshall as solicitor general.

At Marshall's swearing-in ceremony at the White House, U.S. Supreme Court justice Hugo Black, an old friend of Marshall's, administered the oath of office. President Johnson, Cissy Marshall, and their two boys stood nearby. The people attending also included family members from Baltimore, led by his brother, Aubrey; FBI director J. Edgar Hoover; and U.S. Supreme Court justice Tom Clark. It was a proud moment for the president and all of the Marshall family. After the ceremony, the president had a specific request of Marshall. He insisted Marshall move his family to Washington and not commute back and forth. Johnson did not want Marshall's family in one place and Marshall living part time in Washington. Consequently, Marshall and Cissy went house hunting and eventually found a place in Southwest Washington. They also enrolled their boys in Georgetown Day School, which pleased President Johnson. He did not want any implications that Marshall was not fully dedicated to the job.

President Johnson planned to highlight Marshall's importance to him and to the nation by including Marshall in several high-profile activities. When the president signed the Voting Rights Bill, he ensured Marshall had a prominent place among the observers of the event. Johnson also had Marshall head a delegation to a United Nations Congress on the Prevention of Crime and Treatment of Offenders in Stockholm, Sweden. A spokesman for the president said that having Marshall head the delegation indicated the deep concern Johnson had about the problem and his interest in finding solutions. Thurgood Marshall quickly became an important symbol for rational nonviolent change for the president. Marshall's belief in the law and nonviolence stood in contrast to the emerging Black Power Movement among African Americans and the avocation of the use of violence by some. In the face of riots like the one in Watts in Los Angeles, the president saw Marshall as an alternative path to follow based upon "the belief that human rights must be satisfied through the orderly process of law" (Williams, 1998, p. 317).

As Marshall settled into his role as solicitor general, the Department of Justice staff had to make adjustments as well. They had never had an African American hold such an important position before and were not sure what to expect. The only African American who worked in the office at the time was a courier. But Marshall quickly overcame the concerns of even the most skeptical. Prior to his arrival, one of the secretaries from South Carolina had deep concerns about working for an African American. She even considered resigning. However, these worries disappeared not long after Marshall's arrival. He began his tenure as solicitor general by greeting each of the staff individually with a handshake and a warm hello. It paralleled his style when running the LDF and quickly set the office at ease. The South Carolina secretary consequently not only stayed but told others how much she enjoyed her job. The staff also wondered if Thurgood's knowledge of the law extended beyond issues associated with civil rights, given his reputation in that sphere. However, they found that his understanding of legal issues extended beyond that realm. The years spent researching and writing opinions as a circuit judge had helped fill in many of the gaps that might have once existed.

The atmosphere in the office under Marshall greatly differed from the operating style of his predecessor, Archibald Cox. As solicitor general, Cox, a former Harvard Law School professor, ran a tightly organized office. He was described as one of the best solicitor generals in the history of the office. Cox believed in long hours and an authoritative management approach. His years as a professor at Harvard and in the office of the solicitor general under Franklin Roosevelt provided him with an experienced breadth of knowledge of the law and in the operation of the solicitor's office. Thurgood Marshall had neither the previous experience in the office or the breadth of knowledge of the laws possessed by Cox. His management style differed as well. Marshall followed a more informal approach in which he encouraged and valued the ideas of the members of his staff. He recognized gaps existed in his knowledge of the law, which others knew better. As he had with the LDF staff, Marshall encouraged lively, probing conversations with his new staff. From these discussions he gained a deeper sense of the issues and how to think about the many cases that came to his office for consideration to take before the U.S. Supreme Court.

The most important task of the solicitor general's office was deciding which of the, sometimes, thousands of cases heard in lower federal district courts should be appealed to the U.S. Supreme Court. A majority of the cases heard each session by the court results from decisions made by the solicitor general. Final authority over choosing the cases allowed to go forward rested with Marshall, which made his role a critical one. For a man who believed in the power of the court to shape society, it was a responsibility Marshall both relished and took seriously.

After working in the relative isolation of the Second Circuit Court, Marshall enjoyed the role of solicitor general. Marshall described it as the best job he ever had. He was back in the middle of exciting daily activities and interaction with the members of his sizeable staff. His new staff was much larger than the one he ever had at the NAACP. Twenty-three lawyers reported to Solicitor General Marshall. He also had access to many more resources than he had while with the NAACP. He could call upon the legal staff or the legal resources of any agency in the federal government. In addition, representing the federal government gave his voice before the court more impact than when he was an NAACP lawyer. Given the variety of cases he personally presented to the court, his opportunities to impact issues connected to human rights and other questions of due process increased dramatically.

There were members of the Supreme Court and other individuals who questioned how well Marshall performed his duties. A large part of that perception revolved around his following the much-respected Archibald Cox, who was in many ways his polar opposite. Cox worked long and late hours at the office. Marshall did not. He went home to spend time with his wife and his two boys, who meant so much to him, although when he did so, Marshall often took work with him to review later. Cox was formal and austere while Marshall was relaxed and informal. For example, he brought a ceremonial leopard-skin he had received when made an honorary Kibiyu tribal chief by Kenyan officials to the office and draped it over his chair. Thurgood also had the reputation of enjoying a drink or two on a regular basis, which he did not refute. When asked by a reporter about the stories of his often having a few drinks at lunch, Marshall replied, "Well, not when I am working, just one, but maybe two more before dinner" (Davis & Clark, 1992, p. 252). For his doubters, this just added to their skepticism of a man they thought not up to the job. Even President Johnson expressed frustrations with Marshall at times, calling him "lazy" and not a very good administrator.

But the people who worked with Marshall on a daily basis had a different perspective. One of his senior people, Louis Claiborne, described Marshall as an outstanding administrator and advocate. In his view, Marshall was generous and kind with a strong sense of justice. Marshall believed in delegation and trusting his staff but did not abdicate his responsibility as the chief administrator. Marshall closely read all the reports his staff produced and quickly digested and understood them. As a leader, according to Claiborne, Marshall did not shrink from making the big or tough decisions. But he also supported the decisions of his staff even when they did something without having gotten his approval beforehand.

The other contrast between Marshall and Cox was their presence before the U.S. Supreme Court. Observers described Cox as professor-like in his presentations. He was formal, well prepared, and understood the nuances of the cases he presented. He spoke in low, controlled tones and had a subtle wit. The justices were regularly impressed by the breadth of his knowledge. The number and variety of cases he presented in the course of his time in office also impressed. He might flawlessly give well-informed presentations on three or more cases in a week on very different issues. Cox set a hard standard for anyone who followed him, and for Marshall, who had a much different courtroom presence, the contrast was stark. Marshall was less formal and more personable in the courtroom. He was apt to look at the human impact of the cases he presented. Marshall sought to make personal contact with the justices, not to tutor them. Marshall spoke in a forceful voice and, at times, used humor that almost brought the justices to laughter to make his points. He did not make as many presentations to the court as Cox had, and there were moments when he had to depend on his staff to pass him notes to respond to some of the more technical issues raised by the justices. This, at times, happened because Marshall chose to present cases where he was not as familiar with the intricacies of the related law but felt were challenging cases that were his responsibility to present and not to pass off to another member of his staff. While Cox was a scholar of the law, Marshall was a practitioner who had spent many years working to reshape the application of the law. This made him less of a theoretician than Cox, but more knowledgeable about the real-life ramifications of decisions made in the courts. Their differing public personalities caused some people to unfairly disparage Marshall's time as solicitor general in comparison to Cox. Looking back at his time in that office, a fairer assessment is that he ran an efficient operation and made a normal number of presentations to the court during his tenure. Over the two years he held the position, Marshall appeared before the court nineteen times and received a positive verdict fourteen times. Marshall saw his record in the office "about as good as anybody else's, maybe better than some" (Zelden, 2013, p. 139).

For Thurgood, one of the big changes as solicitor general was in his private life. He could enjoy time with friends and the social opportunities associated with life in New York as a member of the circuit court. Poker nights and sometimes raucous gatherings with friends and socialite events were part of his routine there. In his new high-profile position in Washington, DC, he had to cut back on any activities that might cast him in a negative light. It was important not to do anything that might embarrass him or the president. Marshall knew there were people watching and hoping he'd do something to prove that he did not deserve the position or any future important offices. Consequently, other than attending official functions, Marshall did not get out as much as he once did. He might host small dinner parties for close friends at his home, but that was largely the extent of his social life. This quieter existence resulted in his putting on weight. A *New York Times Magazine* article called him not fat but "comfortably thick" (Williams, 1998, p. 322). He also began to drink more and chain-smoke cigarettes. His friends and work colleagues also noticed he became a bit grumpier. His revamped regime, though not the lifestyle he preferred, succeeded, and not a touch of scandal swirled around him during the time he served as solicitor general.

While most African Americans took pride in Marshall's success, he did face criticism from some quarters. As nonviolent civil rights protesters increasingly met with violent responses from law officials and local white citizens, alternative ideas about how to improve conditions for African Americans grew in popularity. Malcolm X (1925–1965) of the Nation of Islam raised doubts about nonviolence and the goal of integration advocated by King and others. He suggested separatism and self-defense as alternative ways for improving the challenges faced by African Americans. His ideas gained interest, particularly among student activists in organizations like the Student Nonviolent Coordinating Committee (SNCC) who felt they faced condoned local official violence and slower change than they desired. Stokely Carmichael, then head of the SNCC, gave voice to this growing frustration when at a 1966 protest rally in Greenwood, Mississippi, he captured the enthusiasm of the crowd when he advocated the need for a new way of thinking. He told the crowd, "We been saying 'freedom' for six years. What we are going to start saying now is, 'Black Power'" (Stokely Carmichael). What the phrase "black power" entailed varied depending upon who used the term. Marshall worried about the aspects of it that advocated the use of self-defense and violence. He thought that wrongheaded and not sensible. He took the position when speaking at a meeting of the national African-American fraternity Alpha Phi Alpha that black power offered nothing to African Americans except violence. He believed that it was "Jim Crow thinking" and would set back the efforts of African Americans, in part, because of its avocation of the use of physical force. He did not believe in breaking the law. In his mind, that led to anarchy, for which there was no good excuse. Marshall consistently opposed breaking the law no matter the reason and repeated that belief when he added that, for him, "Lawlessness is lawlessness" (Zelden, 2013, p. 139). Marshall did speak to what aspects of black power he found acceptable: "If black power means the Negro should use his right to vote, then I am for it" (ibid., p. 140). But if it condoned violence, he took the position that "violent protests that destroy property and disobey the law were counterproductive . . . You just can't build yourself by disobeying the law" (ibid., p. 140). This position did not endear Thurgood with Carmichael or others demanding more aggressive actions to bring about change. They considered Marshall a part of the mainstream establishment and much too conservative in his views. It prompted some of these individuals to testify against the nomination of Marshall to the U.S. Supreme Court during his senate hearings.

The description of Marshall as more conservative in his views was not wrong. He was an important part of the federal government hierarchy. As solicitor general, he represented the highest-ranking African American in the Johnson administration or any previous administration. Lyndon Johnson appointed Marshall, in part, because he believed in the rule of law and nonviolence. Johnson felt he could depend on Marshall to support him in his efforts to advance civil rights through legislation and aggressive enforcement of the law. Johnson's belief in Marshall led to a growing camaraderie between them. Marshall became a regular visitor to the White House, where he and Johnson discussed political issues of concern to the president and exchanged information about behind-the-scenes intrigues taking place around the capital. The president came to value Marshall's thoughts both on civil rights matters and other issues. At times they had their discussions over a couple of drinks, as they exchanged ideas and stories. They were similar in that they both came from humble beginnings, sought to make a difference through the work they did, and enjoyed a well-told story. Over time, they became good friends.

That friendship and his role as Johnson's solicitor general made Marshall a defender of the policies of the president. In particular, as the war in Vietnam continued to plague the administration, Marshall publicly defended Johnson's decisions. Antiwar critics included African Americans who argued that African-American soldiers were disproportionately represented in the forces fighting in Vietnam. They saw the hostilities as a fight between Asians and African Americans to the benefit of white politicians like Johnson. It was a war they should not be fighting. Some groups encouraged African Americans to refuse to join the army or criticized African Americans already in the military for supporting the war effort.

Marshall came to the defense of both the president and African-American military personnel. He believed the president was the victim of bad advice and information from his secretary of defense and the military. It caused him to make decisions he would not have made otherwise. Marshall further defended African Americans fighting in the war, saying they were patriots battling communism and were prepared to give their lives for their country. No one should criticize them for taking up arms as African Americans had always done for the country.

There were instances when supporting the president was harder for Marshall to accomplish. This was true when he found himself caught in the middle of a disagreement between Hoover and Senator Robert F. Kennedy. The issue concerned the case of Fred Black, a lobbyist who was suspected of working with the Mafia and was convicted of tax evasion. He had appealed his conviction for review by the U.S. Supreme Court. In the process of its evaluation of the case, the Justice Department learned the FBI had wiretapped Ball's conversations, including those with his lawyer. Upon learning this, Attorney General Nicholas Katzenbach and Thurgood Marshall felt they had to inform the U.S. Supreme Court as part of their report concerning the case. FBI director Hoover did not want them to do this, as it reflected poorly on him for keeping this fact secret. When they refused to hide the information, Hoover insisted that they say the former attorney general Robert Kennedy knew about the wiretaps and condoned them, thus placing the blame on him. When asked about the issue, Kennedy claimed he had no knowledge of the wiretaps.

What complicated the situation were Kennedy's plans to challenge Johnson for the Democratic nomination for president. The growing unhappiness in the country over the war in Vietnam made Johnson vulnerable. When Katzenbach and Marshall refused to comply with Hoover's demand, Hoover appealed to the president. The idea of embarrassing Kennedy resonated for Johnson, and he let his men in the Justice Department know he preferred Hoover's plan. This put the two men in a very difficult position. Placing the blame on Kennedy would deeply undermine his presidential nomination bid, but blaming the FBI placed them at odds with both Hoover and the president. As solicitor general, Marshall had to make the report to the justices and try to avoid angering any of the parties. His solution was not to place the responsibility on Kennedy but to say that it was the policy of attorney generals in the past to allow wiretapping in cases involving national safety. This was the case with Ball and why the FBI had employed electronic surveillance of him. Marshall added that Johnson prohibited the use of those devices after coming to office.

The report was a masterpiece of diplomacy. It pleased Kennedy, as he could continue to deny knowledge of the wiretaps. It made the FBI surveillance acceptable and depicted Johnson as an opponent of electronic surveillance. Katzenbach also was pleased that it prevented him from defying the president or hiding the truth from the U.S. Supreme Court justices. Marshall's report also helped Black because the U.S. Supreme Court then decided to review his conviction and ordered a retrial. This time he won acquittal. For his diplomacy, Marshall received an invitation at the personal request of Hoover to a White House party celebrating Hoover's fifty years at the Justice Department.

Unfortunately, President Johnson did not have the same positive feelings about Katzenbach's role in the Black discussions. Johnson decided to replace him with someone he felt more loyal to him and less concerned about Kennedy. He named Ramsey Clark, the assistant attorney general and a personal friend, as acting attorney general. A fellow Texan, Ramsey, who had a law degree from the University of Chicago, shared Johnson's views on civil rights. Not quite forty at the time, Clark looked to Marshall for advice as he took on his new duties. He knew Marshall had the ear of the president, which helped Ramsey as he made policy decisions. The change also added to Marshall's growing prominence as a part of the Johnson administration. What might result from that growing prominence was a question on the minds of many people. *Jet* magazine wrote that Marshall was the most likely candidate to fill the next opening on the U.S. Supreme Court if Johnson planned to appoint "a Negro on the U.S. Supreme Court bench by 1968" (Williams, 1998, p. 328).

During his time as solicitor general, Marshall had not done anything to discourage Johnson from seriously considering him for the U.S. Supreme Court. He was a loyal public supporter of Johnson and had become an important symbol of Johnson's commitment to promoting the progress of African Americans in his administration and on civil rights. The two also had found common ground as friends, and Marshall became an important sounding board for Johnson on African-American issues as well as other matters. Johnson publicly demonstrated his esteem for Marshall when he appeared at a program sponsored by the White House titled "To Fulfill These Rights," which featured Marshall as the opening-night speaker. There were more than twenty-four hundred participants representing the major civil rights groups gathered to discuss strategies for attacking discrimination against African Americans. Johnson's role was to offer remarks about his hopes for the future and to introduce Marshall. His words of friendship and praise brought tears to Marshall's eyes, as the president referred to Thurgood as his friend and a person he was proud to have in his administration. Their budding friendship, the important symbol Marshall became for the president, and his successes as solicitor general all worked to the favor of Marshall in Johnson's eyes.

When Marshall accepted the position of solicitor general, Johnson was very clear about his expectations. Marshall should focus on successfully operating that office and not worry about other future possibilities. There were no guarantees with the appointment. If he did his work well, he stayed, but if he didn't, he was out. Marshall took Johnson's words to heart. He understood that the position of solicitor general was a challenging job. He knew the stories of other solicitor generals who panicked at the idea of presenting before the justices of the U.S. Supreme Court or got sick to the stomach the night before their presentation. During the two years Marshall held the position, he proved himself an able legal advocate for the president and the Justice Department before the U.S. Supreme Court. Marshall admitted his nervousness his first day before the court, as Chief Justice Earl Warren welcomed him, but then began to relax as he realized he could hold his own against opposing lawyers.

Thurgood was not as consistently impressive as his predecessor Archibald Cox, especially when he presented cases focused on corporate mergers, labor disputes, or other areas of business law or taxes. With these cases, he had little prior experience to draw upon and had to rely upon the expertise of his staff and his ability to quickly internalize and present the legal issues. Where Marshall impressed was on cases that dealt with civil liberties, civil rights, and constitutional law. These arguments allowed him to draw upon his years of work with the LDF and its focus on protecting African-American citizenship rights. As a presenter, Marshall was strongest during the exchanges between himself and the justices as they raised questions or offered comments on the proceedings. In those moments, he could draw upon his past experience as an advocate for LDF clients, which demanded quick, accurate answers to questions posed by often hostile Southern lawyers or judges. Marshall also benefited from the many previous presentations he had made before the justices. Few lawyers could match the twenty-nine cases Marshall argued before the U.S. Supreme Court for the NAACP.

NAACP lawyer Thurgood Marshall did not win all of the cases he brought before the U.S. Supreme Court, and neither did Solicitor General Marshall. In fact, he lost the first case he presented. The Texas defendant, Ethel Mae Yazell, did not want to repay the small business loan her husband received after his shop suffered flood damage. Her lawyer argued that, under Texas law, she was not responsible for her husband's debts. For the federal government, Marshall took the position that federal law superseded Texas law, particularly, as this was a federal loan. After his presentation, Marshall said he was nervous but pleased. Unfortunately, the court did not agree with his argument and voted in a split decision in favor of Mrs. Yazell, stating she had not signed the loan contract and thus, under Texas law, was not liable.

The loss of his first case was disappointing but proved the exception to the rule with regard to Marshall's presentations to the court. He followed the Yazell case with a number of successful presentations focused on the protection of civil liberties. The civil liberties cases were the ones that likely excited Marshall the most about accepting the solicitor general position. His leadership role allowed him to bring the resources of the federal government to bear on the type of cases he had initiated for most of his previous career. It was a wonderful change from the underfunded team he oversaw at the LDF. Two cases Marshall supported before the U.S. Supreme Court exemplified the benefits of his new role: *Katzenbach v. South Carolina* and *Harper v. Virginia Board of Elections*.

The South Carolina and Virginia cases each revolved around issues of voting rights and state efforts to restrict access to African-American residents. In Virginia, resident Annie Harper brought suit against the State of Virginia because of the poll tax they charged anyone who wished to register to vote. She took the position that the tax deprived poorer residents of the opportunity to participate in state elections. Her attorneys used the

Fourteenth Amendment and its equal protection clause, as Marshall had on past cases at the NAACP, to argue the Virginia poll tax was unconstitutional. In rebuttal, Virginia argued the poll tax affected state and not federal elections, so they had the right to levy the tax on potential voters.

The South Carolina case also revolved around voting rights but challenged the constitutionality of parts of the newly passed 1965 Voting Rights Act. South Carolina took the states' rights position that the federal government only had limited power over what took place in the individual states. They argued that the federal government exceeded its powers in the creation of the Voting Rights Act and, in the process, unfairly singled out Southern states for scrutiny. They then sought an injunction from the court to prevent the enforcement of its provisions in South Carolina or other states impacted by it. In response, the brief submitted and presented by Marshall rejected the South Carolina position. He countered that nothing in the Constitution gave any state the authority to decide who could or could not vote there. Indeed, the Fifteenth Amendment specifically denied states the authority to deny anyone the vote based on their race, color, or national origin, which gave Congress solid constitutional grounds on which to create the Voting Rights Act. The brief submitted in support of the Virginia lawsuit followed the same general argument with regard to Virginia's use of the poll tax.

The U.S. Supreme Court agreed with Marshall in each case. They voted unanimously with him on the South Carolina case. Chief Justice Earl Warren wrote the opinion for the court. The significance of the case was that it sustained the constitutionality of the Voting Rights Act of 1965 and contributed to the enfranchisement of millions of nonwhite Americans. With the Virginia case, the court, with three dissenting votes, ruled that voting was a fundamental right of citizenship and economic status cannot be used to deny a person that right; to do so violates the Fourteenth Amendment equal protection clause. They believed that all voters should have an equal right to participate in state elections. For Marshall, the ruling of the court represented not only a victory in the immediate cases but also a reaffirmation of the earlier cases he had pursued for the NAACP against Texas and other states creating devices to deprive African Americans of the right to vote.

African Americans were not the only ones to benefit from Marshall's defense of voting rights. Not long after the ruling on the South Carolina and Virginia cases, the court issued a ruling on a voting rights issue in New York. *Katzenbach v. Morgan* focused on the qualifications needed to vote there. The new state constitution included a section that gave voting rights only to individuals who could read and write English. The Voting Rights Act included language that allowed qualified Puerto Rican residents to vote if they had completed the sixth grade, even if they did not write or speak English. A group of registered voters in New York brought suit against the federal government on this issue claiming that the Voting Rights Act violated the right of the state of New York to define voting privileges. The plaintive argued that almost 50 percent of the hundreds of thousands of Puerto Ricans in the state could only communicate in Spanish. This handicapped their ability to truly understand the political issues and to vote intelligently. In light of this fact, restricting voters only to English speakers would help ensure fairer elections. Their argument focused on Puerto Rican citizens paralleled similar arguments about restrictive voting laws offered by South Carolina and Virginia.

In the brief provided by Marshall, he referred to the historical connection between Puerto Rico and the United States going back to the 1890s. He also pointed out that Congress granted citizenship to Puerto Ricans nearly fifty years earlier in 1917. In granting citizenship to residents of Puerto Rico, Congress also retained the power to define their rights as citizens when they relocated to the mainland and most often New York. Most of these individuals were literate in Spanish even though many could not write, read, or speak English. Congress originally made them citizens even with this language gap, and in the Voting Rights Act, they reinforced the concept that a deficit in English did not deny voting rights to this group. He also pointed out that other states faced with similar language issues were obeying the act. The court agreed with Marshall citing the New York English literacy requirement as "an invidious discrimination in violation of the Equal Protection Clause" (Davis & Clark, 1992, p. 261).

Thurgood presented other cases to the court that touched on additional civil rights issues that had defined his career. These included bringing suit against laws preventing fair access to housing, protecting the right of privacy including the use of wiretaps, and protecting the legal rights of prisoners. As Marshall told one friend, he was thrilled that his position allowed him to persuade the U.S. Supreme Court to use its influence to ensure all citizens had access to the benefits that came with that status.

One of the most precious of these entitlements is the right to live without fear for your life. This was an important aspect of one of Marshall's most significant cases while solicitor general: *United States v. Price*. It involved three civil rights workers operating in Mississippi. James Chaney, Andrew Goodman, and Michael Schwerner were killed for trying to register people to vote. They disappeared after driving to investigate the burning of a church. It was Schwerner's first day in Mississippi. Searchers found their bodies several weeks later buried in an earthen dam. After investigating the murders, the U.S. Grand Jury ruled that the men involved in the murders should be indicted. State law officials instead decided to dismiss the charges for all but three of the men. Marshall stepped in to bring the case before the U.S. Supreme Court to have them overrule the district court and have all the men tried. What happened to the three young men angered him. "It hurt," he told a friend to have "their lives snuffed out by racists" (Rowan, 1993, p. 295). It was a clear instance of racial terrorism.

According to one reporter, Marshall was at his best for the presentation. He knew the law, spoke with a strong steady voice, and was relaxed but authoritative. He told the court that Mississippi was ignoring federal laws by "shooting Negroes, by killing, by pressuring them, by burning crosses in public at night" (Davis & Clark, 1992, p. 256). He pointed to portions of the Enforcement Act of 1870 as legal means for bringing the men to trial. For Marshall, the key part of the statute was the section that made "it a felony to conspire to interfere with a citizen in the free exercise or enjoyment of any right secured or protected by the Constitution or laws of the United States" (*United States v. Price*). Consequently, by killing the young men, the accused had deprived them of their civil rights and, therefore, could be charged by the federal government. The counterargument, presented by the Mississippi attorney, was that the case was a state crime not a federal one; consequently, the federal government had no jurisdiction in the matter. The decision of local law officials to dismiss the cases should stand.

The justices unanimously agreed with Marshall and remanded the case back to the lower court for trial. In Mississippi, the federal government eventually brought charges against all eighteen individuals for depriving the young men of their civil rights, the only legal grounds available to charge them. At the trial in Mississippi, the all-white jury found seven men guilty. The remaining men were found not guilty. The young civil rights workers did not receive the justice they deserved, but Marshall helped ensure that at least some of the individuals involved did not escape punishment.

The satisfaction Marshall derived from his success while solicitor general offered balance to aspects of the work he found less satisfying. Those were the cases where he dutifully represented the views of the federal government that did not match his own preferences. It was particularly less satisfying when the court ruled against his argument. The *Miranda v. Arizona* case epitomized the contradictions faced by Thurgood as solicitor general. The case originated when Ernesto Miranda, who only had an eighth-grade education and was mentally challenged, was accused of raping an eighteen-year-old mentally challenged woman. The police brought him to the station where the woman identified him. Miranda was not informed of his rights and after a two-hour interrogation signed a written confession. The confession provided the sole evidence at the trial. Miranda was found guilty and sentenced to up to thirty years in prison. He appealed his conviction based upon violation of his Fifth Amendment right, which protected him from being forced to incriminate himself.

Marshall, representing the government, held that Miranda's rights were not violated. It was not required that the police inform him of his rights before questioning. The interpretation of the Fifth Amendment offered in Miranda's lawyers' brief did not apply. The state had not denied him the right to silence or to representation of an attorney. They merely remained silent on those issues, which did not constitute a violation his constitutional rights. It was not a powerful position and likely reflected Marshall's conflicting feelings about the case. In many ways, this had to be a hard argument for Marshall to put forth, in light of his past experiences connected to similar issues. As a lawyer with the NAACP, he was involved in numerous cases where forced or coerced confessions were generated in order to try and convict innocent African Americans. In many instances, the resulting verdict generated a death sentence for the accused. Marshall witnessed this happening often and was impacted by his inability to save them. While Miranda did not face a death sentence, the circumstances of his arrest, confession, and trial must have resonated for Marshall.

The justices were conflicted over the case as well. They ruled against Marshall in a close 5–4 decision. The minority opinion held that neither legislative history nor legal precedent connected to the Fifth Amendment supported a requirement to specifically tell suspects their rights. They believed the ruling of the majority would handicap the future work of law enforcement authorities. The majority opinion, written by Chief Justice Earl Warren, held that the Fifth Amendment, which protects against self-incrimination, and the Sixth Amendment, which guarantees the right to an attorney, applied in the case. The police had violated that right, and Miranda deserved a new trial. Unfortunately for Miranda, he was found guilty at his retrial, based this time upon the testimony of his accuser. His case did impact how police officers interacted with suspects after the court ruling. As solicitor general, the adverse court decision must have disappointed Marshall. But, the civil rights lawyer in him must have quietly approved of the court's decision, which provided more protection to defendants, the people he had spent so many years trying to protect from biased police treatment.

During the two years Thurgood Marshall served as solicitor general, President Johnson maintained his desire to nominate an African American for the U.S. Supreme Court. Marshall was the front-runner, but Johnson also considered other candidates. They included: William Hastie, who sat on the Third Circuit Court of Appeals, and A. Leon Higginbotham Jr., also a judge on the Third Circuit Court. Both were Ivy League law school graduates and highly respected. Both men likely were better students of the law, but neither had the national presence possessed by Marshall. The arguments advanced to Johnson not to select Marshall ranged from criticism of his intellect compared to other possible candidates to the belief he carried too much past political baggage. They thought his NAACP work would increase resistance from Southerners and conservatives. Johnson understood that Marshall was not the most outstanding African-American lawyer in the country, but he also knew how well loved he was by African Americans and supporters of civil liberty. An award he received from the Conference of Prince Hall Grand Masters of America, an African-American Masonic organization, illustrated the high regard that existed for Marshall. They gave him the Distinguished Service Award for his skill "far beyond the average American lawyer in his presentations to the courts of the nation" (Rowan, 1993, p. 264). It was recognition that Marshall produced positive results through his work in the courtroom, and that is what mattered most to them and other African Americans. This was why the selection of Marshall to the Supreme Court carried more symbolic weight than the other individuals under consideration. He was "Mr. Civil Rights" and deserved the position in the eyes of the people Johnson particularly wanted to impress with the nomination. Selecting someone else might have been academically better but not politically wiser. Lyndon B. Johnson was a political animal.

This trait particularly came through as he manipulated an opening on the U.S. Supreme Court to allow him to nominate a new justice. After the controversy over the FBI wiretaps, Johnson decided to replace attorney general Nicholas Katzenbach with Ramsey Clark. The decision to select Clark was a calculated political move. Ramsey Clark's father was U.S. Supreme Court justice Tom C. Clark. Johnson understood that Ramsey Clark, as head of the Justice Department, created an apparent conflict of interest for Tom Clark in light of the many cases brought before the court under the name of the attorney general. To avoid the conflict of interest, either Tom Clark had to resign or his son had to refuse the promotion. Justice Clark decided to resign to allow his son to have the job. His decision created an opening on the U.S. Supreme Court for President Johnson to fill. Thurgood Marshall was his choice.

While Marshall hoped Johnson would select him, Johnson kept his decision a secret. In fact, at the retirement reception for Tom Clark, President Johnson took Marshall aside and told him not to expect the job. But on June 13, 1967, Ramsey Clark came to Thurgood's office and told him to go to the White House because "the boss" wanted to see him. When he arrived for the meeting, several of his friends were there at the request of the president. When Marshall came into the room, they all guessed why they were there. Johnson then told Marshall he intended to nominate him for the vacant U.S. Supreme Court seat. Marshall accepted the offer and stayed with the president as he called key members of his cabinet, Congress, and the U.S. Supreme Court to let them know his intentions.

After the calls, Marshall and the president went to a press conference in the Rose Garden, where Johnson announced his selection of Marshall. In describing why, he chose Marshall, Johnson noted, "He is best qualified by training and by . . . service to the country. I believe it is the right thing to do, the right time to do it, the right man and the right place" (Ball, 1998, p. 193). Afterward, Marshall called Cissy to let her know the good news. According to one version of the events, Cissy was not surprised by the decision. When Johnson had her called and put on the speakerphone, Cissy asked, "Did we get the Supreme Court appointment?" While she had hoped this would happen, Cissy, along with Thurgood, was thrilled with the decision. Marshall told people that it was every lawyer's dream to have the opportunity to serve on the court and to serve the country.

As expected, reactions to Marshall's nomination varied widely. Some of the criticism focused on what was described as his "intellectual shortcoming" in comparison to an Archibald Cox. Others questioned his past activities with the NAACP and what they saw as his liberal views. Positive reactions praised the vast experience he had as a lawyer and with the U.S. Supreme Court. They saw him as a brilliant and forceful advocate. They also praised the symbolism of his nomination and the important statement it made about Johnson's administration. Reaction from the African-American community was jubilant. Martin Luther King Jr. and Roy Wilkins, among others, praised both Johnson's decision and Marshall. Wilkins wrote an article for the *New York Amsterdam News* in which he highlighted the numerous contributions made by Marshall that qualified him for the job. He also found criticism of Marshall's "intellectual mastery" wrongheaded and missing all that Marshall brought to the court. Chief Justice Earl Warren also called it an excellent appointment. Few men, he believed, came to the court with more experience or sounder preparation for the work (Ball, 1998, p. 195).

The challenge before both President Johnson and Thurgood Marshall was ensuring his successful confirmation by the Senate. This was not a foregone conclusion, as Southern senators, in particular, were either silent in their opinions about Marshall or openly hostile to his nomination. Opposition to his appointment also existed in more radical portions of the African-American community. SNCC, under the leadership of Stokely Carmichael, did not support Marshall because they perceived him as too moderate and middle class. Marshall often spoke against the idea of black power, promoted by Carmichael and SNCC, which alienated them. They felt Marshall's conservative views and support of law and order made him unacceptable as the first African-American U.S. Supreme Court justice. President Johnson needed to use all his political savvy to ensure the nomination process ended positively.

10

New to the Court

Thurgood Marshall did not let the criticism of his selection for the U.S. Supreme Court bother him. The important point was that the president had nominated him. This was a significant fact unto itself. The U.S. judiciary had been the preserve of white males for nearly all its history. For more than 150 years, no African American had served on a federal appellate court until the appointment of William Hastie by President Truman in 1949. When Marshall became judge for the Second Circuit Court of Appeals, it marked only the second appointment of an African American at the federal judiciary level. Consequently, President Johnson's desire to place Thurgood on the U.S. Supreme Court was monumental. Neither Johnson nor Marshall wanted the nomination to fail, so both did all they could to make it successful.

The president wasted no time trying to smooth the way for Marshall's senate hearing and hoped for confirmation. In advance of the hearings, he began personally contacting members of the Senate, especially those from the South, to persuade them not to oppose Marshall's appointment. Lining up support for this position was much more difficult than the challenge he faced when he appointed Marshall as solicitor general. Marshall prepared himself for the process with the hope it would not take as long as his previous judicial hearings. Those had stretched out over several months and had been very unpleasant. As was the case then, it was important that Marshall not say anything during the hearings that might help the politicians attempting to build a case against him.

This time, the hearings for Marshall took place a month after the announcement of his nomination. Three Southern Democratic members of the committee worked overtime to undermine Marshall's appointment: John McClellan of Arkansas, Samuel J. Ervin Jr. of North Carolina, and J. Strom Thurmond of South Carolina. They were long-standing opponents of Marshall's civil rights activism and disliked the idea of having an African American on the U.S. Supreme Court. In the course of the hearings, they looked for ways in which they might paint Marshall as unfit to sit on the court.

Senator McClellan sought to show Marshall was soft on crime and encouraged lawbreakers. The main issue he grilled Marshall about was his views on the *Miranda* ruling of the court. McClellan believed the ruling caused crime to increase and furthered urban unrest. He wanted to know if Marshall supported it or opposed it. If Marshall supported that ruling, in the eyes of McClellan, it made Marshall a judicial activist not properly interpreting the Constitution and unfit to serve. McClellan knew there was rising concern in the country about the urban rebellions occurring in African-American neighborhoods. He hoped to connect Marshall to those outbreaks as a way of turning public opinion against his nomination. Thurgood avoided getting drawn into that issue by refusing to answer. He offered the explanation that it was an issue that might come before the U.S. Supreme Court in the future and that it was improper for him to speak about it in advance of the court considering the question should it arise. But he did say he did not think there was proof of any connection between the ruling and the crime rate.

Senator Ervin grilled Marshall about his views on the proper way to interpret the Constitution. He wanted to know whether Marshall believed the Constitution was a "living document." What Ervin hoped to show was that Marshall wrongly supported the belief that the interpretations of that document could change over time as societal circumstances evolved. Ervin believed that the role of the justices on the court was not to interpret the current meaning of the document but only to figure out what the founding fathers intended when they created it. For Ervin, this was the difference between justices correctly interpreting the law and those improperly making law through new interpretations. Marshall again refused to get drawn into that trap by stating only that he believed it the task of a judge to interpret the Constitution using their best judgment on a case-by-case basis. Beyond that, he felt again he should not offer further comment. This did not please Ervin who stated that, without more of a response from Marshall, he could not support his nomination.

Strom Thurmond took the questioning in a different direction. He hoped to expose Marshall as ignorant of the law and history connected to the constitutional amendments he used to achieve many of his civil rights victories. Thurmond used his time to question Marshall about obscure issues related to the creation of the Thirteenth and Fourteenth Amendments. He had his staff spend time researching background information that he then sprang on Marshall, hoping to embarrass him. One question was "What committee reported out the Fourteenth amendment and who were its members?" Throughout the questioning, which some observers found similar to the questions asked by white registrars to keep African Americans from voting, Marshall remained calm. Most often, he answered by saying he didn't know or that he would need to do some research to provide the answer. For supporters of Marshall, Thurmond embarrassed himself with these questions. When another senator asked Thurmond for the answer to his question about the members of the Fourteenth Amendment committee, Thurmond did not have the answer himself.

After five days of hearings, the committee recommended confirmation by the full Senate. The five Southern senators voted against confirmation while the remaining eleven on the committee voted in favor. The following month the full Senate voted to confirm Thurgood Marshall by a vote of 69–11. Very pleased with the vote, Marshall issued a statement in which he mentioned how honored he was by the appointment and that he had great faith in the people of the nation and embraced his "obligation to the Constitution and to the goal of equal justice under the law" (Davis & Clark, 1992, p. 275). He then called President Johnson to thank him for the appointment and his help in the process. Johnson was pleased with the outcome, but during their conversation, Johnson gave Marshall a sense of just how tough the process was for him as well. Johnson's words were, "Well, congratulations, but the hell you caused me . . . I never went through so much hell" (ibid., p. 276). In the eyes of African Americans, any hell either Marshall or the president had to go through to get Thurgood confirmed was worth it. They hoped Marshall sitting on the court would add greater momentum to their efforts to obtain equal justice.

For African Americans and the Marshall household, the morning of October 1, 1967, was a special moment. It was the day Thurgood would begin his role as U.S. Supreme Court justice Marshall. Getting ready to go to the ceremony, everyone in the Marshall house was excited. Asked to describe how she felt, Cissy Marshall said she was thrilled because "This is something you hope for but think will never happen" (ibid., p. 277). Marshall's oldest son said that day his father was "kinda jumpy," which was not normal for him. But it was not a normal day. They were on their way to the U.S. Supreme Court building for the public swearing-in ceremony.

The family was excited, even though this was the second swearing-in ceremony for Marshall. A month previously, Justice Hugo L. Black, a long-time friend of Thurgood, had volunteered to administer the oath of office in his chambers with Cissy and the boys present. That was a very emotional moment for all of them and particularly for Marshall, who wished his father could have joined them. Marshall knew he would have been very proud. After Black swore him in, Marshall sent a note to President Johnson, thanking him for all he had done and promising to justify the president's trust in him.

The public ceremony at the U.S. Supreme Court building was important as well since it signified Marshall's first official day as a justice. Family and friends as well as President Johnson would be there to take in the historic moment. When the opening session of the court began, it was crowded with observers. They all watched as Marshall entered with the other justices. Chief Justice Warren began the morning by announcing Marshall's appointment and offering remarks in praise of the newest justice. The clerk of the court followed up by administering the oath of office and then escorted Marshall to his seat behind the bench with the other justices. The court then went into its normal routine. It was a simple procedure often done at the court, but this time it marked a historic occasion. Once sworn in, Thurgood Marshall became the first African American to serve on the U.S. Supreme Court. It only took the United States 178 years from the first session of the U.S. Supreme Court in 1789 to have an African American join its ranks. His place on the court was very meaningful for Marshall.

Thurgood Marshall did not have a difficult time fitting in on the court. Both as an NAACP lawyer and as the solicitor general, he had appeared before its members many times. They were very familiar with one another. In fact, a number of the justices admitted they had anticipated Marshall's appointed for some time. He and Chief Justice Warren quickly became good friends and developed a close personal relationship. Marshall described Warren as "one of the greatest persons who ever lived and . . . probably the greatest Chief Justice who ever lived" (Ball, 1998, p. 210). It was not surprising that Marshall turned to Warren for advice about what to expect in his new role.

Warren had important perspectives to offer. He had been serving as chief justice of the court since 1953. Under his leadership, the court set forth rulings that altered the social landscape of the nation in terms of the protections provided its citizens. *Brown v. Board* was only one of many decisions that sought to live up to the portion of the oath of office they took, which promised "I will administer justice without respect to persons, and do equal right to the poor and to the rich." The *Miranda* ruling; the *Loving v. Virginia* case striking down laws prohibiting interracial marriage; and *Reynolds v. Simms,* which mandated one person one vote in creating voting districts in local and national elections, were among their important rulings.

These decisions did not come without negative reactions from conservatives. They saw the actions of the Warren court as judicial activism. By doing this, the conservatives believed the court was interfering in areas that should be left to the states to decide. They also believed the court should only narrowly interpret the Constitution based on what the founding fathers said at the time. It was not the job of the court to take into account changing human conduct and outlooks over time, which they believed the courts had done. By following the path of judicial activism, the U.S. Supreme Court, in the eyes of conservatives, was aiding criminals, encouraging civil rights activism, and undermining long-held traditions. They viewed Thurgood Marshall as another addition to a liberal-leaning court.

The judicial activism of the court, as described by conservatives, made Marshall's transition onto that entity easier, as he shared the perspective of many of its members. Among the more liberal members of the court supporting Warren were justices Hugo Black, William O. Douglas, William J. Brennan, and Abe Fortas. Thurgood developed good working relationships with most of them, but the closest to his own legal views was Brennan. They both believed in the ability of the law to serve as a source of change through which to better society. They both also believed in the importance of recognizing the human dignity of every person no matter their station in society. This shared vision enabled them to quickly bond. It also resulted in them often voting similarly on cases brought before the court. Cissy Marshall described their relationship as so close they behaved like brothers. Their law clerks also remarked about the close collaboration between the two men, as the flow of ideas and exchange of information were constant between their two adjoining offices. His close philosophical compatibility with Brennan and Chief Justice Warren meant that Marshall most often found himself voting with the majority, and when writing for the court, usually writing opinions for that group.

But it would be a mistake to see Marshall as solely echoing the views already on the court. As was the case when he joined the Second Circuit Court, Marshall brought the element of practical experience to the court. He had been a civil rights attorney who had gone to the jails where his clients were held, who understood the bias that existed in society and in the courtroom, and who had seen the impact that judgments had on the lives of the individuals involved. He used this perspective to enlighten his colleagues and to craft opinions that got to the heart of the issues and the impact court decisions would have on individuals and the larger society. His goal, according to one of his law clerks, was to serve as "a filter through whom the issues could be presented to the Court" (Ball, 1998, p. 198). An early opinion he wrote for the court illustrated the value of his insights.

The case *Mempa v. Rhay* involved a teenager convicted of stealing a car and going joyriding. He received probation for this crime and committed burglary while on probation. At that probation hearing, he did not have counsel, pled guilty to the burglary, and had his probation revoked. On appeal, his counsel protested the sentencing on the basis that the teenager did not have legal representation at the second hearing. The majority of the court agreed that the defendant must have counsel at every step. The one holdout was Justice Black. But after reading Marshall's draft opinion, he decided to vote with the majority. He gave credit to Marshall, praising his opinion for its "brevity, clarity and force" (Williams, 1998, p. 340).

Not all of the liberal justices on the court were pleased with Marshall's addition. Justice William O. Douglas resented Marshall's appointment. He questioned Marshall's intellectual ability. In his view, Marshall only received the nomination because he was African-American, not because he was deserving. As a result, he was abrupt with and, at times, contemptuous of Marshall. Douglas wrote private memos in which he belittled Marshall's contributions. This particularly came through when Marshall clashed with Douglas during the discussion of cases. After one such disagreement, Douglas characterized Marshall as a nice person but overly opinionated and not very well trained in the law (Ball, 1998, p. 212). They often clashed over American involvement in Vietnam. As opposed to Douglas, Thurgood thought American involvement was proper and that Johnson acted properly under the Constitution as commander-in-chief in conducting the war. Douglas's treatment of him was not a new experience for Marshall. He had experienced similar behavior in other situations during his time as a civil rights lawyer. Rather than recognize his abilities and contributions, derogatory comments and disrespectful treatment ensued because he did not conform to their vision of a proper lawyer or judge. In his mind, it was another form of racism, which was disappointing but not necessarily surprising. Supreme Court justices were not immune to discriminatory behavior. Fortunately, Douglas's behavior was not the normal experience of Marshall. The majority of the justices treated him as a colleague and valued his contributions.

This sense of respect for Marshall and collaboration among the justices supporting Warren characterized the first few years of Marshall's time on the court. During that time, the justices passed down numerous rulings protecting the civil liberties of citizens from undue interference from the federal or state government. He voted with the majority on a number of landmark cases. They included: ruling that Southern school boards had to cease using manipulation of local law to avoid desegregation (*Green v. New Kent County*), preventing discrimination in the sale or leasing of private property (*Jones v. Alfred H. Mayer Co.*), expanding the authority of the 1965 Voting Rights Act (*Allen v. Board of Elections*), and approving school busing and racial quotas as permitted measures to help assure racial balance within school districts (*Swann v. Charlotte-Mecklenburg Board of Education*).

Marshall also wrote opinions for the majority that had important consequences. One case in particular, *Benton v. Maryland*, must have been especially satisfying for him. The ruling gave protection against double jeopardy to defendants at the state level. The decision overruled a 1937 U.S. Supreme Court decision that had ruled that double jeopardy was not a constitutional right. While on the Second Circuit Court, Marshall had written a decision that protected against double jeopardy at the state level. The *Benton* case allowed Justice Marshall to reinforce the opinion written by him as circuit judge.

The same year of the *Benton* case, Marshall also wrote the majority opinion for a right to privacy lawsuit, *Stanley v. Georgia*. While searching the home of Robert Eli Stanley with a federal warrant for suspected bookmaking, authorities found pornographic films in a drawer. They then charged him with the possession of obscene material, which was a crime in Georgia. Stanley appealed his conviction on the grounds that he had the material in the privacy of his home, not for general public consumption. On behalf of the court, Marshall overturned Stanley's conviction declaring that citizens had a fundamental right to protection from "unwanted governmental intrusions into one's privacy," particularly the "right to satisfy [one's] intellectual and emotional needs in the privacy of his own home." (Starks and Brooks, 2012, p. 73).This meant the government had no business trying to control what a person may read or watch in his own home.

Interestingly, as part of the process of examining the case, the justices held film sessions in the basement of the building to view the confiscated films. An important aspect of their task was to attempt to figure out a reasonable definition for obscenity. They had to balance constitutional guarantees of free speech with protecting community values. Marshall used the occasions to have fun with his fellow justices. He often sat in the front row and offered comments on the performance. He even teasingly asked if anyone had learned anything new from the films. To help Justice Harlan, who was nearly blind, Marshall volunteered to describe the scenes for him. While Marshall made fun of everyone's discomfort at watching the films, he took the case seriously in terms of curbing government interference in the private lives of citizens (Rowan, 1993, p. 341).

Thurgood did not always agree with his brethren on the court. As opposed to the majority of the justices, he remained staunchly unsympathetic to forced confessions. He had seen too many of them during his NAACP days and was wary of instances when these confessions provided the basis for a criminal conviction. Consequently, he wrote a dissenting opinion in the case of Robert L. Johnson whom authorities accused of killing a policeman. After his capture, officials never read Johnson his rights, and he confessed only after extended questioning that left him in need of brain surgery. Johnson claimed he gave his confession under duress and wanted his conviction and death sentence overturned. The majority of the court disagreed and denied his request. Marshall, in dissent, with Warren and Fortas, took the position that a confession obtained under such circumstances should not be admissible. Marshall opposed both the forced confessions and the death penalty, for as he noted, "death is irrevocable; life imprisonment is not. Death, of course, makes rehabilitation impossible, life imprisonment does not" (Zelden, 2013, p. 149).

As Thurgood adjusted to his new life as a U.S. Supreme Court justice, Cissy made sure everything ran smoothly at home. She organized the family social calendar, ensured the boys got to school on time, shepherded them to various activities, and maintained the house. Keeping the boys in line fell primarily on Cissy's shoulders. Thurgood told her he refused to punish them for doing the same things he did as a youngster. The problem for Cissy was that Thurgood had been a mischievous child so there was little the boys did that he had not also done when young. The result of that rule, as Cissy later explained, "So he never punished them because he had done everything" (Williams, 1998, p. 345).

Cissy not only had to watch the boys but she also had to monitor Thurgood when he came home. Because Marshall had to carefully restrict his outside activities and social engagements, he did not have opportunities to decompress with his friends as he had while with the NAACP. Having a few drinks with friends was one way to relieve the constant pressure he must have felt during those years. Without that outlet, Marshall increasingly turned to drinking to fill the gap. Having a drink or two over lunch and additional ones at home became more and more frequent. On occasion, he was known to leave the house when drunk and go for a walk. The walks, at times, resulted in embarrassing behavior, which forced Cissy to intervene to protect him. One evening he made unwanted comments to a woman he did not know. These incidents made Cissy think that life in the close quarters of the city exposed him to potentially harmful rumors by the neighbors. Her solution was to sell their home in the city and move to the suburbs where there was more space for the boys to play and increased privacy for Thurgood.

She turned to the wife of Ramsey Clark, Georgia, to help her look for a new house. Cissy and Thurgood had visited the Ramseys' home and liked the community in which they lived. They identified a place near the Clark's home in Falls Church, Virginia. It was in the Lake Barcroft community, not too far from the city. It took about an hour to make the drive back into Washington. The Marshalls faced two challenges upon deciding to make

Lake Barcroft their new home. First, Lake Barcroft did not have any African-American residents living there. The Marshalls would be the first. On the positive side, Fairfax County had an open housing ordinance that encouraged diversity. Marshall's U.S. Supreme Court victory with the NAACP more than twenty years previously, which overturned restrictive covenants, paved the way for ordinances like the one in Fairfax County to the benefit of the Marshalls. Even though he was a U.S. Supreme Court justice, not everyone welcomed the Marshall family with open arms. One potential neighbor was not happy because the arrival of the Marshalls might open the door to more African Americans moving into the community. But Clark and the other friends of Marshall living in Lake Barcroft encouraging the Marshalls' move did not look upon the relocation as a planned strategy to desegregate the community. They recognized their community was not integrated as was the case with many suburban areas around the country at the time. Doing something about that certainly was on the radar for the Justice Department, but his friends saw the move as finding a place for a respected friend whose family needed a new and better place to live.

But before they could move, Marshall had to secure a mortgage to buy the property. Many banks at the time did not readily give large loans to African Americans seeking to purchase a home. The Marshalls wanted to acquire a five-bedroom, three-bathroom ranch and needed a loan of fifty-two thousand dollars in order to purchase it. With the help of the Clarks, they found a bank willing to loan them the funds, and they moved to Lake Barcroft. Cissy was happy about the decision. She found the neighbors friendly and helpful. Soon after they moved in, a group of kids came by and welcomed her sons into the neighborhood. Georgia Ramsey said neighbors warmly received the Marshalls. In fact, she worried the neighbors might overwhelm the Marshalls with their hospitality. When reporters questioned Marshall about his move and the adjustment to being the sole African-American family in the complex, he refused to answer their questions. He told them, "It's a private matter where I make my home" (Davis & Clark, 1992, p. 292).

Cissy quickly organized their new home to meet their needs. She turned one of the bedrooms into a study for Thurgood. She furnished it with bookcases filled with legal books, awards, and photographs. It became a place to which he could escape when mulling over cases before the court. They also set up a barbeque area where they cooked all kinds of fragrant foods for friends and neighbors. Among the invitees were old friends like Lena Horne and Harry Belafonte. According to Horne, she ate the best pig's feet in the world at the Marshall home. Thurgood also frequently hosted his colleague and good friend from the court, William Brennan. But Marshall did not host friends from the legal profession to visit. He wisely wished to avoid any future conflicts of interest that might arise if they brought a case before the court. Since many of those legal friends were civil rights lawyers, he did not want to have to recuse himself from cases of great interest and importance to him.

The backyard in the new house became an area where Marshall could play catch or touch football with his sons and the neighborhood children. He said, jokingly, it was the only exercise he got. Marshall also enjoyed watching Western movies and sports on television. He closely followed the Baltimore Orioles and the Washington football team. Marshall enjoyed listening to jazz, which began when he lived in Harlem, as well as visiting the nearby racetracks. He often would meet his college classmate, Cab Calloway at Pimlico, Laurel, or Bowie. They did not bet much but enjoyed watching the horses run and each other's company.

The tranquillity the Marshalls found living at Lake Barcroft was counter to the turmoil faced by President Johnson and the nation at the time. As unrest in African-American urban communities and unhappiness about the war in Vietnam increased, the popularity of the president decreased. These incidents hurt his chances for reelection to a second term. In particular, the campaign by Robert Kennedy for the Democratic nomination for president seemed to be gaining momentum. Johnson hoped the appointment of Marshall to the U.S. Supreme Court and his other civil rights efforts would win him support with African-American voters. Johnson continued to value Marshall's views on these and other issues. As he had as solicitor general, Marshall made visits to the White House to confer with Johnson. The president also invited Marshall to prayer breakfasts, luncheons, and other White House events. When Liberia inaugurated a new president, William Tubman, Johnson sent Marshall along with Vice President Hubert Humphrey to attend the event.

Unfortunately, none of the steps taken by the president quelled the discontent with his presidential policies. Discouraged by what he saw, Johnson decided to withdraw from consideration for a second term. That announcement startled the nation, but the country suffered a greater shock when in April 1968, Martin Luther King Jr. was assassinated in Memphis, Tennessee. He was there supporting a strike by local garbagemen. The following morning, Marshall attended a meeting with the president, other high-ranking politicians, and key civil rights leaders. They discussed the rioting taking place in Washington, DC, and other cities. They worried that the words of Stokely Carmichael and other militants might inflame people even more. When asked to speak to the gathered group, Marshall said he hoped they could find ways to end the flare-ups and try to change the mood of the country. He especially was disheartened by the uprisings in the nation's capital.

While saddened by King's death, Marshall's views on demonstrators or militants advocating violence did not alter. For example, he was not sympathetic to the occupants of Resurrection City, a temporary tent city assembled on the national mall in Washington, DC. Even though it was sponsored by King before his death, Marshall did not support their efforts. When a contingent from there demonstrated outside the Supreme Court, Marshall refused their request to speak to them, saying he never spoke to people who were breaking the law, no matter how they rationalized what they were doing. This further estranged Marshall from the more militant African-American voices demanding change. Later that summer, while speaking at the University of Wisconsin, Marshall found himself threatened and interrupted by a group of Black Panthers and antiwar protestors. Thurgood felt intimidated enough to contact the FBI after his return to Washington, DC, to report the incident and to ask them to look into it.

With Johnson's decision not to run for a second term, the contest for the Democratic nomination heated up, with Vice President Hubert Humphrey, Senator Robert Kennedy, and Senator Eugene McCarthy as the frontrunners. Then tragedy struck again, as after winning the California primary, Kennedy was assassinated in Los Angeles. To add to the negative news, that same month, Chief Justice Earl Warren, after telling the president of his plans months earlier, officially left the court. This was a deep loss for Marshall, who had developed a strong personal relationship with Warren. Marshall especially appreciated Warren's willingness to move the court in the direction of protecting the rights of all citizens. He agreed with Warren's view that "when the rights of any individual or group are chipped away, the freedom of all erodes" (Sabin, 1999, p. 124). The selection of the next chief justice would be critical. What had unexpectedly made Warren's departure more troublesome was the effort to name his successor by the president.

Johnson's original plan was to nominate a new chief justice before the fall election. He selected a sitting justice, Abe Fortas, to send to the Senate for confirmation. Fortas joined the court in 1965, after Johnson appointed him. Fortas represented Johnson in a legal challenge to his election in Texas to the U.S. House of Representatives. They remained close friends from that point onward. Johnson thought Fortas one of the best lawyers he had ever met. While on the court, Fortas met frequently with Johnson to offer advice about the war in Vietnam and economic policy. This relationship proved detrimental to Fortas's nomination, as key senators saw this as ethically improper. They thought it violated the idea of separate spheres of government operating independently from each other. The fact that Fortas advised Johnson on issues that came before the court and did not recuse himself from those cases hurt his integrity in the eyes of the judiciary committee. These issues, along with improper financial dealings, caused the nomination process to drag out longer than expected. Thurgood, having suffered through a prolonged confirmation process himself, encouraged Fortas to proceed despite his critics. But this time Johnson did not have the political influence to push through Fortas's nomination as he had Marshall's. He was forced to withdraw Fortas's name from consideration. The failure of this effort meant the selection of the new chief justice had to wait until after the fall election.

The outcome of the fall election, therefore, became even more important for Marshall and the court, as the perspectives of the two candidates were quite different. Hubert Humphrey won the Democratic Party nomination while Richard Nixon represented Republican Party hopes. Their views on the future direction of the nation and the U.S. Supreme Court were quite different, especially in the realm of civil rights. Humphrey supported the efforts of Johnson to make more opportunities available to African Americans and other groups facing discrimination. According to his campaign brochure, as president he sought to "create a nation where human equality and human opportunity not only exist side by side, but nourish and reinforce each other—a nation where every citizen may participate on equal terms in every aspect of being and doing that which relates to self-respect" (Humphrey for President). For U.S. Supreme Court chief justice, he likely would nominate someone similar in philosophy to Warren.

Richard Nixon saw the direction of the country much differently. He sympathized with Americans troubled by the direction of the Warren court. They did not like its efforts to expand civil liberties and to support racial as well as social justice. They believed this an improper role for the court to assume. These Americans did not want change. They took a very conservative view, which saw the court's decisions as the source of the social and civil upheavals faced by the nation. Liberal court rulings only encouraged antiwar protests, civil rights activism, and urban rebellions. These unhappy citizens believed a court more protective of the rights of law enforcement and less tolerant of civil disobedience would put a stop to the turmoil currently faced by the nation. Nixon sought to leverage this discontent within the nation to his political advantage. He promised, if elected, to appoint to the courts judges who promised "to interpret the Constitution and not put themselves above or outside of it" (Zelden, 2013, p. 150).

Thurgood Marshall thought highly of Hubert Humphrey. As a senator from Minnesota, when Truman ran for his second term, Humphrey played a key role in shaping the civil rights planks in Truman's campaign. And as vice president, he supported Johnson's civil rights efforts. During the presidential campaign against Nixon, Humphrey refused to criticize Johnson concerning the war or his other policies. Marshall felt this handicapped his campaign. Whatever the cause, Nixon narrowly defeated Humphrey by 500,000 votes and became the thirty-seventh president.

The election results upset Marshall. It represented the culmination of a series of setbacks felt by him. President Johnson decided not to run, Warren left the court, and Humphrey lost the election. The political and legal landscape was changing, and the signs did not point to changes that Marshall looked forward to. The retirement event for Warren was bittersweet for Marshall as was the farewell party for Johnson hosted by African Americans appointed to office by him. Thurgood presented the president and his friend a desk set as well as words of appreciation. Marshall saluted Johnson for his role in the passage of both the Civil Rights Act and the Voting Rights Act. He further thanked Johnson for his actions in aggressively appointing African Americans to important government positions. In turn, Johnson thanked Marshall and the others for their praise and characterized them as leaders in the movement for civil rights.

Thurgood and Johnson were of similar minds on that last issue. Thurgood saw the adults in the movement, not the younger generation, as the true leaders. He said as much in a later speech he gave at Dillard University in New Orleans for the celebration of its centennial. In it he characterized demonstrations as having little impact other than getting television coverage. He wasn't even sure the demonstrators knew what they wanted. He felt they needed to channel their energy more constructively. Thurgood also had derisive comments for black power militants calling for separatism. He likened them to the Ku Klux Klan who argued for "rigid separation, from cradle to grave" (Williams, 1998, p. 343). In his eyes, future success in obtaining equal rights lay with educated African Americans. They had the real tools to compete and to have success. Education and obeying the law were most important to him. Marshall ended by saying, "It takes no courage to get in the back of a crowd and throw a rock. Rather, it takes courage to stand up on your two feet and look someone straight in the eye and say, 'I will not be beaten'" (Hunter & Clark, p. 289). The speech received a positive response from the mainstream media. They applauded Marshall for speaking out against militant black power advocates whose endorsement of self-defense and the use of violence troubled many in the nation. They believed he set an example other African-American leaders should follow.

While Marshall spoke out against the tactics of the militants, he understood their frustration with the resistance to change that characterized the nation with regard to civil rights. There was a growing backlash among whites to the turmoil taking place. In fact, the results of the recent election reinforced that fact as the new president, Richard Nixon, came into office, in part, by promising to slow down the changes wrought by the Warren court. He promoted the need for greater "law and order" and promised to appoint conservative "strict constructionist" jurists who would not weaken and restrict law enforcement activities, as he believed the Warren court had done. Nixon professed to represent the "silent majority" in the country who wanted this change.

Soon after he took office, Nixon began the process of reshaping the U.S. Supreme Court. With the withdrawal of Fortas's nomination as chief justice during the last days of the Johnson administration, the selection of the new chief justice belonged to the new president, Richard Nixon. He selected Warren E. Burger, a thirteen-year veteran judge on the District of Columbia U.S. Court of Appeals who had a reputation as a "law and order" magistrate. He was very conservative about protecting the rights of law violators and had criticized the U.S. Supreme Court for its rulings defending those rights. By appointing Burger as chief justice, Nixon hoped to slow down the liberal rulings of the Warren court, which he and conservatives saw as judicial activism.

President Nixon had the opportunity to appoint a second new member to the court when Abe Fortas was forced to resign. Fortas was accused of improperly taking money from a client before he joined the U.S. Supreme Court in exchange for helping to seek a presidential pardon for the client. Fortas initially fought the charges, but when the Senate threatened to impeach him, Fortas decided to resign. He was the first U.S. Supreme Court justice to resign under threat of impeachment. In his search to find a replacement, Nixon ran into problems with the first two men he selected. Clement Haynsworth, as a circuit court judge, had voted on cases in which he had an economic interest rather than recusing himself. Nixon's next selection of G. Harrold Carswell failed, in part, because of allegations of racist activities in his past. Nixon's third choice, a conservative judge from the Eighth U.S. Court of Appeals, Harry A. Blackmun, was successful. He, too, had a law and order reputation. Nixon hoped the appointment of Burger and Blackmun, who were good friends, would shift the court in a more conservative direction.

During the time it took to appoint Burger and Blackmun, Thurgood had health issues. He developed a case of pneumonia in May 1970, which required his hospitalization. His habit of chain smoking, drinking, and avoiding exercise did not help matters. The treatment of antibiotics prescribed by the doctors did not improve his health, and his slow progress became a source of concern. There was some fear he might not survive. Upon learning of Marshall's condition, Warren Burger sent a note to the White House indicating Marshall was much sicker than people realized. According to Marshall, he spent thirty days in the hospital in precarious health. Near the end of his stay, as he recovered, hospital administrators informed Marshall that President Nixon wanted a report on him. The hospital asked Marshall if he approved sharing his medical records. Marshall knew Nixon wanted to determine if he might have to replace Marshall because of his poor health. Marshall gave permission to release the information to the White House but insisted the hospital include the note "Not yet" in the package.

Health issues continued to plague Marshall over the next couple of years. The year following his bout with pneumonia, Marshall returned to Bethesda Hospital. He was not feeling well and was taken to see a doctor. Eventually, they discovered his appendix was ailing and had to remove it. During the summer of 1972, while visiting the U.S. Virgin Islands with his family, Marshall had an accident while driving a Jeep. The vehicle rolled over with him and his oldest son in it. Marshall ended up pinned beneath the car. He suffered a fractured ankle, injured finger, and several bruises but otherwise survived without major injury. According to a newspaper report, Marshall's foot got stuck on the gas pedal, which caused him to lose control. At age sixty-four, he was fortunate to come out of the accident so well. When President Nixon learned of the accident, he had the air force send a plane to bring Marshall home. By 1972, these health issues led to rumors that Marshall was considering leaving the U.S. Supreme Court, perhaps as soon as the next term of the body. Nothing was further from the truth. Marshall had no intention of stepping down. He sent a sharply written letter to the editor of the African-American magazine *Jet* to set the record straight. Marshall wanted to know what caused the magazine to write that he might leave without double-checking its sources. Rumors like the one in *Jet* finally caused him to issue a statement through the court that he was in fine health and was not stepping down.

A few months after the Jeep accident, Thurgood's brother, Aubrey, died. They were not very close, though Aubrey attended Thurgood's swearing-in ceremony for solicitor general and for the supreme court. Aubrey struggled with Thurgood's success compared with his own uneven life as a doctor. He suffered from tuberculosis, developed a drinking problem, divorced, remarried, and lost his job before obtaining a position as medical director at a sanatorium. They rarely communicated, so it was more out of a sense of duty that Marshall traveled to Wilmington, Delaware, for the funeral. Thurgood was the only member of his natal family remaining after Aubrey died.

The arrival of Warren Burger probably added to any physical or emotional distress Marshall might have been feeling. He and Burger had very different views on many legal issues, which created a strained relationship between the two. Whereas under Warren, Marshall received opportunities to write the majority opinion on important decisions, under Burger, these opportunities largely disappeared. Burger tended to block Marshall from writing on issues concerned with constitutional rights, which he cared about deeply. Instead, Burger usually gave writing the majority opinion to Marshall on less important decisions that limited his impact. In addition, Marshall could see the group of justices who were his colleagues as part of the Warren court dwindling in number. By 1971, both Hugo Black and John Marshall Harlan decided to retire. To replace them, Nixon continued to identify conservative candidates and nominated Lewis Powell from Virginia to replace Black, and from Arizona, William Rehnquist. With their arrival, the liberal perspective of the court dissipated. Burger, Rehnquist, Powell, and Potter Stewart constituted a conservative core on the court, often joined by Byron White and Blackmun on key decisions. For Marshall, it meant the values and issues he cared deeply about and fought for throughout his life no longer held sway. His role switched from a part of the majority views of the court to consistently finding himself in the minority on key decisions. The challenge for Marshall was how to be most effective in his new circumstance. At sixty-five years of age, he had to rethink his role on the court.

The challenge to having an impact was that Marshall was an outsider on many levels in the Burger court. The newly arrived justices generally did not value his skills as a jurist or the perspectives he brought to their discussions. The views expressed by one highly respected scholar of the Supreme Court, Charles Whittaker, that Marshall was the least able of the judges on the Warren court, certainly reflected the thoughts of the new Nixon appointees. This unfair and biased criticism disappointed Marshall, as it discounted his brilliance as a civil rights lawyer and his successful roles as a circuit court judge and solicitor general. But the disrespect he felt did not stop Marshall from using whatever influence he had to impact cases of significance to him.

School desegregation and capital punishment were two of the areas in which Marshall impacted the thinking of the court. Despite growing public pressure on the court to curtail desegregating schools and the use of busing, Marshall influenced his colleagues to take a strong stand supporting it in *Swann v. Charlotte-Mecklenburg* (1970). There the Charlotte school board protested federal district court interference in devising their desegregation plan. The court ruled against Charlotte and, at Marshall's urging, made it clear that busing was an appropriate tool to use.

With regard to capital punishment, Thurgood stood firmly against it and lobbied his colleagues to oppose it as well. His strong feelings on this issue came out in the *Furman v. Georgia* case (1972). At issue was Georgia's decision to execute William Furman for accidently killing a homeowner while attempting to rob their home. Marshall saw this as violating Furman's rights under the Eighth and Fourteenth Amendments and constituted cruel and unusual punishment. The decision was a tough one for the court. Marshall took the time to visit each of the other justices to try and convince them to rule against Georgia. His efforts had an effect, as the court ruled 5–4 in support of Furman.

The other case in which Marshall had an impact was *Roe v. Wade*, which deliberated the right to an abortion for women. The case came to the court accompanied by animated protests on both sides of the issue. The plight of poor women shaped Marshall's views on the issue. He knew how the ban on legal abortions left these women at the mercy of back-alley medical personnel, who put the women's lives in jeopardy. He reminded the other justices of how the ban had a greater impact on the poor than the rich, who could find ways around the law by going to other countries where abortions were legal. He argued that an abortion should be a legal right for women. In the end, the court voted 7–2 in support of legalizing abortions. In his majority opinion, Blackmun also advocated a position suggested by Brennan and Marshall to make abortion legal not for just the first three months but until the fetus could survive viability outside the mother's body. He also included the position that a pregnancy that threatened the health of the mother might also be terminated. The *Roe* case and the others previously mentioned provided a diminishing list of positive moments for Marshall during that year.

The reelection of Richard Nixon in 1972 did not please Marshall, as it meant the turn toward greater conservatism in the court would continue well into the future. In his own form of protest, Marshall gave away his tickets to the inauguration of Nixon. A bigger blow hit Marshall when soon after he learned that Lyndon Johnson had died. Thurgood and

---

ROE V. WADE SUPREME COURT CASE

In 1970, "Jane Roe," a fictional name protecting the real identity of the plaintiff, sued the Dallas County, Texas district attorney, Henry Wade. She sought to have her pregnancy terminated through an abortion, which was illegal in Texas. Roe argued that a woman had the right to choose what happened with her body, including having an abortion. The state of Texas, represented by Wade, disagreed. In January 1973, the Supreme Court ruled 7–2 that a woman's right to have an abortion during the first trimester was a right of privacy protected by the Fourteenth Amendment. After the first trimester, other interests came into play that allowed the states to influence the decision. It was a landmark ruling that established the right of woman to have an abortion. Before the *Roe* ruling, only four states permitted straightforward access to an abortion. Justice Thurgood Marshall saw this ruling as equalizing access to safe abortions for poor women who lacked the options available to their wealthier counterparts who could travel to places where abortions were legal.

Johnson had talked the week before he died. During their talk, Johnson reminded Marshall of the sacrifice he felt he had made in putting Marshall on the court. Johnson told Marshall that the decision hurt him politically more than had the Vietnam War. It might have cost him reelection. In effect, he let Marshall know how important his presence on the U.S. Supreme Court was and the need for Thurgood to remain there despite its changes. Marshall was the only Johnson appointee remaining on the court, which also must have been important for Johnson. As Marshall himself noted, Johnson rarely said or did anything with political implications without advance planning. In all likelihood, Johnson's goal was to bolster Marshall for the many court struggles that lay before him. Johnson's words must have echoed in Marshall's mind over the decades that followed as he became increasingly isolated on the court. The position he had accepted so enthusiastically when offered by President Johnson became his cross to bear after Johnson died.

11

The Loyal Opposition

After the reelection of Richard Nixon, Thurgood Marshall began a twenty-year struggle to protect the civil liberties of all Americans. In particular, he sought to protect the poor and minorities. He did it through thoughtful interpretations of the law, which he saw as the cornerstone for change in American society. He hoped sharing his experiences and perspective might allow the other justices to see issues in a new light. Unfortunately, his views became increasingly marginalized as the court became more conservative. While he refused to back down from his principles, the effort took its toll on him emotionally, physically, and legally. The legal impact was most evident, as his ability to influence decisions made by the court weakened over time.

Trying to forge a coalition of votes to support issues important to Marshall became more difficult as older members of the court retired. During Marshall's twenty-four years on the U.S. Supreme court, conservative-leaning Republicans occupied the White House the majority of the time. Besides Lyndon Johnson, the only other Democratic president elected was Jimmy Carter, who served just one term. These presidential election results meant the majority of justices selected to join the court tended to have a conservative outlook. In particular, the desire to support law officials and to limit the rights of offenders increasingly shaped court decisions. Also, support for the protection of the civil rights of minorities lessened in importance as objections to busing and desegregation of school districts presented themselves. These issues were key parts of the legacy built by Marshall as a civil rights lawyer, and their possible demise worried him as they came under attack before the court. The potential existed that the work of thirty years might erode away. Marshall refused to allow that to happen without resisting however he could.

Initially, he had limited success sharing his experiences and insights with other justices while in conference or during individual conversations. He knew the upbringing of many of them had not exposed them to poverty or many minorities. He hoped to make the issues under discussion less abstract and more concrete by illustrating the everyday obstacles faced by these individuals for things most justices took for granted. But that proved a difficult proposition as illustrated in the *United States v. Kras* case. In this instance, Robert Kras hoped to file for bankruptcy but could not afford the fifty-dollar fee to do so. He sued, claiming the required fees deprived him of his due process and equal protection. While a lower court agreed with Kras, the justices ruled 5–4 against him. The majority decision took the position that charging a filing fee was not unfair and the option to pay it in installments made it even less oppressive. In the eyes of the judges, the installment option made the process very easy, as it was cheaper than the cost of a movie ticket or one or two packs of cigarettes.

What Marshall hoped to have his colleagues understand, as he pointed out in his dissent, were the realities of poverty. He first argued that no one should be denied the right to judicial action because they lacked the funds. For the poor, fifty dollars was a significant sum even when spaced out over installment payments. Going to a movie or buying cigarettes was an infrequent luxury, especially if they had to care for hungry or gravely ill family, which Kras had to do. Marshall found it horrible that a court decision involving interpreting the Constitution should depend upon unfair assumptions on how people live. He understood what it meant to struggle daily for enough money to survive and wanted the other justices to have more empathy for Kras and others like him.

The dissenting opinion, written by Marshall in *Kras*, became the path he took most often as the court became more conservative. He believed that dissenting was an essential duty of a justice. Thurgood saw the creation of these opposing opinions as important issues of discussion within the court for future reference. He embraced the belief that yesterday's dissent might become tomorrow's law. The dissent may not impact the case at hand, but it might influence the thinking of justices on future cases. As a result, he eventually produced more dissenting opinions than majority opinions during his time on the U.S. Supreme Court.

One of his strongest dissenting opinions opposed the majority decision in *San Antonio Independent School District v. Rodriguez*. The case examined public school funding in Texas. There, the state provided 80 percent of the monies needed by each district to run their schools. The districts had to raise the remaining 20 percent themselves. In application, this resulted in the richer districts raising more funds than the poorer districts. When Mexican-American parents in the less affluent districts protested this school funding formula saying it discriminated based on wealth, the federal district court agreed with them because of the requirements of the Fourteenth Amendment. The San Antonio school district appealed, and the U.S. Supreme Court voted 5–4 to reverse the lower court ruling. The majority opinion written by Justice Powell held that education was not a fundamental right guaranteed by the Constitution. Consequently, there were no constitutional guarantees concerning education requiring "absolute equality or precisely equal advantages" for everyone (Zelden, 2013, p. 153). Therefore, the state of Texas did not need to provide a justification for its educational formula.

Marshall could not have disagreed more. He believed the 1954 *Brown v. Board* case created an important connection between education and essential constitutional values. Therefore, the system established by Texas was discriminatory and violated the Fourteenth Amendment. He said the majority in its decision looked too narrowly at how to distinguish and judge violations of equal protection cases. Marshall believed that multiple judging standards were necessary to tell if discrimination existed. If the court allowed itself to expand how it judged discrimination under the Fourteen Amendment, the bias in the Texas formula was obvious. In this instance, Marshall's well-written and argued dissent did have a longer-term effect. In later cases brought before the Burger court involving Fourteenth Amendment equal protection issues, the justices did expand how they examined these cases. They did not embrace the multilevel approach Marshall advocated, but they moved away from the narrow views they previously used.

The unfortunate fact for Marshall was that his analysis did not sway the position of the court on a subsequent school desegregation case that involved busing. This issue had become a volatile sore point in the nation by the 1970s. In the past, the Warren court viewed busing as one tool in many to employ when seeking to desegregate schools. But as it was exercised, resistance to its use grew, especially among white parents, and became a political issue exploited by Nixon. The president adopted the public position that he believed in equal educational opportunity but was "opposed to busing for the purpose of achieving racial balance" (Rowan, 1993, p. 371).

In the Detroit metropolitan area, busing became a focal point of a suit brought by African-American parents against the state of Michigan. In the suit, *Milliken v. Bradley,* a student with the help of the NAACP sued Michigan's governor, William Milliken. They claimed that school district lines were setup in a discriminatory way depriving African-American students equal educational opportunities. Essentially, the existing plan funneled African-American students into schools within the city limits of Detroit and kept them out of schools in surrounding white suburbs. The school board plan included rules that allowed the busing of white Detroit children to white suburbs and the busing of African-American students only to other predominantly African-American schools. They further argued that the Michigan state legislature discriminated by refusing to supply funds for busing and underfunding Detroit public schools. Upon review, the federal lower courts agreed with Bradley and ordered the creation of a new plan. Their guidelines called for greater intermixing of suburban and urban students. They viewed metropolitan Detroit, which included surrounding suburbs, as a single educational environment for the purposes of school desegregation. The courts called for busing and other devices to create a better integrated educational system for the region.

The lower court's guidelines for the use of busing between suburbs and the inner city ran counter to the views of Nixon and Americans resistant to aggressive desegregation. Indeed, Solicitor General Robert Bork, representing the federal government, argued against the lower court's plan. Marshall recognized the significance of the court's plan and made a concerted effort to convince the other justices to support it. Thurgood cited previous court precedents and legal and intellectual rationales supporting the court plan as well as illustrations of the negative impact of segregated education in an effort to influence the thinking of the other justices. His efforts had only limited success. Marshall did convince three justices of the importance of including surrounding suburbs in the desegregation plans for metropolitan areas.

But the majority of the justices felt otherwise and refused to support the idea of intradistrict busing as a strategy for Detroit. Chief Justice Burger believed the district court judges went far beyond what was appropriate. The other Nixon appointees agreed with Burger, and Justice Powell called the court plan a "monstrosity." In their ruling, the majority directed the lower court to restrict any desegregation plan to within the boundaries of Detroit. They believed this was an interdistrict issue in Detroit that did not need an intradistrict solution including surrounding communities. They did not believe state officials had used restrictive housing or zoning laws to reinforce segregation as the lower courts suggested.

Marshall and the other dissenting justices disagreed. They thought the state did in fact act to bolster segregation. Each of them wrote a separate dissenting opinion. Marshall, having dedicated years of his life attacking segregated schools, was particularly disappointed. He saw the majority ruling as a step backward in that fight. It represented a roadblock in efforts to allow all children to reach their full potential. In his mind "unless our children begin to learn together, there is little hope that our people will ever learn to live together and understand each other" (Ball, 1998, p. 235). He worried that the ruling set the country and the court on a path that adopted a much narrower standard of what constituted discriminatory segregation and what steps were appropriate to remedy it.

Marshall's concerns were well warranted. In important school segregation cases over the next two decades, the court became more tolerant of educational segregation. The majority found segregated schools in Pasadena, California, the consequence of changing residential patterns, not state-sponsored discrimination. As a result, they felt the courts had done all they could to prevent discriminatory actions by the state and had the lower court cease any further actions. The majority ruled similarly in 1990, in an Oklahoma City case. A judge there created a five-year plan for desegregation of its schools, which was successful. At that time, the judge suspended but did not halt court oversight. When left on their own, the school board installed a "Student Reassignment Plan" that revived the old neighborhood-school pattern. They claimed they did it to ease the amount of busing done by African-American students. A racially segregated school population resulted, where the majority of students at most schools were either white or African-American. In addition, school funding apportioned greater resources to white schools. African-American parents protested and demanded the revival of the old plan. The school board protested and appealed to the U.S. Supreme Court. They argued that the old plan should not be revived, as the judge had ended his supervision of the school system.

The court, now under the leadership of Chief Justice William Rehnquist, ruled against reviving the old desegregation plan. They felt the school board was not acting in a discriminatory fashion and the old plan need not return. In the court's view, the Oklahoma City Board of Education had obeyed the law for a reasonable amount of time, and the lower court should continue to monitor their actions but should not bring back the previous plan for desegregation.

For Thurgood Marshall, the ruling represented another in a long list of decisions by the court undermining equality of educational opportunity. He felt the original monitoring plan ended too soon. Further, the U.S. Supreme Court needed to look more closely at what was truly taking place in Oklahoma City. From what he found, restrictive housing agreements kept African Americans confined to certain areas of the city, which allowed for segregated schools if a neighborhood-school format was followed. This he believed drove the "Student Reassignment Plan" of the Board of Education. He also believed the school board reinforced segregationist beliefs when adopting the position that the public opposed further desegregation. He had heard these same words often during his days at the NAACP and recognized how they were used to resist change. He also recognized that his view increasingly was an isolated dissenting voice on a court that was moving away from a true commitment to equal educational opportunity for all children.

Adding to Marshall's disappointment, the court also sought to reduce the rights of individuals accused of a crime. Under the *Miranda* decision, the police had to advise an accused individual of their rights against self-incrimination and for legal representation. The more conservative Burger and Rehnquist courts increasingly were more interested in broadening the options of law enforcement. On several cases, including *Fare v. Michael C.* and *Duckworth v. Eagan*, the majority took the position that despite law officials not following *Miranda* guidelines, the confessions or evidence obtained from the accused could be used against them during their trials. In each instance Marshall strongly objected to the rulings. For him, the court overlooked the lack of legal sophistication of poorer citizens and the ability of law officials to take advantage of their ignorance and frighten them into self-incriminating statements or actions. In the *Fare* case, the accused juvenile asked for his probation officer rather than his attorney. Since he did not specifically request an attorney, the police continued questioning him after denying access to his probation officer. Eventually, the young man confessed. That coerced admission of guilt became a critical piece of evidence in his trial and conviction. This clearly represented police manipulation to Marshall. They used a legal technicality to avoid the young man obtaining proper legal representation, which was dishonest.

Thurgood further believed that the shift away from a faithful interpretation of *Miranda* was a violation of the intention of that ruling and a debasement of the precedent set by the Warren court. When the police did not inform the accused or used deceitful interpretations of the ruling to entrap individuals in their custody, Marshall believed this to be a breach of the legal guidelines prescribed by *Miranda*. In his eyes, the Rehnquist court, in particular, was making a mockery of the intent of *Miranda* in the name of law and order. The legal rights, particularly, of poor or uneducated individuals, diminished as a consequence.

This outcome especially worried Marshall when this "liberal" interpretation of police powers by the conservatives on the court involved a possible death sentence for the accused. Justices who supported use of the death penalty saw it as a way of deterring possible offenders and as the proper punishment for certain crimes. In the early days of the Burger court, Marshall and Justice William Brennan led the way in convincing a majority of their colleagues to rule the death penalty unconstitutional. They saw it as cruel and unusual punishment. However, as more Nixon appointees joined the court, the majority shifted on the topic, and by 1976, in *Gregg v.*

Georgia, only Marshall and Brennan voted against Georgia's desire to execute Troy Gregg for murder. The majority cited capital punishment as a longtime accepted practice and refused to interfere in the decision of a state on the issue.

As they watched the views of the court shift, Marshall and Brennan first dissented using the argument that the Eighth Amendment forbade the cruel and unusual punishment that characterized the death penalty. When they found that viewpoint had no impact on the thinking of the other justices, they followed a different line of argument. Marshall, again worried about the disproportionate numbers of African Americans and the poor sentenced to death, looked at the application of the penalty. He believed more consistent rules were needed to ensure equal and fair sentencing in death penalty cases. The rules in place, in his view, were capricious and unevenly applied to the detriment of certain sectors of the population. The lack of access to adequate counsel very often resulted in these deadly sentences, according to Marshall. But even when Marshall pointed out that African Americans were much more likely to get death sentences than whites for similar crimes, the Rehnquist court still supported its use. For Marshall, the refusal of the other justices to recognize the racism implicit in death penalty sentencing patterns was inexcusable. It marked another step backward away from protecting individual rights, which was an essential role of the courts for Marshall.

The issue of race played an important role in another significant case that came before the court. It involved the concept of affirmative action and the application of a white veteran, Allan Bakke, to the medical school of the University of California at Davis. He applied twice to the program and was not accepted either time. He then sued the school because it had set aside sixteen seats for African-American, Hispanic, or Native American applicants. Bakke had higher scores than some of the students admitted thru those slots and claimed the affirmative action program of the university discriminated against him under the equal protection portion of the Fourteenth Amendment. The university had illegally established a quota system that he wanted dismantled. The lower courts agreed that the affirmative system established by the university was problematic and illegal, but they did not require the school to admit Bakke. Dissatisfied with that decision, both Bakke and the university appealed the case to the U.S. Supreme Court.

When the case came to the justices, Marshall hoped to guide them to an understanding of why affirmative action was necessary. He felt there were several factors they needed to consider. They included the continuing aftereffects of the legacy of slavery, the use of the Constitution to impede progress for African Americans through discrimination as endorsed by practices like separate but equal, and the appropriateness of affirmative action as a necessary remedy to past roadblocks placed in the way of African-American progress. The discussions he had with the other justices were passionate and insightful. As Justice White reported, Marshall spoke with great conviction based upon his experiences with related issues. He could "embellish his points with examples that would scare you to death, experiences he had trying cases in the South" (Williams, 1998, p. 365). Marshall wanted the justices to see the actions of the university as not excluding certain students but enabling other students and a group of people seeking to improve themselves. He did not want the justices to think that the civil rights movement's successes meant that "Negroes had arrived" and were no longer held back by discrimination. There remained many obstacles still to overcome, and the University of California program sought to provide help. As the discussion unfolded, Marshall hoped to get one of the undecided justices in a group divided over the issue to support him and uphold the program of the university.

Marshall did not get the vote he needed, as Chief Justice Burger made a personal appeal to wavering colleagues and secured a 5–4 vote against the university and for admitting Bakke. For Burger and the justices firmly opposed to affirmative action, as used by the university, any race-specific strategy employed in the admission process was prohibited by a strict reading of the Fourteenth Amendment. The key issue for justices who understood the need to take race into account in the admissions process was the idea of a fixed quota controlling the process. In the past, quota systems excluded certain groups, such as Jewish applicants from admittance to colleges or other opportunities. The association of quotas with that past practice prevented their support for its use by the university, even though the context was different. The compromise majority opinion supported the use of race as a factor in the admission process but rejected the use of quotas as part of the process.

Thurgood gathered some solace from the decision, as it recognized that race was an important element for consideration in the application process for a university. It also upheld the use of affirmative action but not quotas. What Marshall resented was the opposition to the use of quotas as a way of ensuring past inequities were consistently addressed. From his viewpoint, there was nothing wrong with guaranteeing that a certain number of "disadvantaged minority students" would gain admittance. It was a way of balancing the scale for the many years in which an arbitrary exclusionary policy at many institutions barred minority candidates from admittance no matter how good their qualifications. In those instances, considerations of race applied but to the detriment of minority applicants. For Marshall, affirmative action could not be viewed simply in a legal context. To address it properly, a broader context of historical racial practices in the nation and its resulting long-term impact had to be considered. That history had to be addressed and amends made for the damages it created. Affirmative action and quotas offered a reasonable strategy to address the issue and needed to be upheld. In addition, the position taken in the majority opinion, that time had run out for race-specific solutions through using the guarantee of equal protection clause struck Marshall as illogical and racially insensitive. In his view, racial discrimination ruled in the nation for several hundred years and that the justices now claimed, after less than thirty years, time had run out to use the Constitution to balance the scales made no sense. For him, it was a sign that the court and the country were no longer willing to work to support equality of opportunity.

The majority's opposition to affirmative action did not end with its use by a university in its admission policy. They also found fault with its use by governmental agencies as illustrated in their ruling in the *City of Richmond v. Croson* case. In Richmond, the city council adopted regulations that required companies receiving city contracts to subcontract 30 percent of their work to minority-owned businesses. Their goal was to attempt to remedy a historical pattern of discrimination in allotting public contracts by the city. One half of the city population was African-American, but only 1 percent of city contracts went to minority businesses. The city used a set-aside program that had been ruled as valid in the past by the courts. The J. A. Croson Company sued the city after it lost its contract when it did not meet the 30 percent goal of including minority subcontractors.

The court under Rehnquist had a different view. They ruled against Richmond's set-aside regulation and reversed the court's validation of the use of such plans nine years earlier. The view, core to the majority opinion, was that past history by itself could not justify the use of a rigid quota system in the awarding of contracts in Richmond. They did not believe that Richmond had proven the need for such remedial action in awarding public construction contracts so that in creating the set-aside requirement, it violated the equal protection clause. Racial neutrality for them was an essential requirement of the Fourteenth Amendment, which the Richmond law violated.

For Marshall, the ruling represented another deliberate and giant step backward on the part of the court. He was flabbergasted by the dismissal by the majority of the testimony of Richmond elected officials concerning the long history of racial contracting bias by the city. Their failure or unwillingness to understand the true issues in Richmond was extremely disheartening to Marshall. In effect, they were discounting and minimizing the impact of racial discrimination in Richmond and, by inference, in other settings. They saw racial discrimination as a phenomenon of the past that no longer needed addressing by governmental bodies. In Marshall's view, the decision was "a full-scale retreat from the court's long-standing solicitude for race conscious remedial efforts" (Ball, 1998, p. 279). For him, it represented the "civil rights massacre of 1989." It was a painful blow for Marshall that "scarred his heart," according to one of his clerks. In Marshall's mind, the "court has gone to pot, that's for sure," which saddened and enraged him (ibid., p. 279).

His deteriorating relationship with the other justices on the court added to Marshall's disappointment. When he first joined the court, Marshall found a core group of welcoming justices. They did not always see things in the same way, but there was receptiveness to the experiences and perspective that Marshall brought to the group. Led by Warren, their general preference for judicial activism and the protection of civil rights allowed for lively discussions but in an environment Marshall found cordial. Justice William O. Douglas was not a fan of Marshall or his appointment, but his views did not make Marshall feel he was not taken seriously as a member of the court.

But Marshall felt his standing decline and his opinions less respected as other justices retired and the court became more conservative. The new court opposed judicial activism and the expansion of civil rights, which made Marshall an outsider in the group. He did not have as good a relationship with Chief Justice Burger as he had with Chief Justice Earl Warren. In assigning the writing of majority court opinions, Burger minimized Marshall's impact by limiting his assignment to less important, technical decisions. Marshall also felt stung by the actions taken by Burger, which seemed to show little respect for him as a fellow justice. In particular, Marshall was angered when he requested the postponement of a conference meeting of the court so he could attend the funeral of a relative. Initially, a new date was scheduled, and Marshall left for the funeral. He returned to find the meeting took place at the original time during his absence. The reason he was told this was done was to allow other justices to attend the funeral of former U.S. Supreme Court justice and avowed segregationist James F. Byrnes. For Marshall, this decision indicated little respect for him or for his African-American aunt.

Burger was not the only justice with whom Marshall had a poor relationship. The replacement for Justice Harlan, William Rehnquist, approached legal issues for minorities differently than Marshall and did not have high regard for Marshall or his perspectives. As a law clerk for Justice Robert Jackson in 1952, Rehnquist wrote a memo to Jackson opposing the overturning of *Plessy*. He opposed judicial activism then and held to that belief as a member of the court. He also seemed to have little sympathy for the quest for equal rights through the courts by African Americans or other minority groups. His personal history included charges of harassing African-American voters while a poll watcher in Arizona and buying a home with a contract that included restrictive covenants. As a consequence, he and Marshall were opponents on numerous issues that came before the court. In particular, Marshall viewed Rehnquist as seeking to roll back the impact and gains generated by the *Brown* decision, which he had opposed when it was made. He also felt Rehnquist had little understanding of the struggles faced by the poor in society and offered dispassionate theoretically based decisions divorced from the realities of life of common people. When Rehnquist became chief justice, his views concerned Marshall even more because of the increased influence Rehnquist gained in that role. In fact, Marshall found out the chief justice was not above using his position against Marshall. After his retirement, Marshall maintained an office at the U.S. Supreme Court and because of his infirmities requested access to a driver and car occasionally to drive him between home and the court. He had done this regularly while still serving, but Rehnquist refused, claiming this did not qualify as official business and he could not allow it. For Marshall, it was another in a long list of things done by Rehnquist to undermine him.

Marshall also found his relationship with Justice Lewis Powell a difficult one. His antipathy toward Powell sprang, in part, from Powell's Virginia heritage and his opposition to busing and school desegregation. Powell had filed a friend of the court brief opposing busing when a case from Virginia came to the court early in Marshall's tenure there. Powell's continued opposition to equal protection and affirmative action cases when he became a justice further reinforced Marshall's concerns. They came from such different backgrounds that it was difficult for Marshall to relate to Powell more than on a casual basis. They might speak when they passed one another in the building, but that was the extent of their relationship. Other members of the court noticed Marshall's attitude, as one colleague remarked that Marshall held Lewis at a distance.

Other than William Brennan, Marshall had few solid relationships among the other justices. He did have a good opinion of Sandra Day O'Connor, despite her conservative views. They both understood the importance of their place on the court as the first woman and first African American to serve as justice. O'Connor admired Marshall for his many accomplishments and pioneering legal efforts. She frequently found the perspectives he offered when the justices were in conference instructive and sobering. They also were experiences to which she could connect from her own life. As she noted, Marshall affected her with his stories because at the base of those stories "was a relevant legal point" (ibid., p. 204). His words did not always influence how she voted on issues, but they did cause her to carefully reflect on the impact of her decisions.

Unfortunately, O'Connor was one of the few justices who found Marshall's commentary instructive. More members of the court could not relate to Marshall's words and saw him as wasting their time. Rehnquist referred to them as "tall tales." They felt he was oversensitive on issues of race and was too quick to lambast them when they disagreed with his point of view. And there was some truth to their view. Marshall became bitter as more and more cases connected to civil rights and affirmative action came before the court with rulings that undercut past progress. His discussions with the other justices became straightforward and critical. Even his good friend Justice Brennan worried that Marshall, in expressing his anger and disappointment, carried things too far. Marshall refused to compromise his beliefs, which put him constantly at loggerheads with the conservative majority. He would rather produce a dissenting opinion than to allow what he felt were insensitive and sometimes racist perspectives gain any currency in an opinion of which he was a part. This stubbornness caused other justices to view Marshall as confrontational and sullen. It also impacted their opinion of him and his work.

These views became more public in a critical book written by Robert Woodward and Scott Armstrong titled *The Brethren: Inside the Supreme Court*. They based the content on interviews with former clerks to the justices to develop what they said was a peek into the inter-realms of the U.S. Supreme Court. The book did not treat Marshall well. It depicted him as lazy and not engaged with the day-to-day work of the court. According to the authors, Marshall spent long hours watching TV, telling jokes and stories, and having his law clerks write his opinions for him. They pointed out how Justice Stevens had gone to see Marshall about a case and, after talking to him, decided Marshall did not really understand its issues. In Steven's mind, Marshall was totally dependent upon his law clerks to do his work. The book's conclusion was that Marshall lacked the energy and will to do the work and perhaps the intellect required of the office. The authors were, in effect, resurrecting attacks his opponents had raised against Marshall since he came on the court.

The book only increased Marshall's belief that he was not appreciated or respected by the other members of the court. The book sought to hurt his public reputation and to question his fitness to continue serving on the court. He believed much of the information directly or indirectly came from members of the court or people close to them. He remained angry about its implications for years after its publication. As one of his law clerks pointed out, Marshall operated like the other justices, who had their clerks perform the research and write a first draft after conferring with the justice. Like the other justices, Marshall then went over the draft and had it reworked according to his instructions. The Marshall his clerks knew was hardworking and devoted to his work. Thurgood felt that Woodward and Armstrong looked for ways to paint a negative picture of him and people associated with the court helped them do it. He believed his strong views, which ran counter to those of the conservative majority on the court, and his growing isolation from them helped fuel the negative stories.

In turn, his resentment toward the court caused Marshall to begin expressing his views and frustrations more openly in public settings. He saw the rulings of the conservative members of the court as dangerous, wrong, and sometimes racist. One of the strongest comments he offered took place in a speech given in Hawaii. That address marked the bicentennial of the Constitution. The speech was widely reprinted and commented upon in numerous journals and publications. In it, Marshall offered a stinging criticism of the efforts of the conservatives on the court and elsewhere to refuse to see the Constitution as a living document whose original perspectives were meant to evolve over time. For Marshall, the Constitution was a flawed document from its inception, as it condoned slavery and the exclusion of certain members of society from full participation in that society. He thought it wrong to focus on the moment of its creation, but more appropriate to focus on how it had enabled changes in the way American society operated, over the years. This was the result of the pressures brought to bear by individuals excluded who demanded their place at the table. For Thurgood, it was not strict adherence to the original words penned by the founding fathers but the flexibility inherent in those words that was most important to celebrate. The protection the Constitution provided for individual freedom and human rights as well as the inclusion of a Bill of Rights was what should be the true focus of any celebration of that document. These things allowed American society to evolve and become more inclusive. The true importance for Marshall was not the birth of the document but its evolution in the decades that followed. For him the task of jurists was to continue to allow the Constitution to live, not to let its original words predominate in a constantly changing society.

He also criticized the decisions of the court at speeches he gave before judges of the Second Circuit Court, where he once served. In those speeches, he discussed topics ranging from civil rights to the death penalty to the violation of constitutional rights. The court, in Marshall's view, was shirking from its responsibilities in these areas and needed to do more to protect the rights of individuals. He believed that "when rights are violated, courts should normally craft remedies that attempt to make victims 'whole' and deter future violations" (Tushnet, 2001, p. 198). If the courts fail to do this, he believed, people will lose faith in them and look to alternative means of redress. The present court refused to take appropriate actions when these violations occurred and was undermining the Bill of Rights. This was wrong, and Marshall was determined to point this out, with his last breath, if necessary.

The challenge was that his declining health made the role of the loyal opposition increasingly harder on him. He suffered several medical incidents in the late 1970s and the years that followed. While traveling to Las Vegas, he developed pneumonia and spent time recuperating at Bethesda Naval Hospital. A couple of years later, just before his sixty-eighth birthday, he woke up to chest pains that turned into several mild heart attacks. His constant smoking as well as enjoyment of drinking and good food did not help his health. Neither did the stress of his role as the voice of the common man on the court. It left him increasingly isolated, angry, and tired. The doctor prescribed bed rest and a change in lifestyle. Marshall got more rest but could not stop the other things. The impact of the heart attack was one of the reasons he started to come to work a little later and to leave a little earlier. But as Cissy pointed out, he regularly brought paperwork home with him and was lost in thought about cases as he sat in his den with the television on in the background.

The heart attack increased speculation that Marshall might retire, but when asked, he told reporters he had no intention of stepping down. His position did not change with the election of the Democratic candidate Jimmy Carter to the presidency. Although people connected to Carter suggested Thurgood should consider allowing Carter to name a liberal justice to continue Marshall's fight on the court, Thurgood refused to resign. Marshall was determined to remain a justice until he was physically unable to perform the duties. This was despite another health crisis, when he fell down the steps of the Capitol, cutting his forehead and breaking both arms.

When Carter lost his reelection bid to Republican Ronald Reagan, he once again approached Marshall about retiring before Carter left office. Once again, Marshall refused to consider stepping down, telling reporters, "I am serving out my term . . . And it's a life term" (Williams, 1998, p. 373).

Although Marshall was able to remain on the court for another decade, his health did not improve, and it impacted his work. He suffered from emphysema and experienced a bout with bronchitis that hospitalized him for several days. Marshall had glaucoma, which made reading difficult. In order to hear, he wore hearing aids in both ears and periodically received treatments of anticoagulants at the hospital to help prevent more heart attacks. As the decade wore on, walking became more difficult, and he had to use a cane to help him get around. He had another mishap in Chicago when his cane got entangled in a sign and he fell, bruising his left shoulder. His memory also began to fail him. It was reported in conference discussion with the other justices that he lost track of the conversations. He also had trouble at times during public sessions of the court. His body was failing him, and the question was how long his strong spirit could keep him going.

The retirement of his good friend William Brennan made life on the court even more challenging. Brennan also suffered from poor health, having experienced a series of strokes. His doctor advised him to retire, and he decided to step down. Marshall and Brennan represented the last of the justices to serve under Earl Warren on the U.S. Supreme Court and the only ones consistently standing against the conservative majority. He, like Marshall, saw the Bill of Rights as the heart of the Constitution and was willing to dissent, even when it was not popular. Brennan's departure left Marshall as the lone consistent voice opposing the Rehnquist led conservative justices. He missed Brennan, and the task of operating without him took its toll on an already physically weak Marshall.

Cissy could see how much life on the court was taking out of Thurgood and, finally, along with his doctor, convinced Marshall it was time to retire. He was eighty-two years old. His last day on the U.S. Supreme Court was on June 27, 1991. Cissy and his sons came that day in part because Thurgood had the opportunity to speak in favor of having his son, John, admitted to the court's bar. They also knew this was Thurgood's last day. It was the final meeting of the court for that session, and Marshall ended the day by reading his dissents with a number of decisions made by the majority. It typified the pattern of his last few years on the court.

Thurgood Marshall sent his letter of resignation to President Bush that same day and announced his intentions to the other justices the following day. In his letter, he told the president that his advancing age and medical condition rendered him no longer able to handle the duties of a U.S.

CLARENCE THOMAS NOMINATION

Soon after Thurgood Marshall announced his retirement from the Supreme Court in 1991, President George H. W. Bush nominated Clarence Thomas to replace him. Thomas was a Yale Law School–educated, conservative African-American federal appeals court judge who had only held that position for nineteen months. When asked to appraise his candidacy, the American Bar Association rated him unqualified to serve on the Supreme Court. Several groups strongly opposed his nomination due to his anti-abortion views and opposition to affirmative action. During his confirmation hearing, law professor Anita Hill, who had worked for Thomas at the Equal Employment Opportunity Commission, offered explosive televised testimony accusing him of sexual harassment. Her descriptions of his inappropriate actions, which Thomas strongly denied, lasted three days and was a media event. Despite the controversy caused by Hill's statements, Thomas, whose views were very different from those of Thurgood Marshall, was confirmed by the Senate and joined the court. His appointment greatly disappointed Marshall, who worried the very principles he advocated while on the court would be undermined by the addition of Thomas to the growing conservative majority on the court.

Supreme Court justice. He expected his resignation to take final effect after a replacement was affirmed by the Senate.

At the press conference, after the public learned of his stepping down, Marshall reaffirmed what he had told the president. When reporters asked him why he finally decided to retire after resisting for so long, his response was, "I'm old. I am getting old and coming apart." When asked about a possible successor to be named by Bush, Marshall remained publicly neutral on that topic. He only noted that race should not be used as an excuse to appoint the wrong person to the position. Privately, he was concerned about who might follow him. He knew a conservative nominee was likely but hoped it would be someone well respected nationally.

The nomination of Clarence Thomas did not please Marshall. Thomas did not bring the same quality of credentials Marshall had brought to the court. He also was much more conservative than Marshall and opposed many of the issues dear to Marshall, such as affirmative action. According to a friend of Marshall, the nomination of Thomas and to think people were comparing Thomas to him deeply hurt him. Marshall felt Thomas lacked ability and a commitment to the plight of African Americans, and it was a travesty to have him take the seat Marshall once held. Despite Marshall's unhappiness with Thomas, he was confirmed in a close vote after a controversial hearing. Marshall spent a couple of hours talking with Thomas the first day he came to work at the court.

Although retired, Marshall maintained an office at the U.S. Supreme Court building. But the continued downturn in his health prevented him from using it as much as he might have wished. He watched the Clarence Thomas hearings there with his friends, and it is there that he had his meeting with the newly confirmed justice. An important decision he had to make was what to do with his papers. The Library of Congress had approached him about getting them many years previously, but he had kept them at arm's length. After retiring, he had a change of heart and decided to make them available to the library. He only asked that the collection remain closed during his lifetime.

Unfortunately, Marshall's health continued to decline. To help his heart, he had a pacemaker implanted but still reached the point that he needed a wheelchair to get around. In one of his last public appearances, he received the Liberty Medal at a Fourth of July celebration in Philadelphia, and he had to be lifted to the stage in his wheelchair by a forklift. People who saw him there noted that he looked weaker than he had a year earlier. His friends and family worried about him as he continued to decline. By January 1993, Thurgood was too weak to leave his home or even get out of bed. When coaxed to sit up, he declined, asking why he should make the effort. He was having a lot of pain and was not happy about his condition. When the newly elected Democratic vice president, Al Gore, asked Marshall to swear him into office, Marshall was too weak to do it.

Gore and President William Clinton were sworn into office on January 20, 1993, and the next day Thurgood Marshall was transported from his home to Bethesda Naval Medical Center. Three days later, he died at the age of eighty-four. Before the funeral, Marshall's casket lay in state in the Great Hall of the U.S. Supreme Court so that the public could pay a last tribute to him. More than eighteen thousand people walked by the casket, some in tears while others left flowers and other mementos. His funeral service took place the following day attended by dignitaries from across the country. It was followed by a private family service at Arlington Cemetery on January 30.

Newspapers around the country and the world paid tribute to Thurgood Marshall after his death. Perhaps the headline that summed his life up best came from *The Washington Post*, which called him an "Unyielding Defender of Individual Rights." Those words captured what he tried to do both as a civil rights lawyer and as a federal judge. What he did was not always popular, but it was consistent. He had the heart of a warrior and the zeal of a reformer, which made an impression on all who came in contact with him. The fact that thousands of people stood in line on a cold January day to file past his casket in tribute to Marshall spoke to the impact he had on the lives of many generations of people. The answer he gave when someone asked him how he wanted to be remembered, "He did what he could with what he had," is an appropriate way to best understand Thurgood Marshall. With often meager resources and frequently under assault, he was able to make a major difference in how this nation thought about race and equity. It, at times, was a lonely battle but one he fervently believed in throughout his career.

Why Thurgood Marshall Matters

Without a doubt, the most celebrated moment in Thurgood Marshall's career was his appointment to the U.S. Supreme Court. This appointment was a major milestone not only for him but also for African Americans. Lyndon Johnson understood its significance when he selected Marshall, and Thurgood recognized its importance when he accepted the nomination. He acknowledged not knowing how his confirmation process would unfold. His earlier appointment to the Second Circuit Court of New York had been a prolonged and arduous process. Southern congressmen and conservatives did not want him appointed as a judge at the circuit-court level, and they certainly were not eager to have an African American, and particularly Thurgood Marshall, appointed to the U.S. Supreme Court. Marshall accepted the opportunity regardless of the possible consequences because he was confident of his qualifications and knew that his successful appointment would open doors for other people of color in the legal field and elsewhere. It was another battle he stood willing to wage because it was the right thing to do, and it was how he had conducted his life for years. He stood ready and willing to accept whatever challenge confronted him as he sought to force the nation to apply the ideals and the promises in its founding document, the U.S. Constitution, to all its citizens.

Thurgood Marshall believed the U.S. Constitution with its Bill of Rights was a unique and singular document. It provided protections and opportunities for its citizens, unmatched by any other governing document in the world. His belief was substantiated by his research on the governing documents of other nations. When asked to prepare a constitution for the new government of the African nation of Kenya, he closely studied governing documents from around the world. This investigation reinforced his admiration for the Constitution of the United States on which he modeled key aspects of his governing document for Kenya. He said publicly at that time that no other documents came close in comparison to the one governing the United States.

Thurgood's admiration for the U.S. Constitution reinforced his belief that African Americans should have the same access to opportunities available to other citizens. The Bill of Rights along with the Thirteenth, Fourteenth, and Fifteenth Amendments dictated as much. Any impediments placed in the way should be attacked and removed. To accept anything less was to allow the biased presumption that African Americans were inferior to their white counterparts to gain credence and justify the discriminatory laws and actions some individuals sought to put in place. Even if large segments of the population believed in discriminatory practices, they should not be allowed to deny the rights of citizenship to other members of society. For Marshall, the law was the vehicle to use to launch counterattacks against these discriminatory practices.

His commitment to this belief and guiding life canon is not surprising in light of his ancestral heritage. His parents and grandparents on both sides took public stands against what they saw as unjust actions. His maternal grandfather led protests against racial profiling by Baltimore police officers, while his paternal grandmother successfully resisted the efforts of the local utility company to build on her property. His grandparents' example was reinforced by the resolve of Marshall's parents who also demanded that he stand up for his rights. His father, in particular, resented disrespectful treatment and was quick to respond when confronted with it. As Marshall often repeated, his father told him that "If someone called you n—, you have my permission to fight them." The family demanded respect and expected their children to have the same attitude.

Thurgood Marshall took this perspective to heart and extended it to his treatment of less fortunate members of the community. As a youngster, he often brought home stray animals and less fortunate friends he made while out playing. Thurgood believed it the right thing to do to provide help or support for those who might need it. His parents and relatives reinforced this instinct by supporting his decisions and offering temporary shelter or aid to these friends he brought home, despite the economic struggles of the Marshall family.

His empathy for the less fortunate strengthened as Thurgood grew older, and he observed the treatment of African Americans by the Baltimore police. From his high school classroom window across from the local police station, he viewed the intimidation and mistreatment of people brought in accused of a crime. Frequently, they were coerced into confessions. He then viewed their sentencing in the courtroom when he accompanied his father to observe the trial system and the decisions rendered by judges. The overall experience provided him with a sense of the positive and negative aspects of the legal system. In particular, he could see the impact a good lawyer could have in the courtroom. These experiences helped lay the first building blocks in the creation of a future civil rights lawyer.

More blocks developed after he graduated high school. Thurgood did not know he wanted to be a lawyer as he headed off to Lincoln University for college. He did know he enjoyed debating, and he did not want to follow his brother into the field of medicine. At Lincoln, he became even more attuned to issues of race through protests he joined against segregation in a local movie theater, conversations with his more activist-minded college friends, and debates over whether Lincoln should hire African-American faculty. By the time he graduated from Lincoln, Thurgood knew he wanted to pursue a legal career.

The logical and most cost-efficient law school for him to attend was the University of Maryland Law School. But its long-standing policy of denying admittance to African Americans blocked that option. Instead, Marshall decided to attend the law school at Howard University. At the time it was a choice he was forced to make, probably resentfully. But it was a decision that would change the trajectory of the civil rights of African Americans and the poor over the next half century. Attending Howard became the launching pad for his life's work and a legacy of courage and unflinching dedication to the use of the law to transform the racial environment in the United States.

It is at Howard that he came under the influence of Charles Hamilton Houston, the dean of the law school. This relationship had a seminal impact on Thurgood and his life choices going forward. While attending Howard, he became a devotee of Houston's philosophy concerning the responsibilities of African-American lawyers. Dean Houston believed that African-American lawyers had a higher calling, which was to reengineer the American social system and, in the process, make it more equitable for everyone. Houston further believed they had to use their legal training for the higher goal of helping their community and not just for personal gain. To accomplish this ambition, dedicated African-American lawyers had to strive for excellence in their training, in their preparation of legal briefs, in their presentations in court, and in the strategies they used to win their cases. This philosophy reinforced the family values that surrounded Marshall during his youth and offered him a platform through which he could help more than the strays he brought home as a child or the people he watched unfairly treated by the legal system in Baltimore. A law career, as defined by Houston, was more than a paycheck; it was a calling to significantly change the American society. Marshall's training at Howard Law School became the springboard for his legacy.

Houston provided not only theoretical classroom training for Marshall but also hands-on experience. He engaged Marshall to provide research on cases Houston was defending for the NAACP and to watch him apply the concepts taught at Howard. Observing Houston present his arguments in defense of African Americans, oftentimes victimized by the legal system, reinforced for Marshall how the law, when interpreted by well-trained lawyers, could benefit individuals as well as the larger community. Through these cases, Thurgood came to understand that the lawsuits a lawyer selected to pursue could create legal precedents, which would change the way similar cases in the future would be decided.

The summer after Thurgood completed law school, Houston further buttressed the need for such legal action for Marshall. Charles invited Thurgood to accompany him on a trip to visit African-American elementary and secondary schools in the South. Their task was to document the deteriorating state of the educational facilities provided to African-American students in comparison to their white counterparts. The trip was a "success" in the sense that it verified what the two men suspected, that African-American students did not have access to "separate but equal" facilities. The better description was that they were "separate but unequal." By this time Houston had joined the legal arm of the NAACP and was considering a strategy to undermine the "separate but equal" proviso of the 1896 *Plessy v. Ferguson* U.S. Supreme Court decision. The trip confirmed Houston's belief that lawsuits brought against unequal, segregated schools could be successful and should be pursued by the NAACP. The trip also allowed the two men to spend extended time together as colleagues, not student and teacher, and for Houston to share more of his thoughts about how the NAACP and its legal arm might revolutionize the racial environment of the United States.

The trip and Houston's influence made a significant impression on Marshall. After graduating with honors from Howard, he had the opportunity to further his education at Harvard University and receive an advanced degree in law. Financially, it was the best choice to make for Marshall and his wife. The scholarship offered them enough money to live comfortably in Boston. But he turned it down. Thurgood instead chose to wait tables as he awaited the results of the Maryland bar exam. He was eager to practice law rather than study it further.

As a new lawyer in Baltimore, Marshall increased his work with the Baltimore branch of the NAACP. The work paid very little but gave Marshall the opportunity to apply Houston's belief that he had a social responsibility as a lawyer. This work also gave him the chance to strike a blow at the discriminatory admission policy of the University of Maryland Law School. In collaboration with Houston, Thurgood identified a qualified candidate to apply to Maryland, Donald Murray, a good student and a graduate of Amherst College. When the school rejected Murray's application based on his race, Marshall took them to court. It was an opening salvo in the NAACP's long-term strategy to force schools denying admission to African Americans to provide equal accommodations or to admit them. The lawsuit was also the first of many cases initiated by Thurgood seeking to change the racial landscape of the nation. In this instance, Maryland lost the case in the Maryland State Supreme Court. More importantly, the decision set a legal precedent that worried other states with similar practices. Thurgood was beginning to build his legacy.

Buoyed by the success of the Murray decision, Thurgood initiated additional lawsuits at the secondary-school level in Maryland. His goal, such as in the suit he brought against the Baltimore County Board of Education, was to force the equalization of educational opportunity for African-American high school students. His objective was the desegregation of the existing segregated schools in the county or the creation of educational facilities for African Americans equivalent to those of white students. His success in this and other cases in Maryland gained the attention of the leadership at the NAACP headquarters in New York and led to Houston hiring Marshall as his deputy. Together they made plans to attack the segregation laws of the country by using litigation to develop legal precedents they hoped would eventually result in granting full legal rights of citizenship for African Americans. This goal became Thurgood's passion and life's work for the next three decades.

As a lawyer at the NAACP, Marshall became an unrelenting defender of the rights of African Americans and the poor. As the highest profile African-American civil rights organization, the NAACP is flooded with requests for help from across the country, but most often from the South. Unable to provide help in every instance, the NAACP and Marshall strategically elected to pursue cases whose outcomes might result in important legal precedence. While Thurgood at the time would not have considered it creating a personal legacy, his work resulted in important legal decisions that had long-lasting implications.

The legal process he pursued at the NAACP took patience and fortitude. Plus, there was no guarantee of success. No matter the outcome, the legal process entailed extensive research into each case to determine the most effective line of argument. If the goal was to get the case before the U.S. Supreme Court, the line of argument had to be positioned to allow for an appeal of a lower court ruling, or if the suit was successful, to anticipate the opposition appealing the decision in the hopes of obtaining a reversal.

Marshall also understood that even an adverse ruling did not necessarily denote defeat. Especially in Southern courts, success was measured in less obvious ways. In a trial where the prosecution sought the death penalty, a final verdict of a life sentence or less provided a measure of solace to the legal team, to the defendant, and to his family. Especially in cases where local officials used intimidation to extract a confession, Marshall felt he had done extremely well when he convinced an often all-white jury to spare the life of his client.

These smaller successes along with similar cases that Thurgood won were what prompted mothers or other family members to write the NAACP and him for help. They knew they had a chance if Thurgood decided to accept the case. His arrival in their community brought the best legal representation they could get. They saw Thurgood as an individual willing to challenge the white legal system and possibly defeat it, despite the unfair methods used against him. Marshall's presence signaled hope because of his well-known past successes.

Cases like these resonated for Marshall because he understood how local authorities manipulated the legal system in an effort to attain the results they desired. Their actions ran counter to the rights guaranteed citizens under the Constitution when they blocked African Americans from serving on juries or contrived evidence in order to obtain a conviction. Equal protection under the law was to apply to everyone rather than selectively excluding segments of the population. It was a principle Marshall firmly believed in and consistently expressed and applied throughout his career.

His belief in justice, and the desire to do whatever he could to help his clients, was what compelled Thurgood to pursue alternative avenues, even when he lost cases. It was this sense of justice that had him use political pressure to save the life of a young man tried and sentenced to death in Groveland, Florida. And it was this same sense of justice that haunted him after he could not save the life of James Gross when he was sentenced to death in Prince George's County, Maryland. The people who wrote to the NAACP understood Marshall's reputation and commitment, which is why they contacted his office when they needed help. If justice had a possibility of ruling the day, Marshall was someone who had a real chance of making that happen.

Thurgood's reputation as a lawyer dedicated to social justice also resulted from cases he took that did not involve the life or death of the client. The issues confronting the African-American community covered a wide gamut of challenges that Marshall also battled. He understood the variety of devices employed to undermine African-American citizenship and looked to use the law to thwart them.

Prominent among these discriminatory gambits were roadblocks created to control housing options available to African Americans and to impede their ability to vote. These were issues of great concern to the NAACP, and Marshall played a major role in the efforts of the organization to have the courts block their implementation. Texas became a key battleground over the issue of voting. Politicians there sought to control who could vote in the Democratic primary, which effectively decided who would prevail in the Texas general election. Thurgood helped plan and execute the legal strategy, which brought the case *Smith v. Allwright* before the U.S. Supreme Court and convinced it to rule against Texas. Marshall saw this victory as one of the most important ones of his career. Its importance for him was captured in words of the *Norfolk Journal and Guide*, when it proclaimed that with the case the NAACP did, "more to translate the U.S. Constitution and laws of this country in their proper perspective for minorities than any other organization" (Williams, 1998, p. 112). The ruling reinforced Thurgood's belief that the legal system, when used effectively, could help reengineer how American society treated minority citizens.

Marshall's efforts in the realm of housing discrimination also proved reinforcing to his faith in the power of the legal system. The idea of restricting where individuals could purchase or rent housing had its early roots in Thurgood's hometown of Baltimore, Maryland. The concept spread and was refined in its use in other localities. The federal government even applied it in its creation of public housing, which it segregated. The application of the concept resulted in confining African-American living options to certain sectors of cities. These locations frequently became African-American enclaves characterized by overcrowding, poor sanitary conditions, and inflated costs. This was not solely a Southern issue but one evident in urban areas across the nation.

With Marshall in the lead, the NAACP used a unique legal approach to undermine housing discrimination contained in restrictive covenants written into mortgage contracts. While mortgages were private individual contracts not under the control of the government, the NAACP argued their enforcement was executed by the government. As a consequence, their application by government agencies violated due process under the Constitution and were thus unconstitutional. The U.S. Supreme Court justices unanimously agreed.

The case *Shelley v. Kramer* brought increased recognition to the NAACP and Marshall for the creative way in which the litigation was successfully presented and won. Charles Houston, who by then had left the NAACP and entered private practice, was part of the team crafting the strategy for the lawsuit. His involvement gave Thurgood the opportunity to work once again with his mentor and to reinforce Houston's expectations of the lawyers he had trained at Howard. Thurgood Marshall was becoming the epitome of the kind of attorney Houston had envisioned. His student was using the law to impact the treatment of African Americans through his work at the NAACP. Marshall accepted this mission despite the physical toll on him, as well as the financial sacrifice. The NAACP could only afford to pay him a salary substantially below what he might have made in private practice. In addition, the train and automobile trips to litigate cases around the country made for long and, at times, uncomfortable travel arrangements. For example, to get to Hugo, Oklahoma, to defend a man accused of murder, Marshall had to travel three days by train and six hours by bus. The Oklahoma trip was difficult but not an extraordinary travel itinerary for him. But Thurgood made the sacrifices necessary for the larger goal of fairer treatment of minorities.

He also was willing to risk the personal danger that came with his duties. Especially in the South, local officials and white residents did not appreciate Thurgood's efforts to thwart local discriminatory actions. Marshall regularly received threats against his life and took a risk each time he traveled, often unescorted, to cities and towns south of the Mason-Dixon line. The effort to intimidate or even stop him came from a variety of sources. Some of the threats came from public officials. The lawyer who Marshall outperformed during the trial told him if he ever came back again, he would have him killed. Or the intimidation attempts might come from angry local residents who resented an African-American "outsider" interfering in their judicial process. This was the case with the crowd gathered by the river in Tennessee who likely would have lynched Marshall had not his friends interfered.

It was not unusual for local residents to fear for Marshall's safety and to take measures to protect him. When Thurgood finally arrived in Hugo, Oklahoma, African-American residents immediately whisked him away and hid his location from local white officials. They had armed guards with him constantly and moved him regularly from location to location for his protection. Steps like these to protect him by African-American members of the community frequently occurred when Marshall arrived to try a case. Thurgood understood the potential for violence but came anyway. He also understood how important what he was doing was for the communities where he traveled. Marshall told his wife and others that the truly brave individuals were the people who had to remain in those communities after having dared to oppose local white officials. In his mind, they truly put their lives and their futures in danger by asking him to come and defend their rights in court. If they were willing to risk so much for fairer treatment, he was ready to support them through his efforts. His answering their many calls for help was part of what made Thurgood such an important figure within the African-American community.

Marshall's importance also lay in his recognition that changes in the racial mores of American society would not come without confrontation.

Thurgood did not condone violence and preferred to use his legal training as his weapon to create change. He believed the education he received at Lincoln and at Howard had equipped him to stand as an equal to the lawyers and public officials he confronted in the courtroom. He understood how valuable a good education was for him, and he sought to provide the same opportunity for African-American children. This was why while many cases he litigated and won were important in their own right, his ultimate goal was to undermine the system of segregation in the nation. Segregated school systems throughout the country became the focal point of that legal attack.

Thurgood's travels with Houston after graduating law school highlighted for him the terrible educational conditions for African-American children across the South. It also solidified for both men that a concerted legal attack on the segregated Southern educational system might provide the wedge to undermine segregation as a policy in various areas of American life. As a result, they sought to identify legal cases in the field of education that could help them achieve that goal. This decision ultimately led to the most significant legal victory for Marshall and the NAACP.

The Donald Murray case against the law school of the University of Maryland was a first step along that path. Its success reaffirmed their belief that the separate but equal edict of the *Plessy v. Ferguson* case of 1896 was vulnerable and could be overturned. The right litigants and the right legal circumstances were needed upon which to build their cases. The goal was to steadily construct a body of U.S. Supreme Court decisions that would result in ruling separate but equal as unconstitutional.

It is to the credit of Thurgood and his colleagues at the NAACP that they had the vision and determination to pursue this strategy. There were no precedents that could have predicted their success. Nor were there previous instances they could turn to that offered guidelines as to the best way to proceed. They knew the law, understood its possibilities, believed segregation was wrong, and hoped that judges who were sworn to protect the rights of all citizens could be persuaded to extend that protection to African Americans. But they had to proceed carefully and patiently if they had any possibility of success.

Patience and adherence to their ultimate goal of desegregation was not always easy. Thurgood faced resistance when he demanded the end of segregation rather than accepting separate and equal alternatives. Confronted by unequal options for decades, there were sectors of the African-American community who saw new equal facilities and opportunities as a victory worth accepting as a compromise. This alternative offered economic and educational opportunities many communities had only dreamed might be possible. They were hesitant to refuse them when offered in exchange for the hope that in the future the rewards might prove even better. Marshall was sympathetic to these worries and recognized what he was turning down when he pushed forward with his legal strategy.

What encouraged Thurgood were the victories he experienced as the strategy built momentum. The rulings in the Gaines case in Missouri, the Sipuel and McLaurin cases in Oklahoma, and the Sweatt case in Texas all indicated an evolving legal mood on the U.S. Supreme Court. At minimum, the justices indicated they expected adherence to the concept of separate but equal in the field of education. When the options offered by local officials fell short, the court insisted on the provision of access for the plaintiffs to existing segregated facilities. As a result, African-American applicants were allowed to attend previously segregated institutions. The hope was that the justices might even be convinced to rule "separate but equal" as unconstitutional.

Thurgood's system for making decisions also encouraged him to stay true to his strategy. Rather than rely solely upon his own perceptions, Thurgood used the experiences and instincts of others to guide him. Typically, Thurgood assembled a group of legal experts to discuss the next steps in their legal efforts. In the meetings he encouraged freewheeling discussions in which every idea was dissected and challenged by the participants. Out of that exchange, Marshall crafted what he believed was the most effective direction to proceed in next.

It was in such a meeting that the controversial idea of making sociological data an important part of the *Brown v. Board of Education* litigation against school segregation emerged. At first, many of the experts present thought the doll study conducted by Kenneth and Mamie Clarke would not impress the justices and might even hurt the case. But as the arguments unfolded, Marshall decided to use the material to heighten the court's understanding of the extent of the harm done to all children by segregation. Clark's work also offered another reason Thurgood would not settle for separate but equal options. That choice would not end segregation or the psychological harm it had on the individuals forced to operate in such a system. Such a compromise would prevent Marshall from attaining his ultimate goal, which, he described in later speeches, was to ensure every African-American child had the same access to a quality education as their white counterparts.

Thurgood's decision to argue for the end of segregation and to include its devastating psychological impact was rewarded by the court. As he hoped, the justices were prepared to reverse the *Plessy* decision and rule against segregation in educational facilities. New justices added to the court under the presidency of Franklin Roosevelt, and the appointment of a new chief justice, Earl Warren, created an environment in the court poised to acknowledge the citizenship rights of African Americans. The *Brown v. Board* ruling was a powerful reinforcement for Marshall of how using the courts and the law could improve the opportunities available to

African Americans. Careful planning and a clear vision of the intended goals could result in the social engineering preached by Charles Houston at Howard. The landmark *Brown* decision was proof.

The Brown ruling also served to further burnish the reputation of Thurgood Marshall. While the contributions of the NAACP legal team and other experts made the decision possible, Thurgood stood as the lead architect of the effort. The media saw him as the spokesman for the team and turned to him when seeking official reactions to the decision. Even before the *Brown* case, Thurgood had earned the reputation of "Mr. Civil Rights" for his tireless dedication to undermining what he called "the legacy of mistreatment," which was the law of the land in the wake of the 1896 *Plessy* U.S. Supreme Court decision. The success of the *Brown* case served to further enhance that title and to make him the most highly recognized African-American attorney in the United States.

At that time, Thurgood had argued and won more cases before the Supreme Court than any other African-American lawyer. Among lawyers in general, he also ranked high in terms of cases argued and won in that venue. While other lawyers often represented a variety of issues before the court, Marshall consistently focused on matters concerned with the civil rights of African Americans. That was the issue of greatest importance to him, and he crafted lawsuits intended to reorient the thinking of the U.S. Supreme Court with regard to those rights. His success in this endeavor was especially celebrated by African Americans and their allies concerned with civil rights.

The accolades directed toward Thurgood after the decision illustrated the high regard in which he was held. Howard University presented him with an honorary degree during which President Mordecai Johnson called him the greatest constitutional lawyer in history. At the NAACP annual convention in Texas, he was hailed as a hero, and speeches he gave across the country drew crowds of people. The *Baltimore Afro-American* gave Marshall the lion's share of the credit for the court victory while other African-American newspapers used the words "brilliant," "resourceful," and "dedicated" to describe him.

Organizations outside of the African-American community also acknowledged Thurgood's accomplishments. The Workman's Circle, the largest Jewish fraternal labor organization, awarded Marshall their human rights award. *Life* magazine, which had followed his career closely, described Thurgood as "the chief counsel for equality." *Time* magazine featured Marshall on its cover in September 1955. Consequently, Thurgood Marshall became a widely recognized national figure and a symbol of how unwavering dedication to a conviction could effect change.

It was his success as a lawyer with the NAACP that brought Thurgood to the attention of Presidents Kennedy and Johnson. Both men understood his iconic stature among African Americans and civil rights supporters for his unwavering championing of equal rights. If they wished to make a statement illustrating their support of African Americans and legislation backing improved civil rights, appointing Thurgood to a prominent position in their administrations was a logical decision to make. A judicial appointment for a prominent lawyer like Thurgood made the most sense. President Kennedy appointed Thurgood to the Second Circuit Court, but for Johnson, the U.S. Supreme Court was where he believed Marshall belonged.

The judicial appointments repositioned Marshall's role with regard to civil and human rights legal issues. As a judge, he no longer brought cases to the courts hoping to convince them to rule in his favor. His conversations now were with other fellow justices as they conferred. Sitting on the bench, he had more direct impact on the final rulings they offered. This was an opportunity Thurgood embraced wholeheartedly. As a federal judge, Thurgood remained a staunch champion of civil and human rights. He took seriously the part of the judicial oath that obligated them to "administer justice without respect to persons, and do equal right to the poor and to the rich." His record on the U.S. Supreme Court, in particular, reflected his commitment to this responsibility.

During his early years on the court, Thurgood felt welcomed and his opinions respected. The rulings of the court led by Chief Justice Earl Warren regularly sought to protect individual rights to ensure everyone received fair and equal treatment. Other justices found Thurgood's experiences as a civil rights lawyer instructive. He provided them with a better understanding of how poverty or race might impact the decisions rendered. In particular, he often successfully urged the court to rebuff discriminatory efforts to undermine school desegregation, voting rights, or access to housing. He also was with the majority on cases related to treatment of prisoners and the death penalty. His experiences with death cases in the past made him wary of its imposition. The death penalty ended any future options for the accused, while a life sentence allowed for the possible discovery of new information that might acquit the defendant or drastically reduce their sentence. For Marshall, the death penalty was cruel and inhumane punishment and more often unequally applied to the poor and African Americans.

Under Warren's administration, Thurgood had the opportunity to write majority opinions that permitted him to reinforce his belief that, properly interpreted, the Constitution was an instrument dedicated to ensuring equal treatment under the law. His hope was that the decisions of the Warren court were influencing the nation to embrace the importance of protecting the rights of individuals from discriminatory treatment by governmental institutions and officials. Its decisions were also making the legal issues to which he had dedicated himself for many years as an NAACP lawyer the law of the land.

Unfortunately, as Warren and other members of that cohort of justices retired, Thurgood found the ideals in which he believed increasingly under attack. More conservative justices gained seats on the court who preferred a strict interpretation of the Constitution and favored the rights of law enforcement above those of the individual. Finding himself increasingly in the minority, Thurgood searched for ways to champion the principles that had defined his public life. Crafting dissenting opinions became the platform he used to accomplish this goal. He wrote twenty or more of them each year during the latter stages of his time on the court. He wrote his dissents with the belief that while they represented a minority opinion at the time, they might provide grounds for the court to change directions in the future. He had seen interpretations of the Constitution altered in the past and hoped his words might influence adjustments in the future.

Thurgood also used his public speeches as opportunities to describe his principles in contrast to his fellow justices with whom he strongly disagreed. In those presentations he spelled out his beliefs about the proper interpretation of the Constitution and the importance of ensuring equal access to the benefits of citizenship for all residents of the nation.

For Thurgood Marshall, the Constitution, as originally crafted, was flawed. Proof of that fact lay in the need to add amendments over the years, three of which specifically redefined the status of African Americans. Consequently, the task of the U.S. Supreme Court was to take the spirit of that document and interpret it in the eyes of the present, not the past. It was a living document, not one irrevocably tied to its origins. That was why the descendants of enslaved Africans who were not among the "We the People" included in the original document were now citizens.

For Thurgood Marshall, the phrase "We the People" applied to all citizens and compelled the courts to ensure that everyone was justly and fairly treated. He had dedicated his career to that principle, and he refused to stop defending it despite his minority status on the court during his last years of service. He began his career seeking fair and equal treatment for African Americans and adhered to that goal throughout his time at the NAACP. As a judge, he broadened this concern to include women, the poor, and others improperly treated by society.

For Marshall, the goal in the 1990s was the same as it was in 1939. In an essay he wrote for the NAACP publication *The Crisis*, he gave it the title "Equal Justice under the Law" and declared that his goal was to strengthen the principles of democracy and "build a body of public opinion in which rights and privileges of citizenship may be enjoyed and in which more brazen as well as more sophisticated attempts at deprivation may be halted" (Tushnet, 2001, p. 77). This was the unwavering ideal, which energized Thurgood Marshall and earned him the title of "Mr. Civil Rights" and what distinguished him as a federal judge. Thurgood Marshall proudly carried that burden and reputation, and it is what made him and his contributions so enduring and meaningful.

Timeline

1895
Charles Hamilton Houston born.

1896
Plessy v. Ferguson Supreme Court decision (Separate but Equal rule).

1908
Springfield Race Riot is first major race riot in a Northern city in fifty years.

1908
Thoroughgood Marshall is born on July 2 to Norma and William Marshall in Baltimore, Maryland.

1909
National Association for the Advancement of Colored People (NAACP) founded.

1910
National Urban League founded.

Baltimore City Council approves one of the first in the national residential segregation ordinances.

1914
Start of World War I.

1915
Beginning of the Great Migration of African Americans from the South to the North in search of better opportunities.

1916
Thoroughgood Marshall shortens his first name to Thurgood.

James Weldon Johnson becomes head of NAACP (the first African American to hold that position).

1917

The United States enters World War I.

Buchanan v. Warley: Supreme Court overrules use of restrictive covenant in Louisville, Kentucky.

1925

Alain LeRoy Locke is given the title of "Father of the Harlem Renaissance" for his publication of the book *The New Negro*.

Founding of National Bar Association for African-American lawyers (in Iowa).

Ossian Sweet arrested in Detroit for murder when attacked for moving into a white neighborhood.

Marshall graduates from Douglass High School in Baltimore at age sixteen.

Marshall enters Lincoln University in Pennsylvania.

1926

Mordecai Johnson named first African-American president of Howard University.

1929

Marshall marries University of Pennsylvania student Vivian "Buster" Burrey.

1930

Marshall graduates with honors from Lincoln University (cum laude).

Charles Hamilton Houston joins Howard Law School.

1931

Walter White named head of NAACP.

Arrest and trial of the Scottsboro Boys.

1933

Marshall receives his law degree from Howard University (magna cum laude), begins private practice in Baltimore.

Nathan Margold delivers his report to NAACP with a strategy to improve the civil rights of African Americans.

Thurgood Marshall investigates African-American Southern schools with Houston.

1934

Marshall works for NAACP in Baltimore.

W.E.B. Du Bois resigns from NAACP.

Second Southern school research trip with Houston.

1935

Charles Houston joins NAACP as special counsel.

Marshall, working with Charles Houston, wins first major civil rights case, *Murray v. Pearson*. Maryland Supreme Court rules against segregation at the University of Maryland Law School.

Norris v. Alabama case: Supreme Court rules the systematic exclusion of African Americans from the jury unconstitutional.

National Council of Negro Women formed.

1936

Marshall becomes assistant special counsel for NAACP in New York.

1937

William Hastie named first black federal court judge.

1938

Missouri ex rel. Gaines v. Canada: Supreme Court rules that a state with a single law school could not discriminate on the basis of race.

Marshall becomes chief counsel for NAACP, replacing Houston, who resigns.

1939

Jane M. Bolin named first African-American female judge in the United States.

1940

Marshall is named first director counsel of NAACP Legal Defense Fund.

Chambers v. Florida reversed the conviction of four black men accused of murder on grounds that excessive police pressure and coercion rendered their confessions inadmissible.

1941

President Roosevelt issues Executive Order 8802, which desegregates war production plants and creates the Fair Employment Practices Committee (FEPC).

Pearl Harbor is bombed by the Japanese, and the United States enters World War II.

1942

Congress of Racial Equality founded in Chicago.

1943

The first class of Tuskegee airmen are trained and fly combat missions.

Marshall investigates Detroit race riot and writes a report critical of Detroit officials.

1944

Smith v. Allwright overthrows the use of the "white primary" as a device to exclude African-American voters.

Gunnar Myrdal publishes *An American Dilemma: The Negro Problem in Modern Democracy.*

1946

Morgan v. Virginia: Supreme Court bars segregation in interstate bus transportation.

1947

Jackie Robinson joins the Brooklyn Dodgers and desegregates major league baseball.

1948

Shelley v. Kraemer: Supreme Court strikes down legality of racial restrictive covenants.

President Harry Truman desegregates the armed forces.

1950

Marshall and NAACP win Supreme Court victories in two graduate-school integration cases, *Sweatt v. Painter* and *McLaurin v. Oklahoma State Regents.*

1951

Marshall visits South Korea and Japan to investigate charges of racism in U.S. armed forces. He reported that the general practice was one of "rigid segregation."

1954

Brown v. Board of Education of Topeka, Kansas is a landmark case; Supreme Court rules against the *Plessy v. Ferguson* concept of "separate but equal."

1955

Emmett Till is murdered in Mississippi.

Vivian "Buster" Marshall dies.

Marshall marries Cecelia "Cissy" Suyat Marshall.

Montgomery, Alabama, Bus boycott.

Supreme Court *Brown II* court ruling, spelling out more information about the court's instructions for the school desegregation process.

1956

Son Thurgood Marshall Jr. born.

1957

Civil Rights Act 1957.

1958
Southern Christian Leadership Conference formed with Martin Luther King Jr. as leader.

1959
Son John W. Marshall born.

1960
Marshall travels to Africa and then to London to assist with creation of the Kenya Constitution; Greensboro, North Carolina, Woolworth's sit-ins.
Civil Rights Act 1960.

1961
Garner v. Louisiana: Supreme Court rules that peaceful sit-in demonstrators protesting segregation cannot be arrested under a state's "disturbing the peace" laws.
Marshall is nominated to Second Court of Appeals by President John F. Kennedy.
Freedom Rides begin.

1963
Marshall is appointed as a judge to the Second Court of Appeals.
Birmingham, Alabama, civil rights marches.
Martin Luther King Jr.'s Letter from a Birmingham Jail.
March on Washington.
Sixteenth Street Baptist Street bombing in Birmingham, Alabama.
John F. Kennedy is assassinated.

1964
Student Nonviolent Coordinating Committee founded.
Civil Rights Act 1964.

1965
Marshall appointed U.S. Solicitor General by President Lyndon Johnson.
Voting Rights Act 1965.

1966
Robert Weaver named head of Department of Housing and Urban Development, first black cabinet member.
Constance B. Motley becomes first female African-American federal judge.

1967
Marshall becomes first African-American Supreme Court justice.

1968
Martin Luther King Jr. assassinated.

1971
Supreme Court guarantees abortion rights in landmark *Roe v. Wade* case.

1978
Supreme Court bars quota systems in college admissions in *Regents of the University of California v. Bakke.*

1991
Marshall retires as associate justice of U.S. Supreme Court.

1993
Marshall succumbs to heart failure at age eighty-four.

PRIMARY DOCUMENTS

University of Maryland v. Donald G. Murray

Donald Gaines Murray initially applied to the University of Maryland School of Law in 1935 and was denied admission because of his race. Represented by Thurgood Marshall, Charles H. Houston, and William I. Gosnell, he sued the university for admittance. After losing the case in the lower courts, the University of Maryland lawyers appealed to the Maryland Court of Appeals where they lost once again. This was one of the first cases won by Marshall contesting segregation.

In the Court of Appeals of Maryland
October Term, 1935
General Docket No. 53.

Raymond A. Pearson, President, W. M. Hillegeist, Registrar, and George M. Shriver, John M. Dennis, William P. Cole, Henry Holzapfel, John E. Raine, Dr. W. W. Skinner, Mrs. John L. Whitehurst and J. Milton Patterson, Members of the Board of Regents of the University of Maryland,
vs.
Donald G. Murray, Otherwise Donald Gaines Murray.

Thurgood Marshall,
Charles H. Houston,
William I. Gosnell,
    Attorneys for Appellee

Appellee's Brief

Statement of the Nature of the Case.
This is an appeal by Raymond A. Pearson, President of the University of Maryland; W. M. Hillegeist, Registrar of the Baltimore Schools of the University, and George M. Shriver et al., constituting the Board of Regents of the University, from an order of the Baltimore City Court entered the 25th day of June, 1935, granting a Writ of Mandamus, and ordering the above named appellants to admit Donald G. Murray, appellee, as a first year student in the Day School of the School of Law of the University of Maryland for the academic year beginning September 25, 1935, upon his paying the necessary fee charged first year students in the Day School of the School of Law of the University of Maryland, and completing his registration in the manner required of qualified and accepted students in the first year class

of the Day School of the School of Law of the University of Maryland, to wit, that he be not excluded on the ground of race or color (R. 41–42).

The trial Court rendered no formal opinion.

Questions for Decision.
Question No. 1.
Whether the refusal of the appellants to admit appellee, a qualified student, to the first year class of the day school of the School of Law of the University of Maryland solely on account of his race or color was in violation of the Constitution and laws of the State of Maryland.

The trial court held that appellants had violated the Constitution and laws of the State of Maryland in refusing to admit appellee to the School of Law of the University of Maryland solely on account of his race or color.

Appellee contends that there is no statutory authority for excluding him from the School of Law of the University of Maryland solely on account of his race or color; that in the absence of statutory authority the attempted administrative regulation by the executive officers and agents of the University of Maryland and by the Board of Regents excluding appellee from the School of Law of the University of Maryland solely on account of his race or color is void; and that appellants having conceded of record that appellee was qualified from an educational standpoint to be admitted into the Day School of the School of Law of the University of Maryland (R. 44), and basing their refusal to admit him solely on account of his race or color (R. 18–22), the trial court was correct in issuing the writ of mandamus herein.

Question No. 2.
Whether appellants' attempt to exclude appellee, a qualified student, from the day school of the School of Law of the University of Maryland solely on account of race or color was a denial to him of the equal protection of the laws within the meaning of the Fourteenth Amendment to the Constitution of the United States.

The trial court held that appellants could not exclude appellee from the School of Law of the University of Maryland solely on account of his race or color.

Appellee contends that the acts of the executive officers and agents of the University of Maryland, and the Board of Regents, in attempting to exclude appellee, a qualified student, from the School of Law of the University of Maryland was state action within the meaning of the Fourteenth Amendment to the Constitution of the United States; that the State of Maryland having established a state university supported in part from public funds and under public control, appellee, if otherwise qualified, could not be excluded therefrom solely on account of his race or color; that the State of Maryland has provided appellee no equivalent in opportunities for legal education equal to the opportunities and advantages offered him in the School of Law of the University of Maryland; and that the attempt by appellants to exclude him from the School of Law of the University of Maryland solely on account of his race or color in the absence of equal opportunities and advantages in legal education otherwise furnished him by the State of Maryland is a denial to him of the equal protection of the laws within the meaning of the Fourteenth Amendment to the Constitution of the United States.

Statement of Facts.
Appellee, Donald G. Murray, a Negro citizen of the State of Maryland and a resident of the City of Baltimore, on January 24, 1935, made application in due form for admission as a first year student in the Day School of the School of Law of the University of Maryland (R. 6, 18). His application was rejected by the appellant President of the University and the appellant Registrar solely on account of his race (R. 30–32). He appealed from this ruling to the appellants, the Board of Regents of the University (R. 32–33), who ratified the rejection (R. 60–61).

Murray is a graduate of Amherst College with the degree of Bachelor of Arts conferred upon him in 1934 after successful completion of a four-year residence course (R. 6). Appellants stipulated that he was educationally qualified to enter the Day School of the School of Law of the University of Maryland (R. 44).

The University of Maryland is an administrative department of the State of Maryland, performing an essential governmental function and supported in part out of funds derived from taxes collected from the citizens of the State (R. 4, 17). The powers of governing the University are by law vested in the Board of Regents; the President and Registrar of the University act as agents of the Board. The charter of the University provides that it shall be maintained "upon the most liberal plan, for the benefit of students of every country and every foreign denomination" (R. 4).

Under its charter the University conducts in the City of Baltimore a School of Law as an integral component part of the University. The School operates in two divisions: a day school and an evening school, having the same entrance requirements, to wit, the completion of at least one-half of the work acceptable for a Bachelor's degree granted on the basis of a four-year period of study by the University of Maryland or a principal college or university in the State (R. 5). The School of Law of the University of Maryland is the only State institution which affords a legal education to Maryland citizens, and is the only law school in Maryland approved by the American Bar Association and a member of the Association of American Law Schools (R. 5, 18, 54).

All racial groups except Negroes, if otherwise qualified, are admitted to the University. Resident Negro citizens are excluded; non-resident whites, Filipinos, Indians, Mexicans, Chinese, et al., are admitted (R. 54–59).

When Murray applied for admission to the School of Law he was advised that the University of Maryland did not accept Negro students except at Princess Anne Academy, the so-called Eastern Branch of the University of Maryland (R. 30–32). No instruction in law is offered at Princess Anne Academy (R. 47). Murray was further referred to Chapter 34 of the Acts of 1933 which purported to create scholarships for Negro students who desired to take professional courses or other work not given at Princess Anne Academy (R. 21, 31). No money was ever appropriated or allocated for scholarships under said Act of 1933, nor was any scholarship under it ever awarded (R. 62–65).

Ten thousand dollars were appropriated for Negro scholarships under Chapter 577 of the Acts of 1935, approved April 29, 1935 (R. 20, 109). The administration of the Act was placed in the hands of a specially created Maryland Commission of Higher Education of Negroes. The administrative interpretation of the Act was that the scholarships provided covered tuition only (R. 112); and there were so many applications for scholarships that the Commission was not in position to satisfy all qualified applicants (R. 110–111).

Murray does not want an out-of-state scholarship (R. 48). He desires to attend the School of Law of the University of Maryland in Baltimore where he is at home and room and board cost him nothing (R. 45, 50). The nearest out-of-state law school with a general standing comparable to that of the School of Law of the University of Maryland, which he could attend, is the Howard University School of Law in Washington, D.C. To attend this School Murray would be put to the expense of commuting daily from Baltimore to Washington and return, with attendant loss of time; or of paying for room and board in Washington (R. 49–50).

Murray further desires to attend the School of Law of the University of Maryland for professional advantages. He is preparing himself to practice law in Baltimore, and attending law school in Baltimore would give him the opportunity to observe Maryland courts and to become acquainted with other Maryland practitioners (R. 45). Ninety-five percent of the enrollment in the School of Law of the University of Maryland comes from the State of Maryland (R. 84), and the School of Law lays emphasis on Maryland law (R. 85). A majority of its faculty is made up of judges and practicing attorneys of Maryland (R. 85).

Finally Murray desires to attend the School of Law of the University of Maryland in exercise of his rights as a citizen to share equally the advantages offered by a public tax supported state university (R. 45).

Murray renewed the tender of his application and examination fee in open Court (R. 87), and submitted himself to be fully able to meet all legitimate demands of the School of Law of the University of Maryland (R. 46). The tender was refused (R. 87).

Source: *Murray v. Pearson*, 169 Md. 478, 182 A. 590 (1936).

Thurgood Marshall's 1953 Oral Argument before the Supreme Court on Behalf of *Brown v. Board of Education*

As one of the lead attorneys in the groundbreaking Supreme Court case of Brown v. Board of Education, *Thurgood Marshall delivered the oral argument. In it, he argues against the legality of segregation and unequal treatment. Marshall presents a powerful statement against the decades-long Supreme Court endorsement of the concept of "separate but equal."*

IT FOLLOWS THAT with education, this Court has made segregation and inequality equivalent concepts. They have equal rating, equal footing, and if segregation thus necessarily imports inequality, it makes no great difference whether we say that the Negro is wronged because he is segregated, or that he is wronged because he received unequal treatment . . . .

I would like to say that each lawyer on the other side has made it clear as to what the position of the state was on this, and it would be all right possibly but for the fact that this is so crucial. There is no way you can repay lost school years.

These children in these cases are guaranteed by the states some twelve years of education in varying degrees, and this idea, if I understand it, to leave it to the states until they work it out—and I think that is a most ingenious argument—you leave it to the states, they say, and then they say that the states haven't done anything about it in a hundred years, so for that reason this Court doesn't touch it.

The argument of judicial restraint has no application in this case. There is a relationship between federal and state, but there is no corollary or relationship as to the Fourteenth Amendment.

The duty of enforcing, the duty of following the Fourteenth Amendment, is placed upon the states. The duty of enforcing the Fourteenth Amendment is placed upon this Court, and the argument that they make over and over again to my mind is the same type of argument they charge us with making, the same argument Charles Sumner made. Possibly so.

And we hereby charge them with making the same argument that was made before the Civil War, the same argument that was made during the period between the ratification of the Fourteenth Amendment and the *Plessy v. Ferguson* case.

And I think it makes no progress for us to find out who made what argument. It is our position that whether or not you base this case solely on the Intent of Congress or whether you base it on the logical extension of the doctrine as set forth in the McLaurin case, on either basis the same conclusion is required, which is that this Court makes it clear to all of these states that in administering their governmental functions, at least those that are vital not to the life of the state alone, not to the country alone, but vital to the world in general, that little pet feelings of race, little pet feelings of custom—I got the feeling on hearing the discussion yesterday that when you put a white child in a school with a whole lot of colored children, the child would fall apart or something. Everybody knows that is not true.

Those same kids in Virginia and South Carolina—and I have seen them do it—they play in the streets together, they play on their farms together, they go down the road together, they separate to go to school, they come out of school and play ball together. They have to be separated in school.

There is some magic to it. You can have them voting together, you can have them not restricted because of law in the houses they live in. You can have them going to the same state university and the same college, but if they go to elementary and high school, the world will fall apart. And it is the exact same argument that has been made to this Court over and over again, and we submit that when they charge us with making a legislative argument, it is in truth they who are making the legislative argument.

They can't take race out of this case. From the day this case was filed until this moment, nobody has in any form or fashion, despite the fact I made it clear in the opening argument that I was relying on it, done anything to distinguish this statute from the Black Codes, which they must admit, because nobody can dispute, say anything anybody wants to say, one way or the other, the Fourteenth Amendment was intended to deprive the states of power to enforce Black Codes or anything else like it.

We charge that they are Black Codes. They obviously are Black Codes if you read them. They haven't denied that they are Black Codes, so if the Court wants to very narrowly decide this case, they can decide it on that point.

So whichever way it is done, the only way that this Court can decide this case in opposition to our position, is that there must be some reason which gives the state the right to make a classification that they can make in regard to nothing else in regard to Negroes, and we submit the only way to arrive at that decision is to find that for some reason Negroes are inferior to all other human beings.

Nobody will stand in the Court and urge that, and in order to arrive at the decision that they want us to arrive at, there would have to be some recognition of a reason why of all of the multitudinous groups of people in this country you have to single out Negroes and give them this separate treatment.

It can't be because of slavery in the past, because there are very few groups in this country that haven't had slavery some place back in history of their groups. It can't be color because there are Negroes as white as the drifted snow, with blue eyes, and they are just as segregated as the colored man.

The only thing can be is an inherent determination that the people who were formerly in slavery, regardless of anything else, shall be kept as near that stage as is possible, and now is the time, we submit, that this Court should make it clear that that is not what our Constitution stands for.

Thank you, sir.

Source: Marshall, Thurgood. "Argument before the U.S. Supreme Court." *Brown v. Board of Education of Topeka*, 347 U.S. 483 (1954).

United States v. Kras (1973)

In this case in which Robert Kras, because of poverty, asks for relief from paying court fees to file for bankruptcy, Marshall dissents from the court's ruling against Kras. A strong defender of the rights of the poor, Marshall criticizes his fellow justices for their lack of understanding and compassion for the plight of the impoverished. This is one of Marshall's most forceful dissents as a Supreme Court justice.

MR. JUSTICE MARSHALL, dissenting.

The dissent of MR. JUSTICE STEWART, in which I have joined, makes clear the majority's failure to distinguish this case from Boddie v. Connecticut, 401 U.S. 371 (1971). I add only some comments on the extraordinary route by which the majority reaches its conclusion.

A. The majority notes that the minimum amount that appellee Kras must pay each week if he is permitted to pay the filing fees in installments is only $1.28. It says that "this much available revenue should be within his able-bodied reach." Ante, at 449.

Appellee submitted an affidavit in which he claimed that he was "unable to pay or promise to pay the filing fees, even in small installments." App. 5. This claim was supported by detailed statements of his financial condition. [409 U.S. 434, 459] The affidavit was unchallenged below, but the majority does challenge it. The District Judge properly accepted the factual allegations as true. See, e.g., Poller v. Columbia Broadcasting System, 368 U.S.

464 (1962); First National Bank of Arizona v. Cities Service Co., 391 U.S. 253 (1968); 35B C. J. S., Federal Civil Procedure 1197 n. 4 (1960). The majority seems to believe that it is not restrained by the traditional notion that judges must accept unchallenged, credible affidavits as true, for it disregards the factual allegations and the inferences that necessarily follow from them. I cannot treat that notion so cavalierly.[1]

Even if Kras' statement that he was unable to pay the fees was an honest mistake, surely he cannot have been mistaken in saying that he could not promise to pay the fees. The majority does not directly impugn his good faith in making that statement. Yet if he cannot promise to pay the fees, he cannot get the interim relief from creditor harassment that, the majority says, may enable him to pay the fees.

But beyond all this, I cannot agree with the majority that it is so easy for the desperately poor to save $1.92 each week over the course of six months. The 1970 Census found that over 800,000 families in the Nation had annual incomes of less than $1,000 or $19.23 a week. U.S. Bureau of Census, Current Population Reports, series P-60, No. 80; U.S. Bureau of Census, Statistical [409 U.S. 434, 460]. Abstract of the United States 1972, p. 323. I see no reason to require that families in such straits sacrifice over 5% of their annual income as a prerequisite to getting a discharge in bankruptcy.[2]

It may be easy for some people to think that weekly savings of less than $2 are no burden. But no one who has had close contact with poor people can fail to understand how close to the margin of survival many of them are. A sudden illness, for example, may destroy whatever savings they may have accumulated, and by eliminating a sense of security may destroy the

---

1. The majority also misrepresents appellee's financial condition. It says that $1.28 "is a sum less than the payments Kras makes on his couch of negligible value in storage." Ante, at 449. Nowhere in the slender record of this case can I find any statement that appellee is actually paying anything for the storage of the couch. He said only that he "owed payments of $6 per month" for storage. App. 5 (emphasis added). He also stated that he owed $6,428.69, but I would hardly read that to mean that he was paying that much to anyone.

2. The majority, in citing the "record of achievement" of the bankruptcy system in terminating 107,481 no-asset cases in the fiscal year 1969, ante, at 448 n. 7, relies on spectral evidence. Because the filing fees bar relief through the bankruptcy system, statistics showing how many people got relief through that system are unenlightening on the question of how many people could not use the system because they were too poor. I do not know how many people cannot afford to pay a $50 fee in installments. But I find nothing in the majority's opinion to convince me that due process is afforded a person who cannot receive a discharge in bankruptcy because he is too poor. Even if only one person is affected by the filing fees, he is denied due process.

incentive to save in the future. A pack or two of cigarettes may be, for them, not a routine purchase but a luxury indulged in only rarely. The desperately poor almost never go to see a movie, which the majority seems to believe is an almost weekly activity. They have more important things to do with what little money they have—like attempting to provide some comforts for a gravely ill child, as Kras must do.

It is perfectly proper for judges to disagree about what the Constitution requires. But it is disgraceful for an interpretation of the Constitution to be premised upon unfounded assumptions about how people live.

B. The majority derives some solace from the denial of certiorari in In re Garland, 402 U.S. 966 (1971). Reliance [409 U.S. 434, 461] on denial of certiorari for any proposition impairs the vitality of the discretion we exercise in controlling the cases we hear. See Brown v. Allen, 344 U.S. 443, 491–492 (1953) (opinion of Frankfurter, J.). For all that the legal community knows, Mr. Justice Harlan did not join the dissent from denial of certiorari in that case for reasons different from those that the majority uses to distinguish this case from Boddie. Perhaps he believed that lower courts should have some time to consider the implications of Boddie. Most of the lower courts have refused to follow the First Circuit's decision in Garland, 428 F.2d 1185. See ante, at 453 n. 5 (STEWART, J., dissenting). Perhaps he thought that the record in that case made inappropriate any attempt to determine the scope of Boddie in that particular case. Or perhaps he had some other reason.

The point of our use of a discretionary writ is precisely to prohibit that kind of speculation. When we deny certiorari, no one, not even ourselves, should think that the denial indicates a view on the merits of the case. It ill serves judges of the courts throughout the country to tell them, as the majority does today, that in attempting to determine what the law is, they must read, not only the opinions of this Court, but also the thousands of cases in which we annually deny certiorari.[3]

C. The majority says that "[t]he denial of access to the judicial forum in Boddie touched directly . . . on the marital relationship." It sees "no fundamental interest [409 U.S. 434, 462] that is gained or lost depending on the availability of a discharge in bankruptcy." Ante, at 444, 445. If the case is to turn on distinctions between the role of courts in divorce cases and

---

3. That one of us undertook to write a dissent, even a "pointed dissent," from the denial of certiorari should suggest, again, nothing at all about the views of any other Members of the Court on the merits of the petition. Surely each of us has seen many cases in which a colleague's dissent from the denial of certiorari pointed to an issue of great concern that we thought should be decided by this Court, but in which we did not join because we did not consider the case to be an appropriate vehicle for determination of that issue.

their role in bankruptcy cases,[4] I agree with MR. JUSTICE STEWART that this case and Boddie cannot be distinguished; the role of the Government in standing ready to enforce an otherwise continuing obligation is the same.

However, I would go further than MR. JUSTICE STEWART. I view the case as involving the right of access to the courts, the opportunity to be heard when one claims a legal right, and not just the right to a discharge in bankruptcy.[5] When a person raises a claim of right or entitlement under the laws, the only forum in our legal system empowered to determine that claim is a court. [409 U.S. 434, 463] Kras, for example, claims that he has a right under the Bankruptcy Act to be free of any duty to pay his creditors. There is no way to determine whether he has such a right except by adjudicating his claim.[6] Failure to do so denies him access to the courts.

The legal system is, of course, not so pervasive as to preclude private resolution of disputes. But private settlements do not determine the validity of claims of right. Such questions can be authoritatively resolved only in courts. It is in that sense, I believe, that we should consider the emphasis in Boddie on the exclusiveness of the judicial forum—and give Kras his day in court.

Source: *United States v. Kras*, 409 U.S. 434 (1973).

---

4. I am intrigued by the majority's suggestion that, because the granting of a divorce impinges on "associational interests," the right to a divorce is constitutionally protected. Are we to require that state divorce laws serve compelling state interests? For example, if a State chooses to allow divorces only when one party is shown to have committed adultery, must its refusal to allow them when the parties claim irreconcilable differences be justified by some compelling state interest? I raise these questions only to suggest that the majority's focus on the relative importance in the constitutional scheme of divorce and bankruptcy is misplaced. What is involved is the importance of access to the courts, either to remove an obligation that other branches of the government stand ready to enforce, as MR. JUSTICE STEWART sees it, or to determine claims of right, as I see it.

5. The majority suggests that no such right is involved, because Congress could have committed the administration of the Bankruptcy Act to a nonjudicial agency. Ante, at 447. I have some doubt about the proposition that a statutorily created right can be finally determined by an agency, with no method for a disappointed claimant to secure judicial review. But I have no doubt that Congress could not provide that only the well-off had the right to present their claims to the agency. As should be clear, the question is one of access to the forum empowered to determine the claim of right; it is only shorthand to call this a question of access to the courts.

6. It might be said that the right he claims does not come into play until he has fulfilled a condition precedent by paying the filing fees. But the distinction between procedure and substance is not unknown in the law and can be drawn on to counter that argument. [409 U.S. 434, 464]

Reflections on the Bicentennial of the United States Constitution

Thurgood Marshall gave this speech in Hawaii at the annual seminar of the San Francisco Patent and Trademark Law Association. In it, he highlights the shortcomings of the founding fathers, who created a defective document that condoned slavery and excluded rights for women. It took years of struggle to correct these shortcomings through the addition of amendments and new legislation. Marshall offers this view, in part, as a criticism of jurists who believed in a strict interpretation of the Constitution based upon the original intentions of the founding fathers.

The year 1987 marks the 200th anniversary of the United States Constitution. A Commission has been established to coordinate the celebration. The official meetings, essay contests, and festivities have begun.

The planned commemoration will span three years, and I am told 1987 is "dedicated to the memory of the Founders and the document they drafted in Philadelphia." We are to "recall the achievements of our Founders and the knowledge and experience that inspired them, the nature of the government they established, its origins, its character, and its ends, and the rights and privileges of citizenship, as well as its attendant responsibilities."

Like many anniversary celebrations, the plan for 1987 takes particular events and holds them up as the source of all the very best that has followed. Patriotic feelings will surely swell, prompting proud proclamations of the wisdom, foresight, and sense of justice shared by the framers and reflected in a written document now yellowed with age. This is unfortunate—not the patriotism itself, but the tendency for the celebration to oversimplify, and overlook the many other events that have been instrumental to our achievements as a nation. The focus of this celebration invites a complacent belief that the vision of those who debated and compromised in Philadelphia yielded the "more perfect Union" it is said we now enjoy.

I cannot accept this invitation, for I do not believe that the meaning of the Constitution was forever "fixed" at the Philadelphia Convention. Nor do I find the wisdom, foresight, and sense of justice exhibited by the framers particularly profound. To the contrary, the government they devised was defective from the start, requiring several amendments, a civil war, and momentous social transformation to attain the system of constitutional government, and its respect for the individual freedoms and human rights, that we hold as fundamental today. When contemporary Americans cite "The Constitution," they invoke a concept that is vastly different from what the framers barely began to construct two centuries ago.

For a sense of the evolving nature of the Constitution we need look no further than the first three words of the document's preamble: "We the People." When the Founding Fathers used this phrase in 1787, they did not have in mind the majority of America's citizens. "We the People" included, in the words of the framers, "the whole Number of free Persons." On a matter so basic as the right to vote, for example, Negro slaves were excluded, although they were counted for representational purposes—at three-fifths each. Women did not gain the right to vote for over a hundred and thirty years.

These omissions were intentional. The record of the framers' debates on the slave question is especially clear: the Southern states acceded to the demands of the New England states for giving Congress broad power to regulate commerce, in exchange for the right to continue the slave trade. The economic interests of the regions coalesced: New Englanders engaged in the "carrying trade" would profit from transporting slaves from Africa as well as goods produced in America by slave labor. The perpetuation of slavery ensured the primary source of wealth in the Southern states.

Despite this clear understanding of the role slavery would play in the new republic, use of the words "slaves" and "slavery" was carefully avoided in the original document. Political representation in the lower House of Congress was to be based on the population of "free Persons" in each state, plus three-fifths of all "other Persons." Moral principles against slavery, for those who had them, were compromised, with no explanation of the conflicting principles for which the American Revolutionary War had ostensibly been fought: the self-evident truths "that all men are created equal, that they are endowed by their Creator with certain unalienable Rights, that among these are Life, Liberty and the pursuit of Happiness."

It was not the first such compromise. Even these ringing phrases from the Declaration of Independence are filled with irony, for an early draft of what became that declaration assailed the King of England for suppressing legislative attempts to end the slave trade and for encouraging slave rebellions. The final draft adopted in 1776 did not contain this criticism. And so again at the Constitutional Convention eloquent objections to the institution of slavery went unheeded, and its opponents eventually consented to a document which laid a foundation for the tragic events that were to follow.

Pennsylvania's Governor Morris provides an example. He opposed slavery and the counting of slaves in determining the basis for representation in Congress. At the Convention he objected that—

the inhabitant of Georgia [or] South Carolina who goes to the coast of Africa, and in defiance of the most sacred laws of humanity tears away his fellow creatures from their dearest connections and damns them to the most cruel bondages, shall have more votes in a Government instituted for protection of the rights of mankind, than the Citizen of Pennsylvania or New Jersey who views with a laudable horror, so nefarious a practice.

And yet Governor Morris eventually accepted the three-fifths accommodation. In fact, he wrote the final draft of the Constitution, the very document the bicentennial will commemorate.

As a result of compromise, the right of the Southern states to continue importing slaves was extended, officially, at least until 1808. We know that it actually lasted a good deal longer, as the farmers possessed no monopoly on the ability to trade moral principles for self-interest. But they nevertheless set an unfortunate example. Slaves could be imported, if the commercial interests of the North were protected. To make the compromise even more palatable, customs duties would never be imposed at up to ten dollars per slave as a means of raising public revenues.

No doubt it will be said, when the unpleasant truth of the history of slavery in America is mentioned during this bicentennial year, that the Constitution was a product of its times, and embodied a compromise which, under other circumstances, would not have been made. But the effects of the framers' compromise have remained for generations. They arose from the contradiction between guaranteeing liberty and justice to all, and denying both to Negroes.

The original intent of the phrase, "We the People," was far too clear for any ameliorating construction. Writing for the Supreme Court in 1857, Chief Justice Taney penned the following passage in the *Dred Scott* case, on the issue of whether, in the eyes of the framers, slaves were "constituent members of the sovereignty," and were to be included among "We the People":

We think they are not, and that they are not included, and were not intended to be included . . . .

They had for more than a century before been regarded as beings of an inferior order, and altogether unfit to associate with the white race . . . ; and so far inferior, that they had no rights which the white man was bound to respect; and that the negro might justly and lawfully be reduced to slavery for his benefit . . . .

Accordingly, a Negro of the African race was regarded . . . as an article of property, and held, and bought and sold as such . . . . No one seems to have doubted the correctness of the prevailing opinion of the time.

And so, nearly seven decades after the Constitutional Convention, the Supreme Court reaffirmed the prevailing opinion of the framers regarding the rights of Negroes in America. It took a bloody civil war before the thirteenth amendment could be adopted to abolish slavery, though not the consequences slavery would have for future Americans.

While the Union survived the civil war, the Constitution did not. In its place arouse a new, more promising basis for justice and equality, the

fourteenth amendment, ensuring protection of the life, liberty, and property of all persons against deprivations without due process, and guaranteeing equal protection of the laws. And yet almost another century would
pass before any significant recognition was obtained of the rights of black
Americans to share equally even in such basic opportunities as education,
housing, and employment, and to have their votes counted, and counted
equally. In the meantime, blacks joined America's military to fight its wars
and invested untold hours working in its factories and on its farms, contributing to the development of this country's magnificent wealth and
waiting to share in its prosperity.

What is striking is the role legal principles have played throughout
America's history in determining the condition of Negroes. They were
enslaved by law, emancipated by law, disenfranchised. And segregated by
law; and, finally, they have begun to win equality by law. Along the way,
new constitutional principles have emerged to meet the challenges of a
changing society. The progress has been dramatic, and it will continue.

The men who gathered in Philadelphia in 1787 could not have envisioned these changes. They could not have imagined, nor would they have
accepted, that the document they were drafting would one day be con-
strued by a Supreme Court to which had been appointed a woman and the
descendent of an African slave. "We the People" no longer enslave, but the
credit does not belong to the framers. It belongs to those who refused to
acquiesce in outdated notions of "liberty," "justice," and "equality," and
who strived to better them.

And so we must be careful, when focusing on the events which took
place in Philadelphia two centuries ago, that we not overlook the momentous events which followed, and thereby lose our proper sense of perspective. Otherwise, the odds are that for many Americans the bicentennial
celebration will be little more than a blind pilgrimage to the shrine of the
original document now stored in a vault in the National Archives. If we
seek, instead, a sensitive understanding of the Constitution's inherent
defects, and its promising evolution through 200 years of history, the celebration of the "Miracle of Philadelphia" will, in my view, be a far more
meaningful and humbling experience. We will see that the true miracle
was not the birth of the Constitution, but its life, a life nurtured through
two turbulent centuries of our own making, and a life embodying much
good fortune that was not.

Thus, in this bicentennial year, we may not all participate in the festivities with flag-waving fervor. Some may more quietly commemorate the
suffering, struggle, and sacrifice that has triumphed over much of what
was wrong with the original document, and observe the anniversary with
hopes not realized and promises not fulfilled. I plan to celebrate the bicentennial of the Constitution as a living document, including the Bill of

Rights and the other amendments protecting individual freedoms and human rights.

Source: Remarks of Thurgood Marshall at the Annual Seminar of the San Francisco Patent and Trademark Law Association. May 6, 1987. *Congressional Record.* Volume 133, Part 15. Washington, DC: Government Printing Office, 1987.

Bibliography

Afro-American. Week of June 22, 1935. http://msa.maryland.gov/megafile
/msa/speccol/sc2200/sc2221/000011/000007/pdf/d007071a.pdf

Ball, Howard. *A Defiant Life: Thurgood Marshall and the Persistence of Racism in America.* New York: Crown, 1998.

Bernhard, Berl. Thurgood Marshall Oral History Interview. John F. Kennedy Library #1. April 7, 1964.

Black Worker. Vol. 32, No. 10. New York, October 1, 1961.

Bland, Randall W. *Private Pressure on Public Law: The Legal Career of Justice Thurgood Marshall.* Lanham, MD: University Press of America, 1993.

Bland, Randall W. *Thurgood Marshall: Crusader for Liberalism: His Judicial Biography.* Bethesda, MD: Academic Press, 2001.

Boger, Gretchen. "The Meaning of Neighborhood in the Modern City: Baltimore's Residential Segregation Ordinances, 1910–1913." *Journal of Urban History,* Vol. 35, No. 2 (November 1979), pp. 236–258.

Burks, Mary. "Trailblazers: Women in the Montgomery Bus Boycott," in *Women in the Civil Rights Movement Trailblazers and Torchbearers, 1941–1965,* ed. Vicki L. Crawford, Jacqueline Anne Rouse, Barbara Woods, Boadus Butler, Marymal Dryden, and Melissa Walker. Bloomington: Indiana University Press, 1990, 71–84.

Callcott, Margaret Law. "The Negro in Maryland Politics, 1870–1912." Ph.D. dissertation, University of North Carolina, 1967.

Carter, Robert L. *A Matter of Law: A Memoir of Struggle in the Cause of Equal Rights.* New York: The New Press, 2005.

Crosby, Emilye. Oral interview of Cecilia Suyat Marshall for the National Museum of African American History and Culture and the Library of Congress. July 29, 2013.

Davis, Michael D., and Clark Hunter R. *Thurgood Marshall: Warrior at the Bar: Rebel on the Bench.* New York: Carol, 1992.

DeMille, Arnold. "Thurgood Marshall." *Chicago Defender.* May 8, 1954.

Detroit News. February 10, 1999. http://blogs.detroitnews.com/history /1999/02/10/the-1943-detroit-race-riots/

Donaldson, Madeline, *Ruby Bridges.* Minneapolis: Learner Publishing, 2009.

Dudziak, Mary J. *Exporting American Dreams: Thurgood Marshall's African Journey.* New York: Oxford University Press, 2008.

Edwin, Edward. Interview with Thurgood Marshall. Columbia Digital Library Project. April 13, 1977.

Farrar, Harward. *The Baltimore Afro-American.* Santa Barbara: Greenwood, 1998.

The Fight for African American Teachers in Baltimore City (Part 2). http:// www.watkinseducation.org/uncategorized/colored-teachers-for -the-colored-schools-the-fight-for-african-american-teachers-in -baltimore-city-part-2/

Franklin, John Hope, and Genna Rae McNeil, eds. *African Americans and the Living Constitution.* Washington, DC: Smithsonian, 1995.

Gibson, Larry S. *Young Thurgood: The Making of a Supreme Court Justice.* Amherst, New York: Prometheus Books, 2012.

Goldman, Roger, and Gallen, David. *Thurgood Marshall Justice for All.* New York: Carroll & Graf Publishers, 1992.

Greenberg, Jack. *Crusaders in the Court: How a Dedicated Band of Lawyers Fought for the Civil Rights Revolution.* New York: Basic Books, 1994.

Groves, Paul A., and Muller, Edward K. "The Evolution of Black Residential Areas in Late Nineteenth-Century Cities." *Journal of Historical Geography,* Vol. 1 (1975).

Haygood, Wil. *Showdown: Thurgood Marshall and the Supreme Court Nomination That Changed America.* New York: Vintage Books, 2016.

Hitzeroth, Deborah, and Leon Sharon. *The Importance of Thurgood Marshall.* San Diego, CA: Lucent Books, 1997.

Hubbell, John T. Some Reactions to the Desegregation of the University of Oklahoma. *Phylon* (1960–), Vol. 34, No. 2 (2nd Qtr., 1973). http:// www.jstor.org/stable/273826 (accessed February 4, 2018).

Humphrey for President 1968 Campaign Brochure. "1968—A Time for Hope The New Democracy." http://www.4president.org/brochures /1968/hhh1968brochure.htm

James, Rawn Jr. *Root and Branch: Charles Hamilton Houston, Thurgood Marshall and the Struggle to End Segregation.* New York: Bloomsbury Press, 2010.

Kennedy, Randall. *Race Crime and the Law.* New York: Vintage Books, 1997.

King, Gilbert. *Devil in the Grove: Thurgood Marshall, the Groveland boys, and the Dawn of a New America.* New York: Harper, 2012.

Kluger, Richard. *Simple Justice: The History of Brown v. Board of Education and Black America's Struggle for Racial Equality.* New York: Alfred Knopf, 1975 (revised edition, New York: Vintage, 2004).

Lavergne, Gary M. *Before Brown: Herman Sweatt, Thurgood Marshall, and the Long Road to Justice.* Austin: University of Texas Press, 2010.

Long, Michael G., ed. *Marshalling Justice: The Early Civil Rights Letters of Thurgood Marshall.* New York: Amistad, 2011.

Mack, Kenneth W. *Representing the Race: The Creation of the Civil Rights Lawyer.* Cambridge: Harvard University Press, 2012.

McCain, Delores. Before Rosa Parks There Was Irene Morgan. *Austin Weekly News.* July 11, 2007. https://www.austinweeklynews.com/News /Articles/7-11-2007/Before-Rosa-Parks,-there-was-Irene-Morgan/

McNeil, Genna Rae. *Groundwork: Charles Hamilton Houston and the Struggle for Civil Rights.* Philadelphia: Penn Press, 1984.

Memorandum from Thurgood Marshall, Special Counsel, NAACP, to State Conferences of Branches, NAACP (June 29, 1945), micro-formed on Papers of the NAACP, supra note 3, at Reel 1: 669.

Moreno, Paul D. *The Awesome Power: Harry S. Truman as Commander in Chief.* Baton Rouge, LA: LSU Press, 1999.

Motley, Constance Baker. *Equal Justice under the Law: An Autobiography.* New York: Farrar, Straus and Giroux, 1998.

Ogletree, Charles J. Jr. *All Deliberate Speed Reflections on the First Half Century of Brown v. Board of Education.* New York: W. W. Norton & Company, 2004.

Ordinances and Resolutions of the Mayor and City Council of Baltimore, 1910–1911, p. 378. http://mdhistory.msa.maryland.gov/msaref14 /bca_m1237/html/bca_m1237-0001.html

Pietila, Antero. "History of Baltimore's racial segregation includes a hard look at newspapers' role." *Baltimore Sun* (March 15, 2010). https:// baltimorebrew.com/2010/03/15/history-of-baltimores-racial -segregation-includes-a-hard-look-at-newspapers-role/

Press Release. "Sipuel Victory Brings Educational Equality Step Nearer, Says NAACP" (undated), microformed on Papers of the NAACP, supra note 3, at Reel 14:074.

The Road to Brown. https://50791327-The-Road-to-Brown.pdf

Roberts, Samuel Kelton. "Infectious Fear: Tuberculosis, Public Health, and the Logic of Race and Illness in Baltimore, Maryland, 1880–1930." PhD Dissertation. Princeton University, 2002.

Rowan, Carl Thomas. *Dream Makers, Dream Breakers: The World of Justice Thurgood Marshall.* Boston: Little Brown, 1993.

Sabin, Arthur, J. *In Calmer Times: The Supreme Court and Red Monday.* Philadelphia: University of Pennsylvania Press, 1999.

Shogan, Robert. *Harry Truman and the Struggle for Racial Justice.* Lawrence: University of Kansas Press, 2013.

Smith, J. Clay. *Supreme Justice: Speeches and Writings: Thurgood Marshall.* Philadelphia: University of Pennsylvania Press, 2003.

Smith, Stephen, and Kate Ellis. *Thurgood Marshall: Before the Court.* St Paul, MN: American Radio Works, 2011. http://americanradioworks .publicradio.org/features/marshall/

Stanford, The Martin Luther King, Jr., Research and Education Institute. "Letter From A Birmingham Jail." 1963. http://okra.stanford.edu /transcription/document_images/undecided/630416-019.pdf

Starks, Glenn L., and F. Erik Brooks. *Thurgood Marshall A Biography.* Santa Barbara, CA: Greenwood, 2012.

Stokely Carmichael. https://www.history.com/topics/black-history/stokely -carmichael

Testimony of Clarence G. Cooper. http://teaching.msa.maryland.gov /000001/000000/000056/images/cooper.pdf

Testimony of Joshua B. Williams Jr. http://teaching.msa.maryland.gov /000001/000000/000056/images/williams.pdf

Thirty years of lynching in the United States, 1889–1918. https://archive .org/stream/thirtyyearsoflyn00nati#page/n7/mode/2up

Transcript, Thurgood Marshall Oral History Interview I, 7/10/69, by T. H. Baker. Internet Copy. LBJ Library.

Truman, Harry S. "Address before the National Association for the Advancement of Colored People." Washington, DC (June 29, 1947). http://voicesofdemocracy.umd.edu/harry-s-truman-naacp-speech -text/

Tushnet, Mark V. *Making Civil Rights Law: Thurgood Marshall and the Supreme Court 1936–1971.* New York: Oxford University Press, 1994.

Tushnet, Mark V. *Making Constitutional Law: Thurgood Marshall and the Supreme Court 1961–1991.* New York: Oxford University Press, 1997.

Tushnet, Mark V., ed. *Thurgood Marshall: His Speeches, Writings, Arguments, Opinions, and Reminiscences.* Chicago: Lawrence Hill Books, 2001.

Tushnet, Mark V. Thurgood Marshall Interview. Columbia University. 1989.

United States v. Price, 383 U.S. 787. Appeals from the United States District Court for the Southern District of Mississippi (1966). https:// supreme.justia.com/cases/federal/us/383/787/case.html   (accessed June 19, 2018).

Vose, Clement V. *Caucasians Only: The Supreme Court, the NAACP, and the Restrictive Covenant.* Los Angeles: University of California Press, 1967.

Wattley, Cheryl B., and Ada Lois Sipuel Fisher. "How a 'Skinny Little Girl' Took on the University of Oklahoma and Helped Pave the Road to *Brown v. Board of Education*," 62 *Oklahoma Law Review*, Vol. 449 (2017), pp. 464–465. http://digitalcommons.law.ou.edu/olr/vol62/iss3/6

White, Walter, and Thurgood Marshall. *What Caused the Detroit Riot? An Analysis.* New York: NAACP, 1943.

Wilkins, Roy. "The Role of the NAACP." *Social Problems*, Vol. 2, No. 4 (April 1955), pp. 201–205.

Williams, Juan. *Thurgood Marshall: American Revolutionary.* New York: Times Books, 1998.

Zelden, Charles L. *Thurgood Marshall: Race, Rights, and the Struggle for a More Perfect Union.* New York: Routledge, 2013.

Index

257

About the Author

Spencer R. Crew, PhD, is the Clarence J. Robinson professor of history at George Mason University, Fairfax, Virginia. He is the coauthor of *Slave Culture: A Documentary Collection of the Slave Narratives from the Federal Writers' Project* (ABC-CLIO, 2014) and *Memories of the Enslaved: Voices from the Slave Narratives* with Lonnie G. Bunch III and Clement A. Price (ABC-CLIO, 2015).